Development Management
in Africa

Development Management in Africa

Toward Dynamism, Empowerment, and Entrepreneurship

EDITED BY

Sadig Rasheed
and David Fasholé Luke

Westview Press

BOULDER • SAN FRANCISCO • OXFORD

This Westview softcover edition is printed on acid-free paper and bound in library-quality, coated covers that carry the highest rating of the National Association of State Textbook Administrators, in consultation with the Association of American Publishers and the Book Manufacturers' Institute.

Published in 1995 in the United States of America by Westview Press, Inc., 5500 Central Avenue, Boulder, Colorado 80301-2877, and in the United Kingdom by Westview Press, 36 Lonsdale Road, Summertown, Oxford OX2 7EW

A CIP catalog record for this book is available from the Library of Congress.
ISBN 0-8133-2147-6

Printed and bound in the United States of America

The paper used in this publication meets the requirements of the American National Standard for Permanence of Paper for Printed Library Materials Z39.48-1984.

10   9   8   7   6   5   4   3   2   1

Contents

PART SIX
THE WAY FORWARD

Acronyms and Abbreviations

AAPAM	African Association for Public Administration and Management
AAWORD	Association of African Women for Research and Development
ACBF	African Capacity Building Foundation
AEC	African Economic Community
AfDB	African Development Bank
AI	artificial intelligence
APDF	African Project Development Facility
BCEAO	Banque Centrale des Etats de l'Afrique de l'Ouest
BST	Banque Saoudienne Tunisienne (Tunisia)
CAMPE	National Centre for Assistance to Small- and Medium-Sized Enterprises (Cameroon)
CDG	Caisse de Depôt et de Gestion (Morocco)
CD-ROMs	Compact Disks Read-Only Memory
CFAF	Communauté Financière Africaine Franc
CFAO	Compagnie Francaise Afrique Occidentale
CNAREP	National Commission for the Restructuring of Public Enterprises (Tunisia)
CNCA	Caisse National de Crédit Agricole (Morocco)
COBOL	common business oriented language
CODESRIA	Council for the Development of Social Science Research in Africa
DSE	German Foundation of International Development
EC	European Community
ECA	Economic Commission for Africa
ECOWAS	Economic Community of West African States
EDECO	Economic Development and Cooperation Department (of the OAU)
EFFs	Extended Fund Facilities
ENA	Ecole Nationale d'Administration
EPZ	Export Processing Zone (Mauritius)
ESCAS	Education, Science, Culture and Social Affairs Department (of the OAU)
EU	European Union
FAO	Food and Agricultural Organisation
FAVDO	Forum for African Voluntary Development Organisations

GDP	gross domestic product
GFCF	Gross Fixed Capital Formation
GIS	Graphical Information Systems
IASIA	International Association of Schools and Institutes of Administration
IBM	International Business Machines
ICL	International Computers Limited
IDRC	International Development Research Centre (Canada)
IDS	Institute of Development Studies (University of Sussex)
IFC	International Finance Corporation
IGOs	intergovernmental organisations
IIES	Institut International d'Etudes des Sociétiés (Genéve)
ILO	International Labour Organisation
ILO/JASPA	International Labour Organisation/Jobs and Skills Programme for Africa
IMF	International Monetary Fund
IPA	Institute of Public Administration
KANU	Kenya African National Union
LAN	Local Area Network
LDCs	less developed countries
MDI	Management Development Institute
MFC	Ministerial Follow-up Committee
MMD	Movement for Multiparty Democracy (Zambia)
MPs	ministers of Parliament
NGOs	non-governmental organisations
NICs	newly industrialised countries
NSO	National Security Organisation (Nigeria)
OAU	Organisation of African Unity
OECD	Organisation for Economic Cooperation and Development
ORAP	Organisation of Rural Associations for Progress (Zimbabwe)
PAC	Partnership Africa/Canada
PADIS	Pan African Development Information System
PHSD	Public Administration, Human Resources and Social Development Division (of ECA)
PSDU	Private Sector Development Unit
PTA	Preferential Trade Area
R&D	research and development
REC	Regional Economic Communities
SALs	Structural Adjustment Loans
SAP	Structural Adjustment Programmes

SAPAM	Special Action Programme for Administration and Management
SECAL	sectoral adjustment loan
SIDA	Swedish International Development Agency
SMC	Supreme Military Council (Nigeria)
SME	small- and medium-scale enterprise
SQL	Structure Query Language
TEPCOW	Technical Preparatory Committee of the Whole
UAC	United Africa Company
UMOA	Union Monétaire Ouest Africaine
UN	United Nations
UNDP	United Nations Development Programme
UNDTCD	United Nations Department of Technical Cooperation for Development
UNEP	United Nations Environmental Programme
UNESCO	United Nations Educational, Scientific, and Cultural Organisation
UNICEF	United Nations International Children's Emergency Fund (now UN Children's Fund)
UNIP	United National Independence Party (Zambia)
UNIX	computer operating system
USAID	United States Agency for International Development
UTC	United Trading Company
VAT	value-added tax
VIOs	Vehicle Inspection Officers
WIB	Women in Business
WID	Women in Development

Foreword

This book is being published at a very challenging and exciting time for Africa. It comes after the difficult decade of the 1980s, during which the region experienced a devastating socio-economic crisis. Many African countries have embarked upon serious economic and institutional reforms in response to this crisis and to the relentless forces of economic globalisation. The tide of democratic change in Africa has become more sweeping; the operations of the state and the public sector are being thoroughly scrutinised; and the roles of the private sector, entrepreneurship, and popular participation in development have become more recognised. But this book also comes at a time when poverty has become more pervasive in Africa; when national cohesion seems to be disintegrating in many countries; and when armed conflicts are proliferating.

Against this background, a new meaning has been given to the task of managing development. The analyses here of the context in which new trends concerning the emerging role of the state in society and economy and the practical recommendations delineating priority areas where action should be taken to support these undercurrents have the important function of sending the message that hope in Africa's future can triumph over despair. This message underscores and reinforces the growing confidence of ordinary men and women in all corners of the continent in seizing the initiative to undertake activities outside the framework of the state and, indeed, to challenge the institutions of state power. It is a message that should inspire governments and the state sector at large to work with and through their people to pursue such widely accepted goals as raising living standards, improving life chances, and enhancing sustainable development. The authors send a clear message that the international community should renew its confidence in and commitment to Africa. Students, practitioners, and those interested in socio-economic development processes in Africa and how these processes should be managed will find within these pages many ideas for responding to contemporary problems and challenges.

This book includes as an appendix a seminal document by the United Nations Economic Commission for Africa (ECA): *Strategic Agenda for Development Management in Africa in the 1990s*. Within its mandate and work programme of advisory services, training, research, and advocacy, the ECA stands ready to facilitate the implementation of the *Strategic Agenda*. One of the foremost challenges in the region today is to manage development processes effectively for the benefit of all its peoples. This book contains a wealth of ideas for meeting this challenge.

Layashi Yaker
UN Under Secretary General,
Executive Secretary of ECA,
Addis Ababa

Preface and Acknowledgements

The ideas constituting the main theme of this book are a response to past experiences, emerging challenges, and changing realities in development management in Africa. As such, its authors argue the case for a more responsive development management paradigm in Africa in the 1990s and beyond. They set out to probe this framework by focusing on the imperatives and requirements of change and reform as related to the public policy-making process and the efficiency of the civil service and public enterprise sectors. These imperatives are: building entrepreneurial capacity, promoting private sector development, meeting the challenge of productivity improvement, promoting ethics and accountability in African civil services, ensuring popular participation in development and governance, decentralization for sustainable development, improving the resource mobilisation and financial management capacity of African governments, empowering women managerially and economically, managing development assistance, achieving the African Economic Community, and optimising the use of information technology.

Because it stresses the imperatives of popular participation in development and governance; the growing importance of entrepreneurship, the private sector, and people's organisations in the management of development; and the need for deliberate action to facilitate entrepreneurship and effective measures for empowerment outside the state sector, this book is also a contribution to advancing the thinking on promoting sustainable growth and development in Africa, in a context of greater creativity, participation, and accountability.

The chapters represent edited versions of what was originally submitted, but we have been very careful to preserve the essence of the original contributions. Each chapter has been sufficiently documented and, for this reason, a consolidated bibliography has not been provided. Each contributor has written in her or his personal capacity, and the views presented do not necessarily reflect the official position of the organisation to which any is affiliated, certainly not the United Nations or the United Nations Economic Commission for Africa (ECA).

Reproduced as an appendix is the *Strategic Agenda for Development Management in Africa in the 1990s*, which has been endorsed by the ECA's Conference of Ministers. This important document sets out the basis for multi-actor involvement in the management of development and proposes mechanisms for coordination, exchange of information, and networking among all actors and supporters. The *Strategic Agenda* also identifies ten areas of common concern and priorities for action.

We wish to express our profound gratitude to the authors for their thought-provoking and generous contributions. We are also grateful to the staff of the Public Administration, Human Resources, and Social Development Division at ECA, in particular Asmelash Beyene, Eloho Otobo, and the support staff of the Special Action Programme on Administration and Management Project (SAPAM) for their assistance in the preparation of this book. Finally, we would like to thank Shewaye Woldeyes for word-processing the final manuscript.

Sadig Rasheed
David Fasholé Luke
Addis Ababa

1

Introduction: Toward a New Development Management Paradigm

Sadig Rasheed and David Fasholé Luke

The changing role of the state in society and economy, new orientations in public sector management and reform, and the growing recognition of the part played by people's and voluntary organisations, have given new meaning to the management of development. These trends have challenged traditional public administration paradigms and exposed their limitations. Two decades of economic decline in Africa have been accompanied by a tendency to display much scepticism about the role and performance of the state sector. But dissatisfaction with public sector performance is also part of a worldwide trend. Indeed, it is a matter of universal concordance that the modern state, as a complex organisation, should overcome as much as possible the rigidities of its bureaucratic structures. Irrespective of level of development or official ideology, one of the foremost challenges in today's world is for the state sector to find new and creative ways of exercising governance over populations that are becoming more and more discerning. It is also clear that the modern state must be able to respond imaginatively to such contemporary undercurrents as economic globalisation, persistent poverty or wide disparities in the quality of life, ethnic and associated tensions, and misgivings about environmental degradation and pollution. It is precisely against this background of public dissatisfaction with the response of the state to these and related challenges that private, voluntary, and people-centred initiatives have grown in importance.

1

A Catalogue of Public Sector Distress

As one would expect, however, the extent and specific dimensions of shortcomings in the state sector in Africa do vary from place to place and country to country. But there are some common elements. In forward planning and policy analysis, for example, a paucity of analytical capacity, creativity, and flexibility in response to changing circumstances or emerging challenges is ubiquitous. In financial systems, largely symbolic budgets have been found to be unconnected to actual funds available and to identified priorities. In human resource management, serious pay and performance problems as well as lack of fit between skilled manpower recruited and the needs of public agencies have surfaced. Moreover, the talents and skills of women remain to be fully utilised. In organisation and work processes, the design of organisations and schedule of duties sometimes have little relation to actual responsibilities or established procedures.

Management systems appear to have broken down, with the very predictable consequence of disarray in the flow of supplies and equipment and maintenance of buildings and infrastructure, which are vital for the smooth running of government. Centre-periphery relations (especially in regard to rural services) are characterised by excessive centralisation of decision-making and resources, with little understanding of local needs or commitment of the wherewithal. In fact voluntary or non-governmental organisations (NGOs) have generally replaced government agencies in relevance at this level for both service delivery and imaginative community-building initiatives. Public enterprises, seen at the time of independence as strategic bridgeheads of entrepreneurship, have largely become acute embarrassments, leading to renewed emphasis on complete divestment or at least privatisation of management in reform programmes.

As common understanding of the consequences of mediocrity in the state sector permeated the realm of public consciousness, several African countries—and others elsewhere—have in recent years experienced considerable political turmoil. To be sure the chain of causality between distressing public sector performance and popular reaction is decidedly complex. Yet there are good grounds for believing there is a link. Certain dramatic events—some of them quite extraordinary—in divers African countries since the late 1980s encompassed popular demand for responsive public policies and institutions. "Second liberation" and "second independence" are some of the epithets that have been used to describe the wave of political turbulence that has been sweeping across the region. In conjunction with the emergence of clear signs of terminal decline in the Soviet federation and the momentous events in Eastern Europe during 1989—the "year of revolutions"—the setting of this "second African liberation" can readily be outlined.

This setting is characterised by the harsh realities of a changing global economic order and its demanding regime of economic restructuring, productive efficiency, and international competitiveness. In the new scheme of things, diminishing value is being placed on Africa's commodity exports, and both the limitations of peasant producing economies and the parasitism of the state sector are being exposed. Indeed, structural adjustment programmes, however flawed as a response to the specific requirements of reform in the region, have been designed to provide stopgap financing as much as to restructure public sector agencies and facilitate policy adjustments to the multiple challenges of economic globalisation.

To this extent, public sector reform has become an integral part of current efforts at policy and institutional realignment. This is underscored by a number of initiatives. In March 1990, for example, the World Bank announced the establishment of the African Capacity Building Initiative. A study released about the same time revealed that attention to institutional issues had become an essential component of the World Bank's policy-based lending, with sectoral adjustment loans (SECALs), which are designed to respond to policy and institutional disarray at the sectoral/departmental level, accounting for US$9.4 billion during the 1980s. Fifty-five SECALs were made during this period, nearly half of them to Sub-Saharan Africa.[1] In addition, to a continuing programme of research, training, and technical assistance within the framework of its more limited mandate, a major response of the United Nations Economic Commission for Africa (ECA) was the early 1990 launching of the Special Action Programme for Public Administration and Management (SAPAM). SAPAM has since organised a number of forums for managers and practitioners, drawn from the public, private, and voluntary sectors, as well for as policy-makers, academics, and other experts, to share experiences of the problems and to identify practical solutions.[2] Other multilateral agencies have also made institutional reform in the region a key priority: notably the United Nations Development Programme (UNDP), the United Nations Department of Technical Cooperation for Development (UNDTCD), the International Finance Corporation (IFC), as well as the Commonwealth Secretariat, bilateral donors, and independent organisations, including the Aga Khan and Ford Foundations, and, of course, the African Association for Public Administration and Management (AAPAM).[3]

A New Development Management Paradigm

In the design of these initiatives, fitting recognition is being given to the growing importance of private and voluntary organisations as agents of sustainable development and vectors of institutional capacity. In this regard, it has become clear that the traditional public administration paradigm underscoring only government or public sector responsibility for "bringing development about" is no longer tenable. At the local level in virtually all African countries, NGOs and grassroots organisations are far more relevant than are government agencies in providing vital services and empowering marginal communities. In Mozambique, for example, some 120 national and international NGOs dominate welfare services.[4] Beyond this, it has become more widely accepted that private sector spontaneity, flexibility, and dynamism are among the key building blocks of economic diversification, higher levels of new, valued employment opportunities, competitive exports, rising living standards, and sustainable growth.

This book's editors and contributors take the view that the old paradigm, shared by public administration and its development administration subspecialisation, must now be replaced by a new paradigm that emphasises that development is no longer solely a state or public sector responsibility. Past strategies that favoured only one set of actors need to be replaced by a strategy that underscores the roles that everybody has and can play and that emphasises the interdependence of these roles. This challenge is referred to as development management.

Although the concept of development administration focused mainly on the public sector, development management may connote the involvement of all sectors and institutions in society: state and civil society, public and private enterprises, and NGOs and cooperatives. Thus there is a role for everyone, including external donors and development partners. It is clear that, in the final analysis, these agents and institutions are interdependent. Yet each brings distinctive organisational perspectives, experiences, and even cultures to the development process. Their dynamic interaction is essential in enhancing the prospects of sustainable development.

It should be emphasised here that this is not just a semantic issue. The earlier paradigm was dirigisme, that is plan-oriented, prescriptive, programmatic, and exclusive. This can be seen from the following authoritative formulations. "The term 'development administration' was coined in 1955 or 1956. . . . In some respects it is the counterpart of the term 'development economics' which came into renewed and heightened usage with the growing impact of economic planning in the newly independent countries after World War II. . . . The term used to denote the complex of agencies, management systems, and processes a government establishes to achieve its development goals."[5] Riggs echoed this view, suggesting that "development administration refers to the administration of development programs, to the methods used by large-scale organizations, notably governments, to implement polices and plans designed to meet development objectives."[6]

Hope also underlined the statist orientation of the old paradigm. "Development administration, like development planning in the LDCs (less developed countries), is mainly a postwar phenomenon. It emerged both as a discipline and as a process through which government programs for economic development were implemented and administered in the hope of achieving the best possible results or maximum social gain for society."[7] And, finally, Irving Swerdlow connected development administration to the traditional public administration paradigm. "The term development administration has value in calling attention to the special importance of public administration in the modernisation process."[8]

In contrast to the foregoing characterisations, the proposed new paradigm is society-centred, problem-solving oriented, interactive, and inclusive. It is based on the assumption that, under the right conditions, energies both inside and outside the state sector can be released to find and implement enduring solutions to the multifaceted challenges of development. This is what is meant by development management. To this extent, this concept of development management is concerned with all types of organisational settings—micro-, small-, or large-scale; informal and formal; and public, private, or voluntary. It also encompasses simultaneous initiatives and actions at different levels of society and economy. Moreover, these actions are "grounded" in the daily realities, authentic aspirations and cultural experiences of the people concerned.

It must be further emphasised that this concept of development management does not confine the state and its institutions to a minimalist role. Indeed, in regard to such issues as strengthening policy-making capacity; improving productivity, ethics, and accountability; promoting decentralisation, public enterprise performance, civil service reform, efficient financial resource mobilisation and utilisation, new information technology, and strategies for the advancement of women in public service, several chapters of this book are concerned with practical ways of building public sector capacity and effectiveness.

Accordingly, the authors take the view that an effective and proactive state sector is a fundamental prerequisite for economic transformation. This is one of the main lessons that can be derived from the experience of developmental states, particularly in East Asia, as many students of the subject have correctly observed. But there are few who have not been disappointed by the performance of the public sector in Africa. The catalogue of public sector distress as outlined above provides a reliable estimation of the difficulties. Yet there are many things that only government can and must do to provide what is now fashionably described as an "enabling environment." Private and voluntary actors can thrive only if responsive conditions are provided. The elements of such an environment include peace and political stability; a sound legal framework or appropriate cultural practices for settling disputes equitably and with despatch; competent management of the economy and the provision of basic infrastructure; optimisation of national opportunities in regional economic arrangements and in the wider international economy; and investment in the health, education, training, and other basic needs of the population. On this last point especially, the interconnected requirements for sustained human resource development is a special responsibility of government. The UNDP's well-established series of human development reports have done well to focus attention on these issues.[9] To their credit, researchers at ECA have continued to emphasise the importance of these essentials both for African recovery and development.[10]

Stressing that development is no longer a public sector responsibility alone, the authors offer a deliberate departure from the traditional concerns of public and development administration. They discuss the implications of the growing importance of private and voluntary initiatives for the management of development activities.

As with the public sector, each group's initiative has comparative advantages in specific areas: Voluntary organisations, for example, are beneficial in that they are able to empower and build capacity in local communities; business organisations in that they bear risks that require entrepreneurial dynamism; and the public sector in that it is able to provide an enabling environment as well as actively to oversee the development of human capabilities. Traditional public and development administration managed to accommodate the proliferation of NGO activity at subcentral levels in terms of its strictures on decentralisation. But entrepreneurial activities were deemed to fall outside its ambit and were seen to belong more properly to the sphere of "business administration."

This book's central idea, that the old public administration paradigm is no longer viable, complements current trends and efforts, both in the design of public sector reforms and in training people in institutions and establishments of higher learning to rethink the bonds between public administration, business administration, and management studies, and to rethink their role in development. The validity of applying entrepreneurial practices and concepts to nonprofit settings is increasingly being recognised. In addition, the parallel success of NGOs within the state sector and of such innovations as quality circles and profit centres within private business also require a rethinking of decentralisation strategies. An exceptional enrichment of management practice—and studies—is anticipated as the outcome of a retreat from orthodox approaches to the application of public and business administration concepts.

Elaboration of the Issues

The chapters that follow provide elaboration on the theme that has been advanced. The authors offer a blend of retrospective analyses and practical measures for prospective reform. The book falls into six parts. In Part One, two contributors (in Chapters 2 and 3) reassess thirty years of public administration in Africa. M. J. Balogun traces the factors accounting for institutional decline in governmental agencies in the three decades since 1960 and makes the argument that an effective partnership between the public, private, and voluntary sectors is required to meet the challenges of the 1990s. Ladipo Adamolekun assesses various attempts during the last thirty years to make African state sectors more responsive to development aspirations and illustrates some valuable lessons from the experience.

In Part Two (Chapters 4 through 8) the authors identify some of the main challenges of revitalising institutions and processes of development management. Dele Olowu looks at productivity improvement, and Sadig Rasheed discusses what is required in promoting ethics and accountability in civil service agencies. Peter H. Koehn appraises decentralisation efforts and suggests that local empowerment is a fundamental requirement of sustainable development (that is to say, the ongoing need for community maintenance of institutions, equipment, infrastructure, as well as natural resources). He recommends that governments must reward rather than discourage any impetus for self-reliance generated from "below." Hamadan Benaissa focuses on the role of government in exercising oversight over financial resource mobilisation and utilisation in the public and private sectors. In particular, he identifies policy measures for financial sector development, reform of financial intermediaries, including banks and capital markets, and reform of tax systems. Herbert Girkes draws attention to the falling prices of information technology and to the new possibilities this has opened for their utilisation in enhancing the efficient flow of information and data within and beyond government agencies.

Inclusiveness is one of the characteristics of the new development management paradigm. This extends to the recognition that women constitute a key national resource whose talents, ideas, creative solutions, and concern for the cohesiveness of the social fabric can help change the quality of life and society at large. The authors of Part Three (Chapters 9 and 10) examine ways in which women can become more effectively involved in the development process and its management. To do this, their participation in high-level public policy decision-making roles is essential. Eschewing the debate whether women constitute a uniform group with uniform aspirations, Maria Nzomo reviews the status of women in African public sectors and outlines measures for securing their access to influential positions. Zeinab B. El-Bakry looks at ways in which the capacity of African businesswomen operating at different levels of the economy can be enhanced, thus her chapter compliments that of Nzomo.

The traditional concerns of public administration and development administration have been superseded by the need to purposefully coordinate and integrate private sector initiatives and practices within the overall framework of development; thus the authors of Chapters 11 and 12 in Part Four bring entrepreneurship under focus. David Fasholé Luke tours the labyrinth of concepts characterising African entrepreneurship to distinguish between different levels of business ventures. He assesses the main constraints facing entrepreneurs at each level and distils from this discussion a number of practical insights, policy measures, and recommendations for promoting the private sector at each distinctive level. Mostafa Rhomari is concerned with the challenges of privatisation. Drawing from selected cases, key problems, and possible solutions in transferring public enterprises to private sector ownership and control, he deals with such issues as different techniques of privatisation and associated financial questions, including the role of foreign investors and the pros and cons of debt and equity swaps. He also outlines ways of mitigating adverse post-privatisation effects on employment and income distribution.

Part Five concerns voluntary organisations and related political issues. As previously noted, many African countries have recently experienced considerable political unrest arising from popular awakening to the pernicious consequences of a parasitic and unresponsive state sector. As these voices were being heard, action was being taken to exit or bypass the traditional agencies of public administration in order to establish voluntary organisations as vehicles of popular aspirations. Voluntary organisations have now become not only partners in the development process but also watchdogs of public propriety. The authors of Chapters 13 and 14 examine the implications of these trends for the management of development activities. On one hand, Sadig Rasheed and Getachew Demeke highlight the watchdog activities of popular organisations at a country or national level. Pierre Landell-Mills and Ismail Serageldin, on the other hand, identify the core characteristics of good governance that enjoy wide acceptance internationally, and thus discuss how such attributes may be effectively and legitimately fostered by external development partners.

Part Six is made up of three contributions. In Chapters 15, Goran Hyden advances a model for the disbursement of external assistance. The model is based on recognition of the new reality that private and voluntary organisations have joined the public sector as major players in mobilising resources to meet the multiple challenges of development. Although Hyden is concerned with a new model for external partnerships in development activities, H. M. A. Onitiri in Chapter 16, focuses on inter-African partnerships. African governments have committed themselves to increasing levels of economic cooperation, leading to the establishment of an African Economic Community (AEC) by the year 2025. Onitiri provides a well-informed tour through the organisational and managerial minefield that this commitment implies and argues that the activities of agents in all sectors of society and economy should constitute the basis of implementing the AEC treaty.

Finally, the editors identify the main elements of a strategic agenda for the reform of development management in Africa during the 1990s. This agenda was formulated and adopted by participants at a major regional conference on development management in Africa in March 1993 following debate and discussion of the ideas that have now been assembled in this book.[11] In May 1993, ECA's Conference of Ministers endorsed the agenda, and its full text is reproduced as an appendix.

It is, however, naive not to recognise that development management reform in Africa is, in the final analysis, a political question with a political answer. Nonetheless, the authors take the view that bold and imaginative reforms in less-than-perfect political systems are the first milestones in the evolution of professionalism in public management. For example, the bureaucratic reforms in Japan in the 1870s following the Meiji Restoration were made within a framework of governance that could have hardly been described as democratic. Yet it provided the basis for the emergence, in both the public and the private sectors, of a managerial cadre of good standing and tradition, endowed with a strong sense of duty and an equally strong sense of esprit de corps. Against a background of the constraints of continuing public sector distress, economic globalisation, and other pressures on the contemporary state in Africa, as well as the exciting opportunities provided by current trends in the private and voluntary sectors, this is a lesson that must be taught and learned in the region. The cost of not acting is forbidding.

Notes

1. See Samuel Paul, *Institutional Reforms in Sector Adjustment Operations: The World Bank's Experience* (Washington, DC: World Bank Discussion Papers No. 92, 1990).

2. The reports on these forums provide fascinating insights into the specific dimensions of institutional difficulties. See *Entrepreneurship in Africa* (1990); *Improving the Performance of Public Enterprises in Africa* (1990); *Mobilising the Informal Sector and Non-Governmental Organisations (NGOs) for African Recovery and Development: Policy and Management Issues* (1991); *Improving the Performance of Public Enterprises in Africa: Lessons from Country Experiences* (1992); *Ethics and Accountability in the Public Services in Africa* (1992); *Improving the Productivity of African Public Services* (1992); *Mobilisation and Management of Financial Resources in African Universities* (1992); *Strengthening the Viability of the African University in the 1990s and Beyond* (1992); and *Enhancing the Interface Between Government Policy-Making Entities, Universities, and Research Institutions in Support of Economic Reform and Development in Africa* (1992). All titles published (in English and French) by the Economic Commission for Africa (ECA) in Addis Ababa.

3. The literature on the work of these agencies include United Nations Development Programme (UNDP), *Rethinking Technical Cooperation: Reforms for Capacity Building in Africa* (New York: UNDP, 1993); Gelase Mutahaba et al. *Revitalising African Public Administration for Recovery and Development* (West Hartford, Connecticut: Kumarian Press/United Nations Department of Technical Cooperation for Development [UNDTCD], 1993); Keith Marsden, *African Entrepreneurs: Pioneers of Development* (Washington, DC: International Finance Corporation Technical Paper No. 9, 1990); and M. Jide Balogun and Gelase Mutahaba, *Economic Restructuring & African Public Administration* (West Hartford, Connecticut: Kumarian Press/African Association for Public Administration and Development [AAPAM], 1989).

4. See John Clark, *Democratising Development: The Role of Voluntary Organisations* (London: Earthscan, 1991), 5.

5. George F. Gant, *Development Administration: Concept, Goals, Methods* (Madison: University of Wisconsin Press, 1979), 20.

6. See Fred Riggs (ed.), *Frontiers of Development Administration* (Durham, North Carolina: Duke University Press, 1970), 6-7; also cited in David F. Luke, "Trends in Development Administration: The Continuing Challenge to the Efficacy of the Post-Colonial State in the Third World," *Public Administration and Development* 6 (1), 1986.

7. R. H. Hope, *The Dynamics of Development and Development Administration* (Westport, Connecticut: Greenwood Press, 1984), 64.

8. Irving Swerdlow, *The Public Administration of Economic Development* (New York: Praeger, 1975), 345.

9. See UNDP, *Human Development Report 1993* (New York: UNDP/Oxford University Press, 1993).

10. See, for example, Adebayo Adedeji, Sadig Rasheed, and Melody Morrison, *The Human Dimension of Africa's Persistent Crisis* (Seven Oaks, England: ECA/Hans

Zell, 1990); United Nations Economic and Social Council, *Report on the Eighth Meeting of the Ministerial Follow-Up Committee of Ten of the Conference of Ministers Responsible for Human Resources Planning, Development, and Utilisation* (Addis Ababa: E/ECA/PHSD/MFC/93/6, 1993); and ECA, *From Conflict to Concord: Regional Cooperation in the Horn of Africa: Final Communique* (Addis Ababa: ECA/United States Institute of Peace, 1993).

11. See ECA, *Strategic Agenda for Development Management in Africa in the 1990s* (Addis Ababa: ECA, 1993).

Part One

Thirty Years of Public Administration in Africa

2

A Critical Review of the Changing Role of the Public Sector

M. J. Balogun

Central to our understanding of the protracted debate on the role of government is the question, is there a barrier beyond which any government in Africa must not go? Advocates of structural adjustment reforms, in particular, hold the view that it is fine when a government limits itself to enacting rules and regulations spelling out acceptable norms of social behaviour, but disastrous if the same government deems itself competent to engage in direct productive activity. In other words, it is appropriate for a government to enact and enforce edicts on, say, environmental cleanliness or acceptable business practices, but for it to run a business enterprise is taboo.

Africa's experience is frequently cited to illustrate the difficulties in making the transition from government as a lawgiver to government as an entrepreneur. It is pointed out that the massive government investment in projects, institutions, and personnel (not always in that order) yielded little besides unfulfilled expectations and huge financial losses. Unbridled government intervention in the productive sector is thus largely held responsible for Africa's economic decline in the 1980s.

However, does this overwhelmingly pro-business conclusion fit the facts? Is the private sector's managerial response to Africa's development problem any more imaginative (and so, any less blameable) than the public sector's? Is there not something fundamentally wrong with the contemporary African notion of management—public or private? Finding answers to these complex (sometimes arcane) questions is the first step towards explaining Africa's stubborn socio-economic malaise.

In this chapter, I address contemporary issues of public sector management and look at the role of, and the problems facing, the sector from the colonial period to the present. I then discuss the constraints facing the public sector before I examine the reform strategies. In the last part of the chapter, I discuss the future role of the sector in Africa's development.

African Public Services: The Phase of Institutional Growth

A critical assessment of the role of Africa's public sector over the past three decades reveals a pattern of qualitative decline in institutional capacity. The pre-independence period witnessed the establishment of agencies to handle modest programmes of socio-economic development in addition to the government's traditional regulatory law-and-order functions. On independence, government responded to the popular yearnings for material benefits by creating new institutions and launching new programmes. Apart from the difficulties facing relatively inexperienced officials in managing and controlling a rapidly growing bureaucratic empire, the steady erosion of the inherited values and norms accelerated the pace of institutional decay, which, in turn, undermined the effectiveness (and dented the image) of the public service.

The Law-and-Order Phase

By modern standards, the colonial bureaucracy was very small. It concerned itself largely with maintaining law and order, regulating individual and collective behaviour, and providing basic social and infrastructural services. It was not unknown, but it was rare, for the colonial civil service to engage in manufacturing or trading activities. The civil service merely created an enabling environment for private enterprise to operate. The industrial giants were not the public corporations and state-owned companies of the post-independence era, but private ventures such as United Africa Company (UAC), Kingsway, CFAO, UTC and Leventis (in west Africa), Lonrho and de Beers in eastern and southern Africa, and the petroleum and mineral exploration companies that were active in different parts of the continent. Banking, insurance, and finance were controlled by private institutions, among them, Standard and Barclays Banks.

Whether as a result of an objective and realistic appraisal of its limited capacity and resources or as an ideological preference for nonintervention, the colonial administration focused its attention mainly on the classical role of government. It was in its best form when it came to enacting and enforcing edicts on environmental sanitation, operation of business enterprises or premises, as well as codes governing offenses against person or property.

Compared with the present-day experience, the colonial public service did best what it chose to do. Its corps of sanitary inspectors saw to the cleanliness of the environment and invoked the law against households that were derelict in their sanitary responsibilities. Its police force controlled civil disturbances and, with the support and diligence of the judiciary, made the world unsafe for fraud, embezzlement, and homicide. The traffic branch of the colonial police force (through the Vehicle Inspection Officers [VIOs]) saw to it that motor vehicle driving licences were issued only to those who passed prescribed tests and that such licences were "endorsed" or temporarily withdrawn when holders contravened the road traffic ordinance. The same VIOs helped protect the environment by pasting "off-the-road" stickers on vehicles that were considered environmental hazards, or otherwise not road-worthy. Even minor details such as the possession of valid and up-to-date bicycle licences, were not overlooked by the colonial administration, which decentralised to local or "native" authorities the power to issue such licences.

The colonial administration's efforts in the law-and-order area were complemented with modest achievements in the socio-economic area. For example, in the British colonial territories, officials in the Departments of Education advised on the formulation of the government's education policy and supervised the administration of schools, colleges, and vocational training centres. Departments of Health administered preventive and curative health programmes. Public Works Departments handled the construction and maintenance of roads, bridges, and government housing units. The Departments of Agriculture looked after agricultural extension services, animal health, fisheries, agriculture cooperatives, and forest reserves.

Public utilities and quasi-commercial operations were almost invariably assigned to special agencies, i.e., statutory corporations and state-owned companies. Development corporations supervised the management of the few industrial and manufacturing enterprises established by the government. Marketing boards were responsible for the marketing of export commodities and the management of foreign reserves. Capital-intensive operations, such as railways, electricity, posts and telegraphs, also belonged within the purview of bodies established by law.

If the colonial bureaucracy's achievements in the socio-economic area are considered along with its role in the political transition process, one may conclude, in a manner of speaking that it was as "development-oriented" as were post-colonial regimes. However, in terms of the general orientation of government and the scale of government intervention in economic activities, the colonial public service was a regulatory law-and-order institution.

The Post-Independence Phase

Rapid growth in the size of the public sector became noticeable in the 1960s. For Africa, this was a decade of independence, and for the United Nations it was the First Development Decade. Evidence of this growth is provided by the range of institutions, the number of officials employed, and the sums of money budgeted for capital development programmes and for recurrent services.

Institutional expansion is an indicator of bureaucratic growth during the post-independence period. In Tanzania, the number of ministries increased from ten in 1961 to sixteen in 1985.[1] In Nigeria, the number of statutory corporations and state-owned companies rose from a mere fifty in 1960 to 800 in 1982.[2] Between 1980 and 1984, the number of statutory bodies in Malawi rose from twenty-five to thirty-five.[3] As the data in Table 2.1 indicate, the parastatal sector's share of the national product had become significant by the early 1980s.

Table 2.1
Public Enterprise Contribution to Gross Fixed Capital
Formation in Selected Countries

Country	Year	No. of State-owned Enterprises	Percentage Share of GFCF
Ethiopia	1984	180	36
Tanzania	1984	400	28
Kenya	1982	176	17
Uganda	1985	130	Unknown

Source: Based on data supplied by J. J. Jorgensen "Organisational Life-Cycle and Effectiveness Criteria in State-Owned Enterprises: The Case of East Africa," in A. M. Jaeger and R. N. Kanungo (eds.), *Management in Developing Countries* (London: Routledge 1990), 62.

In many African countries, the decentralised agencies (local government and field administrative units) are, to all intents and purposes, part of the public sector. The rapid increase in the number of such institutions has contributed to the growth of government. Again, Nigeria provides a good illustration of the tendency towards institutional proliferation both at the centre and at the periphery. Up to 1967, there was a federal public service coexisting with four—north, east, west, and midwest—regional public services. With the creation of states in 1967, the number of state administrations rose to twelve. The number further increased to nineteen in 1975. As of today, these are no less than thirty-one state (and one federal) public services. Relative to the arithmetic increase in the number of central government agencies through the creation of new states is the geometric increase in the number of local government councils and of "deconcentrated" agencies of federal and state governments. As recently as 1988, the number of local government areas in Nigeria did not exceed 449. By 1992, there were 589.

Corresponding to the increase in the number of government agencies is the growth in public sector employment. However, before examining the figures, it is necessary to point out that published data on public sector manpower are suspect. In other words, the figures released may not tally with the actual number of people working. After painstaking effort, "ghost workers" have been discovered in different places. A World Bank study revealed numerous nonexistent workers and nonexistent schools in Uganda.[4] Another civil service head-count in the central African Republic turned up 1,300 "ghost workers." Two-thirds of the names on Zaire's civil service manning table in 1978 were fictitious.[5]

All the same, on the basis of the figures released from time to time, one may conclude that the public service in Sub-Saharan Africa grew rapidly between the early 1960s and the late 1970s. Kenya's public service employed 45,000 persons in the mid-1950s, 63,000 in 1965, 84,500 in 1971, and 170,000 by 1980. The Senegalese government employed 10,000 shortly before independence in 1960, 35,000 (an increase of over 300 percent) in 1965, and 61,000 by 1973.[6] Government employment in the Gambia doubled between 1974 and 1984.[7] Ghana's public service employment grew between 1975 and 1982 at a rate five times faster than the growth of the labour market.[8] The number on the public payroll in Cameroon rose from 11,610 in 1970 to 55,100 in 1988. Tanzania offered employment to 113,171 persons in 1970 and 256,754 in 1985.

In Nigeria, the federal public service establishment alone (that is, excluding the states) grew from 50,817 in 1962 to 231,802 in 1980. It is worth noting that substantial increases were recorded after 1970 when the growing oil wealth was ploughed into the post-war programme of reconstruction and rehabilitation. As is to be expected, the rapid expansion in public service institutions and workforce has translated into huge increases in expenditure. In most cases, the wage bill constituted a significant portion of total outlays. In the early 1970s, Uganda's wage bill stood at 40 percent of recurrent expenditure. It is only in recent years that the proportion of the wage bill to total expenditure substantially declined (see Table 2.2).

Table 2.2
Uganda's Total Wage Bill as a Percentage of Recurrent Expenditure (1970-1990)

Fiscal Year	Wage Bill (%)
1970/1971	40
1971/1972	40
1972/1973	40
1973/1974	27.5*
1974/1975	-
1975/1976	-
1976/1977	-
1977/1978	-
1978/1979	-
1979/1980	27.5*
1980/1981	31.2
1981/1982	18.1
1982/1983	15.0
1983/1984	22.2
1984/1985	27.9
1985/1986	17.7
1986/1987	13.1
1987/1988	14.5
1988/1989	18.9
1989/1990	17.9
1990/1991	14.3

* Period Average.
Source: *Report of the Public Service Review and Reorganisation Commission, 1989-1990*, vol. 1, *Main Report* (Kampala: Government of Uganda, 1991), Table 2, 177.

Factors in Bureaucratic Growth

A number of factors account for the rapid growth in public service institutions, workforce and expenditure. Prominent among these are the post-independence revolution of rising expectations, the ideological or policy bias towards central planning, bureaucratic empire-building tendencies, an international environment that was conducive to government intervention in the economy, and objective sociological factors.

The role of the colonial bureaucracy was limited largely because the colonial authorities promised little and delivered even less. In contrast, the indigenous political elites that fought for the transfer of power to Africans were often quick to hold out the prospects of an oncoming utopia. It could not have been any other way. The politics of the nationalist struggles in the 1950s and 1960s had to hinge on the promise of a greater tomorrow. Without this vision of the "promised land" it would have been difficult, if not impossible, to organise diverse ethnic groups and religious faiths behind a common, anti-colonial banner.

Thus after the establishment of the "political kingdom" of Ghana's Kwame Nkrumah, "everything else" (good) was to follow. And Nigeria's Obafemi Awolowo's Action Group appealed to the electorate of the then Western Region of Nigeria with an irresistible offer: "Freedom, Peace, Life More Abundant." Even if these statements were meant to be nothing more than a deft manipulation of language and emotions, they almost invariably came home to roost. As soon as one African country after the other attained independence, the people confronted their leaders with long wish lists. The village roads would need to be tarred, the wells had to be replaced by pipe-borne water, and the herbalists and practitioners of native medicine would have to look for other jobs now that "modern" health care facilities had been included in the ruling party's campaign manifesto.

The new political elites seemed to have fuelled the revolution of rising expectations in other ways. In their words and deeds, they betrayed their bias for an interventionist state even before the attainment of independence. Whether they belonged to one of the diverse schools of socialism or declared no ideological leanings, these leaders were most likely to endorse the idea of development planning and to place a high premium on central government leadership in socio-economic development. As leaders of nations "in a hurry" (nations that could not wait to "catch up" with the Western industrialised economies) they felt that government had a special role to play to bridge whatever entrepreneurial and investment gaps might have been responsible for Africa's economic backwardness.

Institutional expansion may also be attributed to the general, universal tendency on the part of career officials to multiply themselves. Bureaucratic empire-building is a factor in the design and operation of civil service structures, the establishment of parastatal bodies, and the "reorganisation" of local government and decentralised agencies.[9]

In any case, the environment that prevailed during the African public services' formative years was generally conducive to bureaucratic growth. The 1960s, for instance, was a decade of optimism, it was the decade in which many African countries attained independence. But more significant than any other factor was the favourable state of the international political and economic environment. The new states enjoyed a tremendous amount of goodwill in the international community. Foreign investment flows and the commodity export market were "bullish"; external loans (at concessional rates) were readily available, and exchange rates were favourable. When the economic environment changed in the 1970s and 1980s, the philosophy underpinning an interventionist state came under critical scrutiny.

Apart from the preceding explanations, bureaucratic growth in Africa can be attributed to some objective sociological factors. Government intervention is almost invariably a function of the capacity of alternative response mechanisms. Where the culture of entrepreneurship is well established and widely diffused in society, and where the institutions supporting entrepreneurial activity operate effectively, private enterprise is likely to be an active participant in the development process rather than a passive object of public policy. The argument of government interventionists is not necessarily that public enterprise is superior to private enterprise, but that where the latter is dormant, the former has a duty to respond to developmental challenges.

The experience of Africa in the past three decades reveals that if the public sector is weak, so is the private sector. The private sector not only failed to seize the opportunity presented by affluence in the 1960s and 1970s it also proved incapable of responding to the challenges of economic decline in the 1980s. It is a historical fact that a substantial share of the windfall from petroleum in countries such as Cameroon, Gabon, and Nigeria found its way into these countries' private sectors. Yet the same private sectors failed to anticipate difficult days, and took little or no action to invest their earnings in the development of industry and technology. The profits that many private firms declared were, at best, a result of government procurement contracts and, at worst, fictitious surpluses that economic adversity and structural adjustment were to bring to light. It is true that the public sector did live beyond its means, but it is equally true that the role of Africa's private sector, even at the best of times, was essentially that of a "trading post" or "commission" agent.

Even if the public sector was an economic failure—and the private sector's claim to economic success is open to question—it has faced difficult challenges. For example, Nigeria's post-war problems of reconstruction (of war-ravaged infrastructures) and rehabilitation (of displaced persons) would have proved insurmountable but for the timely response of the public sector. Yet the public sector has also experienced institutional decline, the subject of the next section.

African Public Services: The Phase of Institutional Decline

As long as access to external resources remained open, the inherent weakness of the public (and, if one may add, private) sector could be concealed. However, the oil crises of 1973 and 1979 signalled changes in the global economy and spelled trouble for the less developed economies of Africa. The international economic recession of the 1980s brought in its wake a drastic fall in the demand for Africa's major export commodities and, consequently, in commodity prices. Rapid deterioration of Africa's terms of trade followed. In such circumstances, unabated increases in government spending could only be financed through external and domestic borrowing. In fact, it was this method of financing government deficits that set the stage for widening external deficits, increasing debt-service ratios, hyperinflation, the "crowding out" of private investment, and the overvaluation of currencies.

Advocates of structural adjustment reforms—notably the International Monetary Fund (IMF) and the World Bank—have remained largely unimpressed with the performance of Africa's public sector. Critics have noted that instead of the growth the sector was supposed to generate, there was recession. In place of momentum, there was inertia. In contrast to the institutional dynamism of the 1960s and the early 1970s in Africa, the 1980s was characterised by rapid decay of institutions and values. Africa's economic decline in the 1980s and the public sector's culpability for the decline are generally cited as arguments against the expanded role of the state. Indeed, Sub-Saharan Africa's economic performance in the 1980s was the worst of all regions.

The continent's dismal economic performance is matched only by its poor achievements in social and human development. Although Sub-Saharan Africa recorded the highest rate of population growth between 1960 and 1990, its people were generally less educated and more likely (than other people, except those in South Asia) to live below the poverty line.

When viewed at the macrolevel, therefore, the public sector in most African countries has been seen as a parasitic institution. It consumes a huge amount of resources but produces very little in the way of goods and services. A sectoral or microanalytic technique of performance assessment is likely to confirm this negative image.

Ironically, the public sector's inefficiency is most glaring in the elementary area of law-and-order administration—the area in which the colonial bureaucracy acquitted itself creditably. Police protection and the control of crime are among the functions of government that are poorly handled in some African countries—thanks to the increasing incidence of corruption among the police rank-and-file and the general breakdown in service discipline.

The shortfall in the performance of the traditional regulatory functions is confounded by the inadequate handling of the new ones. Bureaucratic red-tape and other man-made obstacles have impaired the ability of the civil service and regulatory bodies to promote private investment and to serve as engines of growth. The unit costs of goods and services produced by civil service agencies tend to be inflated by overinvoicing (padding of bills), overstaffing, elongated decision chains and the resultant paper chases, as well as by the civil service's institutionalised bias against—or inherent distaste for—cost-consciousness.

The inefficiency of the parastatal sector is legendary. High operating costs, declining revenue, poor capacity utilisation, poor service delivery, growing deficits, and corruption are among the discrepancies that audit reports frequently turn up.

Though the performance of the public sector in Africa is in general well below standard, one should guard against its wholesale condemnation. For every ten badly managed public enterprise, there are probably two or more exceptions. Ethiopian Airlines is an example of a state institution whose effectiveness and profitability have not been undermined by ideology, political interference, or managerial ineptitude. Similarly, the Ethiopian Telecommunications Corporation might not regularly post profits or declare dividends, but it at least provides reliable services to its clients. My efforts in combining the public service training role of the Administrative Staff College of Nigeria with effective management of the institution's resources have also been highlighted by an institution evaluation study.[10]

Institutional Decline: Explanatory Variables

If the conclusion is that Africa's public sector is an ineffective agent of development, what explanations can we find for this state of affairs? Is it that the public sector is by its very nature an inappropriate agent of development, or are there certain unique factors that render Africa's public sector prodigal and unproductive? To answer these questions, one can only discuss the related issues of *size* and *reach* of government.

The way out of the present dilemma is to find an optimum role for the public sector. Thus, in response to the argument that government intervention is a hindrance to growth, I counsel a pragmatic approach. "While it is agreed that government intervention in socio-economic life could be carried to a ridiculous extent, nothing is to be achieved by advocating the immediate closure of every government office. Indeed, the level of human happiness might be increased, and the equilibrium of the earth maintained, if government and private individuals do what they are best placed by nature to do."[11] The question then is whether the government in Africa has taken its cues from nature to do what it (government) is capable of doing in the most effective way.

According to a school of thought, bureaucracies in the new states of Asia, Africa, Latin America, and the Middle East cannot be expected to perform as effectively as their counterparts in the technologically developed societies. In fact, long before the advocates of structural adjustment focused on the weaknesses of the public sector, a noted scholar, F. W. Riggs, had pronounced the heavy weight of bureaucratic power as a major obstacle to the modernisation of "prismatic" societies, i.e., societies that are neither wholly agrarian nor industrial.[12] Riggs' conclusion is based on the strategic advantage the bureaucracy has over other social institutions, an advantage that it misuses. The bureaucracy's strength does not lie in its efficiency but in its access to modern technology, its organisational cohesiveness, and its control of vast resources. It alone has a well-articulated ideology (a mix of professionalism, enlightened and not-so-enlightened self-interest), a fairly recognisable command structure, and a body of highly trained officials whose tenure is, at least in law, not subject to changes in political circumstances.

One would have expected the bureaucracy to translate its strategic advantage into an opportunity to serve the people. Instead, it tends to be self-serving. As the sole operator of an alien (mostly Western) institution, it turns even the simplest procedure into a "ritual object" that its clients must worship. It is this "heavy weight of bureaucratic power," the lack of balance between bureaucratic and nonbureaucratic elements in the emerging societies of Africa, that in Riggs' analysis, opens the door to "ego-centric normlessness" and "administrative prodigality." In simple language, the bureaucracy remains corrupt, unaccountable, and unresponsive because it is more powerful than any other social institution.

A Critique of the "Prismatic" Model

There is no doubt that Riggs' prismatic equation sums up the attributes and problems of public sector management in new states. However, although the model seems to have anticipated Africa's current tribulations, it has proved incapable of explaining the "deviations" of some societies—particularly Asian societies—from the prismatic norm. Certainly, Korea, Singapore, Malaysia, and the other nations of the Pacific Rim are not where they were supposed to be, i.e., with the poor and wretched of the prismatic world. Why is this so, and why is Sub-Saharan Africa not up there with the newly industrialised countries (NICs)?

Riggs over-simplified the problems facing new states when he placed the burden of development on one social institution—the public sector. Important as this sector may be, it alone is incapable of removing the deep-seated cultural and institutional obstacles to socio-economic and political transformation. Indeed, Riggs might as well have been describing the entire African society when he focused on the weaknesses of the public bureaucracy. As I have pointed out elsewhere, the traditional African potentate rarely says "no" to power but evades responsibility at every turn.[13] Therefore, whether it is in government or business, or even NGO, there will always be a shortfall in performance until power is checked by responsibility or accountability.

Institutional and Ethical Constraints

In Africa, the problems of public sector management tend to be confounded by institutional and ethical factors. Thus, in contrast to the private sector in which investment decisions are preceded by project feasibility studies and refined by cost-benefit analyses, public sector management decisions tend to be overwhelmed by political considerations. Zaire's hydropower and transmission line project provides a case study of how politics dethrones economics in the decision-making process. The project was constructed at a cost of almost $3 billion in 1990 prices—approximately one-third of the country's external debt. This project has operated at 30 percent of its capacity, and although it was commissioned as recently as 1982, it had to undergo an extensive rehabilitation in 1990.[14]

In other African countries, machinery and equipment imported at high cost are left in open spaces to rust or be vandalised. Expensive infrastructural facilities (such as Nigeria's Trade Fair Complex) are commissioned and then discarded. Cases of "abandoned" (but funded) projects are legion. Huge sums of money are budgeted for the procurement of arms and ammunition even though school laboratories are not equipped and teachers' salaries are not paid on time—if at all.

The attitude of the political leadership is critical both to the quality of investment and allocative decisions and to the capacity and resilience of public service institutions. The merit system, for instance, needs to be restored, particularly in light of the damage wrought by the politicisation of senior-level appointments and by the nepotistic tendencies in public personnel management in general. Career officials are partly to blame for the rapid erosion of merit principles. Some of them have not only succumbed to narrow, ethnic tendencies but have been vague in the definition of organisational objectives and the preparation of individual mission statements. Their negligence is even more unforgivable in the area of personnel records—a fact that is confirmed by the high proportion of "ghost workers" on the public payroll.

Superimposed on the factors of leadership and institutional capacity is that of corruption. Indeed, as one observer notes, corruption is Africa's major obstacle to development: "A leader who vanquishes the corrupt forces in the society is more than half way to the finish line in the economic development race."[15]

Organisational Constraints

Apart from the institutional and ethical factors militating against the effectiveness of the public sector, there is as yet no consensus on the organisational form appropriate to the tasks assigned to the various branches of government. The organisation of ministries and departments, parastatal bodies and decentralised institutions follow the same bureaucratic pattern. As a result, higher premium is placed on hierarchy, seniority, and conformity with established procedures than on creativity, entrepreneurship, and ability to solve problems. Besides, there is still no agreement on the scope and responsibilities of the central government vis-à-vis state-owned business enterprises and agencies of local government.

African Public Services: Perspectives on Institutional Reform and Redynamisation

At least two main strategies have been outlined to meet the challenges of economic recovery and long-term development. The first, structural adjustment, seeks to release the productive forces from the strong grip of the public sector. In plain terms, structural adjustment means not only reducing the size of government but also relieving government of the burden of economic decision making.

The second strategy—structural transformation—proceeds on the basis of the assumption that Africa's development crisis is too deep-rooted to be effectively tackled by occasional shock treatments. According to the proponents of the structural transformation strategy, nothing short of a radical departure from the past could save the continent from economic collapse. It is important to note that in recent years the line separating structural adjustment from structural transformation is becoming increasingly blurred.

The Structural Adjustment Programmes Formula

Structural Adjustment Programmes (SAP) introduced in a number of African countries at the height of the socio-economic crisis were designed to rectify disequilibria in the economy. They are basically short-term measures that are expected to place the countries concerned on a path of self-sustained growth. The main elements of structural adjustment reforms are "privatisation" of public enterprises, reduction in the size of the public sector, reduction of budget deficits, imposition of ceilings on government borrowing from the banking system, removal of price subsidies, elimination of price or rent controls, deregulation and liberalisation of the economy, introduction of production incentives, and devaluation of currency.

The stringent measures introduced as part of SAP may be explained as a desperate last-ditch effort to reform the African public service. After all, the time and resources invested in administrative reform did not bring about substantial improvement in performance. Apart from the sum of US$250 million that the UN, the United States, and the Ford Foundation expended in 1952 alone on the establishment of management training institutes in developing countries, individual African countries between the 1960s and 1970s earmarked considerable amount of resources for the revitalisation of the public service. As noted by Nasir Islam, the comprehensive reform programme initiated in each country "was only partially implemented."[16]

At the early stage of SAP, efforts were made to replace the structural-innovative strategy of the 1960s and 1970s with "a more comprehensive neo-orthodox approach, which assumed deeper causes behind trade and fiscal imbalances."[17] Thus rather than focus on public sector institutions per se, Structural Adjustment Programmes started as an exercise in policy reform. Hence, the early thrusts were towards the encouragement of market-orientation, the dismantling of the expansive state apparatus, and the implementation of fiscal stringency, trade liberalisation, and currency devaluation.

By the 1980s, attention shifted to institutional reform. Under the IMF's standby agreements and Extended Fund Facilities (EFFs) as well as the World Bank-supported Structural Adjustment Loans (SALs), structural adjustment reform took an institutional form. Consequently, in addition to policy reform measures, two types of institutional reform measures were integrated into the implementation of SAP:

- institutional support to specific economic policy measures, (e.g., design of export-incentive systems and procedures for trade liberalisation and introduction of new customs and revenue mobilisation procedures), and
- institutional change warranted by cost-cutting measures (e.g., installation of new personnel information systems and the stream-lining or merger of agencies following retrenchment of staff).

In recent years, issues such as pay, productivity, public service ethics, and the social implications of structural adjustment programmes have started to receive the attention of the advocates of the new reform strategy—particularly, the World Bank.

There is no doubt that any action that is taken to plug resource leaks is justified, particularly at a time when Sub-Saharan Africa is going through a devastating economic crisis. Overstaffing, duplication of effort, and payment for services not rendered are indefensible in a period of boom and are an obscenity in lean times. However, in the attempt to rationalise the system of resource allocation, one must take care not to regard the exercise as a holy war against government intervention in socio-economics. This, in fact, has been the bone of contention between the advocates of structural adjustment and the proponents of structural transformation. The former perceive government intervention as ipso facto bad, but the latter believe that, with the right combination of political and managerial leadership, the innate weaknesses of government may be converted into strengths. In any case, government cannot neglect its responsibility in the socio-economic field. There are signs that the pragmatic position on the role of government, which the Economic Commission for Africa (ECA) and the UN Children's Fund (UNICEF) champion, may yet be vindicated. In a recent cover story, the *Economist* (a magazine noted for its consistent support of conservative ideas) took what amounts to a revisionist view of the Reagan and Thatcher 1980s: Governments (in the 1980s) railed against public spending of most sorts—and, by and large, rightly so. But they sometimes failed to distin-guish between useful spending programmes and wasteful ones, and then went to shrink the former and boost the latter. The inter-connected parts of a country's economic infrastructure—roads, railways, airports and so on—are especially easy to starve of resources, because the costs of neglect mount slowly. But the price, in the end, can be great.[18]

SAP and Human Development

In any case, it is not only in the infrastructural area where the costs of neglect "mount slowly." The new categories of disadvantaged persons (whose conditions were exacerbated by the budget-balancing imperatives of structural adjustment) are a slowly ticking time bomb that only a comprehensive programme of social rehabilitation or poverty alleviation can defuse.

To appreciate the magnitude of Africa's social and human development problem, it may be recalled that per capita income in Sub-Saharan Africa is among the lowest in the world. Although social welfare services (housing, education, health, water supply, and electricity) are concentrated in urban areas, only a few individuals have full, uninterrupted access to them. The bulk of the people live in slums, with large families crowded into a room. Electricity and water supply cannot be taken for granted, and access to proper medical treatment is hampered by the shortage of drugs, diagnostic and recuperative facilities, and medical staff. It is thus not surprising that well over 70 percent of the population in Sub-Saharan Africa are reported to be living below the poverty line.

Apart from the groups that are traditionally acknowledged as underprivileged (peasants, low-income urban dwellers, and women), new categories of disadvantages have emerged. These comprise men, women, and children who are victims of one, or a combination of three, calamities—the deepening socio-economic crises, ethnic conflicts and civil wars, and droughts and desert encroachments.

The victims of the economic crises are the persons who lost their jobs as a result of the retrenchments in both the public and private sectors and the teeming hordes of school dropouts and university graduates who cannot be absorbed by the contracting labour market. In a number of countries in Sub-Saharan Africa, programmes have been designed to train or retrain these people for self-employment.

But if the entrepreneurial development programmes make an effort to address some of the problems facing able-bodied but unemployed personnel, governments in the region appear to be totally silent on the action necessary to improve the lot of the weakest and most disadvantaged groups in society. The "refugees," the "disabled," the "poor and destitute," the "child vagrants" and the "street beggars" as they are variably referred to, do not seem to feature on any clearly articulated social development programme. The train of equal opportunities was delayed long enough for the politically active and significant groups (the urban elites and the well-organised feminist groups) to get on board. Yet those left behind (the physically handicapped and the politically weak) are not as insignificant as the authors of the contemporary policy agenda think. There will be no opportunity—equal or unequal—for anyone if the economy fails to grow. And the economy is not likely to grow if the productive elements hold back on wealth creation for fear of being drowned in a treacherous sea of deprivation and social discontent. Fortunately, the advocates of structural adjustment reforms (particularly the World Bank) have started to acknowledge the need for poverty-alleviation programmes and have tempered the harshness of their reform strategies.

Structural Transformation

The main feature of this reform strategy is its pragmatic approach to the question of role and size of government. W. N. Wamalwa, for instance, begins with a positive assessment of the impact of structural adjustment, but concludes that the public sector still had a vital role to play in the development process.[19] He notes that by taking officials from their bureaucratic fortresses to the marketplace, structural adjustment had promoted cost-consciousness at all levels. The abolition of the system of price control and import licensing also eliminated bottlenecks in commercial transactions. Nonetheless, Wamalwa counsels against measures likely to impair the institutional capacity of the public sector. He argues that "in any case, Africa cannot afford a drained and wobbly public sector, especially, since the private sector . . . is itself far from being an epitome of managerial vitality and efficiency."[20] The pragmatic approach advocated under the structural transformation strategy entails the following measures:

- the restructuring, re-staffing, and reorganisation of policy-making units and the establishment of "open" (homeostatic) policy planning systems;
- the reinvigoration of subsystems in both the public and private sectors (the civil service, public enterprises, "field" administrative and local government units, the "organised" and the "informal" private sector);
- the development of entrepreneurial capacity in the public and private sectors;

- improvement in economic and financial management (including measures designed to instil budget discipline, promote accountability, and eliminate fraud);
- human resource development, management, and utilisation; and
- the dissemination of information about the goals, strategies, and tactics of collective self-reliance.[21]

Towards Public Sector Reform

Implicit in the preceding analysis is the conclusion that a pragmatic view of the role of the public sector is called for if Africa is to surmount the obstacles to growth and meet the challenge of sustainable development. For some time now, the sector has been held responsible for the continent's economic decline. This is to be expected. The sector's immodest approach to developmental problems—an approach that informed its profligate commitment of resources and its undiscriminating acceptance of roles—makes it a perfect scapegoat in bad times.

The Burden of Development

The public sector above anything else needs to temper its ambitions and acknowledge that it cannot single-handedly accomplish the project of developing the economies and societies of Africa. The region's development problems are too deep-seated and the equations too complex to be unravelled by a social institution acting alone.

The way forward therefore lies in the public sector developing the capacity to work with the other institutions whose roles are critical to socio-economic development. It ought to consider, at every turn, the "opportunity cost of intervention" in areas where other institutions (e.g., public enterprises, educational and research institutions, the informal sector, NGOs, or local government) excel in performance. The opportunity cost will be very high if, for example, an agency of the civil service decides to manage chemists and supermarkets when its personnel is trained only to collect taxes, settle chieftaincy or land disputes, and construct infrastructural facilities that the private sector needs but is not prepared to finance.

Cumulative Cost of Neglect

The neglect of governmental responsibilities may prove as costly as bureaucratic overzealousness and governmental responsibilities begin precisely at a point where profit calculations stop. Unless compelled by a government edict or a military decree, a typical business entrepreneur will dump toxic wastes in people's backyards and pretend that no harm has been done. Investors will not consider it as their primary obligation to develop the economic infrastructure, house the homeless, and care for the destitute. Yet, failure to act in any of these areas will prove costly to economic or business growth in the short-run, and to political order in the long-run.

Lessons from NICs

In view of the overwhelming evidence against nonaction, the contention that "big government" was Africa's nemesis needs to be critically reexamined. In fact, when compared with its counterparts in the newly industrialised countries, the typical African government is not "big." If one takes South Korea as an example, one realises that a government-led growth strategy is not a bad idea after all, between 1961 and 1979, the government played a decisive role in every sector of the economy.[22]

The tiny city-state of Singapore is another example of successful government intervention. Its economy prospered in the 1960s and 1970s (at the height of the oil crisis). Much of its economic achievement "has been the result of efficient management of its public enterprises which are actively involved in a wide range of operations in the industrial, commercial and services sectors.[23]

In contrast to Sub-Saharan Africa, where state enterprises were privatised because they were a liability to the exchequer, the recent privatisation efforts in Singapore were a reaction to the success and competitiveness of government-owned enterprises.[24]

What factors account for the effectiveness and efficiency of state-enterprises in NICs? The answer to this question probably lies in what made the superior economic performance of the NICs possible: "the coherence of society, its commitment to common ideals, goals and values . . . (among which are) belief in hard work, thrift, filial piety, national pride."[25]

But the Confucian ethic by itself will not facilitate economic growth or promote managerial excellence. Leadership (particularly, its vision of society) is the decisive factor. Thus South Korea's public enterprises operated efficiently "not because of any exceptional features, but because the (then president) Park Government did not tolerate failure."[26]

If, as suggested earlier, leadership is critical to Africa's development, then it is essential for a group to emerge in each society having as its mission the reformation of values. This group or movement is akin to that commended by the *Holy Qur'an* to the human race—the one "that invites to goodness, enjoins equity and forbids evil."[27]

At the macro-, national level, the leadership group's public sector reform agenda should include the rooting out of the main ethical scourges, the redynamisation of policy analysis, the formulation and implementation of institutions, the review of pay and compensation mechanisms, and the improvement of morale and motivation.

Notes

1. United Nations Department of Technical Cooperation for Development (UNDTCD), *Size and Cost of the Civil Service: Reform Programmes in Africa* (New York: UNDTCD, 1991).

2. Ladipo Admolekun, *Public Administration: A Nigerian and Comparative Perspective* (London: Longman, 1983).

3. M. J. Balogun, "State Capitalist and State Capitalism: An Inquiry into the Conditions of Public Enterprises in Africa," in *Public Enterprises Performance and Privatization Debate* (New Delhi: Vikas/African Association for Public Administration and Development [AAPAM], 1987).

4. World Bank, *World Development Report* 1991 (New York: Oxford University Press, 1991), 140.

5. Ibid.

6. David F. Luke, "Professionalism and the Public Service in Sub-Saharan Africa." Paper presented at the Institute of Development Policy and Management (University of Manchester) International Conference on Managing for Professional Effectiveness, Hulme Hall, University of Manchester, 25-28 June 1991.

7. World Bank, *World Development Report* 1991, 130.

8. Luke, "Professionalism and the Public Service."

9. See M. J. Balogun, "The Nature and Effectiveness of Training for Decentralised Administrative Systems in Africa,"*International Journal of Public Sector Management* 1(1), 1988.

10. George U. Imanyi, "Innovation and Implementation in Nigeria's Public Service: Two Cases from the Administrative Staff College of Nigeria," *Quarterly Journal of Administration* 19 (1 and 2), October 1984/January 1985.

11. M. J. Balogun, "The Role of Management Training Institutions in Developing the Capacity for Economic Recovery and Long-Term Growth in Africa," in M. J. Balogun and G. Mutahaba (eds.), *Economic Restructuring and African Public Administration* (West Hartford: Kumarian, 1989), 231.

12. F. W. Riggs, *Administration in Developing Countries* (Boston: Houghton Mifflin Co., 1964).

13. M. J. Balogun, "Policy and Management Training in Africa," in G. Mutahaba and M. J. Balogun (eds.), *Enhancing Policy Management Capacity in Africa* (West Hartford: Kumarian, 1992), 137-140.

14. See *World Development Report*, 1991.

15. Adebayo Adedeji, "The 'L' and 'M' Factors in Africa's Development," *African Journal of Public Administration and Management* 1(1), January 1992.

16. Nasir Islam, "Managing the Public Service under Structural Adjustment: Politics and Implementation of Administrative Reform," in *The Changing Role of Government: Management of Social and Economic Activities* (proceedings of a Commonwealth Roundtable held in London, 4-7 June 1991, Commonwealth Secretariat, London, September 1991). See also W. N. Wamalwa and M. J. Balogun's contribution to the *African Journal of Public Administration and Management* 1(1), 1992.

17. Islam, "Managing the Public Service"; see also Ladipo Adamolekun, "Public Sector Management Reform in Sub-Saharan Africa: The World Bank Experience," in Balogun and Mutahaba, *Economic Restructuring and African Public Administration*, 67-87.

18. "The Case for Central Planning," *The Economist*, 12-18 September, 1992.

19. W. N. Wamalwa, "The Impact of Structural Adjustment Programmes on the Performance of Africa's Public Services," in Balogun and Mutahaba, *Economic Restructuring and African Public Administration*

20. Ibid.

21. See Economic Commission for Africa (ECA), "Redynamising Africa's Administrative/Managerial Systems and Institutions for Economic Recovery and Development," ECA/EDI Senior Policy Seminar on Development Management (Addis Ababa, 6-10 July 1987) (Ref. ECA/PAMM/PAM/87/1).

22. Tony Michell, "Administrative Traditions and Economic Decision-Making in South Korea," *IDS Bulletin* 15 (2) 1984.

23. Tan Chwee-huat, "International Diversification: Role of the Public Sector in Singapore," *International Journal of Public Sector Management* 4(2), 1991.

24. Ibid.

25. Lee Kuan Yew (former prime minister) in *The Economist*, 16 November 1991.

26. Michell, "Administrative Traditions and Economic Decision-Making."

27. *Holy Qur'an* III: 104.

3

Reassessing Thirty Years of Public Administrative Reform Efforts

Ladipo Adamolekun

During the transition years of decolonisation and immediately after independence, the term "administrative reform" was used loosely in African countries as a synonym for efforts aimed at achieving the "localisation" of staff of the inherited colonial administrative systems. Localisation was of course part of the post-independence phenomenon of expansion in public employment (discussed in Chapter 2). Localisation was also closely related to the establishment of Institutes of Public Administration (IPAs), Management Development Institutes (MDIs), and National Schools of Administration (*Ecoles nationales d'administration,* ENAs) to provide training—a recognition of the deficit of skills and experience—as public employment increased. Subsequently, three new concerns were added to public sector reform efforts: structural reorganisation, improvement of pay and conditions, and the adoption of improved management systems and procedures. For reasons examined later, all of these initiatives have had limited impact in enhancing public sector performance. The most recent phase of public sector reform has coincided with the widespread adoption of Structural Adjustment Programmes (SAPs) in the late 1980s, with administrative reform closely linked to the imperative of fiscal stabilisation and economic adjustment on one hand and concerns that had emerged about increased efficiency, transparency, accountability, participation, and capacity building on the other.

Throughout the different phases of post-colonial public sector reform efforts, three key institutions received particular attention: civil services, public enterprises or parastatals, and local governments. This chapter presents an overview and assessment of these reform activities vis-à-vis each of the three institutions. The concluding section is devoted to some observations on the overall record of administrative reform and on future directions for reform.

Civil Service Reform

As the core institution of the machinery of government, the civil service occupied centre stage in localisation and training efforts of the decolonisation and early post-independence years. In most African countries, the transition to independence was smooth, and administrative institutions continued to be run on the bureaucratic principles and practices that had been introduced under colonial rule. Indeed, some political science and public administration scholars and analysts were so impressed with the continuity in administrative traditions and practices during the early 1960s that they considered the civil service to be stronger than the more recently established political institutions such as legislatures and parties. In reality, this so-called "imbalance thesis" was incorrect because both political and administrative institutions have remained fundamentally weak in virtually every African country.[1] The weakness of the civil service stems from its rapid expansion in size and scope during the 1960s and 1970s—an expansion that was complicated by patronage and other short-term political objectives. Not only did the new training centres fail to cope with the pace of expansion but the very logic of patronage politics undermined conventional approaches to personnel planning, deployment, and career management, of which training is an important part.

Besides training as the main response to localisation and rapid public employment expansion, the improvement of salaries and wages and other conditions of service was the single issue of civil service improvement that received the most attention from the 1960s through the 1970s and right up to the early 1980s. This is particularly true of the anglophone countries (for example, Kenya, Malawi, Nigeria, Tanzania, and Uganda), where a succession of committees and commissions made recommendations on salary increases. The attention given to salary and related issues underlines the role of the public sector as a channel of surplus from peasant commodity producing economies. Significantly, the recommendations made in some of the commissions' reports on institutional strengthening (notably on the rationalisation of structures, clarification of goals and objectives, and the introduction of improved systems and procedures) were virtually ignored at the implementation stage. The Ndegwa Commission Report in Kenya and the Udoji Commission Report in Nigeria are two widely cited examples. It is generally agreed that if the recommendations on institutional strengthening in both reports had received as much attention as those on salaries, the civil services of these two countries would be in much better shape today.

The economic crisis of the 1980s brought into sharp focus two critical problems of civil service management that had been largely ignored in previous reform efforts: (1) the link between the size and wage bill of the civil service and the recurring problem of budget deficits and (2) the extent to which the weakness of the civil service was a drag on development efforts. The latter manifested itself in the inability of governments to formulate and implement development policies and programmes efficiently and effectively. The main advances in rural development, for example, were made by voluntary organisations. However, the rethinking of the role of states in relation to markets, economies, and societies and the near-universal campaign for democratic governance and political pluralism during the 1980s and early 1990s has radically changed the agenda of civil service reform to emphasise responsiveness, accountability, transparency, and participation. Indeed, the concept of development management articulated in this book attempts to capture these new concerns.

Assessment of Civil Service Reform

If the widespread perception that civil service institutions in most African countries were weaker in the 1980s than they had been in the years immediately after independence is correct, then the reform efforts undertaken during the intervening period would have to be considered as having failed. But what are the issues underlying this dismal conclusion?

In most cases an ad hoc approach was adopted and attention was focused on specific pressing issues such as localisation, training, and salaries. Although training and localisation were linked at the earlier stages, no new rationale for training was subsequently articulated. Training came to be largely perceived either as punishment or reward. Staff and trade union pressure led to salary reviews, and hardly any conscious effort was made to relate pay to the performance of public servants. A variation on this ad hoc theme is the arbitrary civil service "purges" that some military leaders carried out in some countries in the late 1970s and early 1980s, notably in Ghana, Guinea, Liberia, Nigeria, and Uganda. However justified some of these purges were in terms of removing corrupt officials from office, they were not carried out as part of an overall effort at improving public service performance. In sofar as some of these purges were used to settle personal and political scores, they undermined the concept of a career civil service and resulted in a sharp decline in officials' morale.

On the few occasions when civil service reform efforts were reasonably comprehensive in scope (addressing all the main issues that could help improve the performance of the entire system), two crucial ingredients were missing: political will and commitment of the civil service leadership. Short-term political considerations and bureaucratic inertia were the main stumbling blocks. Chapter 2 has touched on the importance of competent and committed leadership in effecting and sustaining reform efforts. With the advantage of hindsight, it can now be asserted that the Udoji Commission Report and the Ndegwa Commission Report failed to make significant impact largely because of the absence of political will and committed leadership. In a different context, it is significant that, on one hand, the same factors have been cited as the main causes of the limited impact of the Fulton Report on the British civil service during the late 1960s.[2] On the other hand, a more determined government such as Margaret Thatcher's, was able to effect far-reaching reforms during the 1980s.

Furthermore, in most African countries, there was no serious attempt to anchor civil service reform in prevailing economic realities. The most revealing evidence of this was the inability of many governments (Benin, Liberia, Nigeria, and Sierra Leone, among others) to pay their civil servants regularly during the 1980s. The cumulative result of public sector expansion and periodic salary reviews that were not anchored in economic realities was a situation in which the state could not afford to pay the salaries due its officials. In some other contexts (e.g. in Ghana, Guinea, Tanzania, and Uganda) economic decline, high rates of inflation, and repeated currency devaluations resulted in situations in which salaries had become seriously eroded by the mid-1980s.

Current reform efforts have taken off where the earlier attempts had stopped. As already mentioned, their distinguishing feature is that they are closely linked to fiscal stabilisation and economic adjustment. Accordingly, such concerns as cost containment, retrenchment, and the reduction of the wage bill are among the priorities. The variety of cost-cutting measures used (removal of ghost workers, voluntary departure programmes, etc.) has produced mixed results. Although expenditures on the civil service wage bill has been stabilised in some countries (e.g., Ghana and Uganda), there has as yet been no real change in others (e.g., Senegal).

With regard to capacity building and the promotion of efficiency, few concrete successes had been recorded at the time of this writing. A promising beginning is the support of the multi-donor African Capacity Building Foundation (ACBF) for the establishment of policy analysis units in some countries, with a view to building capacity for policy formulation, implementation and review. Guinea, Senegal, and Zimbabwe are likely to be among the early beneficiaries of this assistance. Finally, the most recent concern with democratic politics and other issues of governance has yet to be tangibly linked to civil service reform. Indeed, it is hoped that this book and the *Strategic Agenda for Development Management in Africa in the 1990s* will contribute to the conceptualisation of the link as a basis of action.[3]

Public Enterprise Reform

In virtually all African countries, the establishment of public enterprises was a crucial symbol of nationhood. Because the private sector was either limited in its capacity to undertake major commercial ventures or was dominated by foreigners, or both, newly independent governments felt obliged to establish state-owned enterprises. For example, in Guinea, the acrimony between the newly independent government of Sekou Toure and the departing French colonial administration made Toure feel uncomfortable leaving the running of public utilities in the hands of French-owned companies and the government proceeded to nationalise them. In Zambia, it was a case of almost total foreign control of economic activities at independence (notably the copper mining industry) so the government embarked on a nationalisation policy. In some other countries, a mixture of welfarism and socialist philosophies was invoked to justify the establishment of public enterprises. The welfarism argument emphasised the need to generate revenues through public enterprises for financing social welfare, but the socialist argument rested on the putative superiority of public ownership of the means of production, with the experience of the former Soviet Union and Eastern Europe as the model. Tanzania is a good example of a country that followed this path.

In most countries, government leaders invoked some combination of the above justifications for the establishment of public enterprises. Significantly, the debate over the rationale for establishing public enterprises continued to dominate attention in some African countries right up to the mid-1980s, with very little attention paid to their actual performance. For example, in the "Fundamental Objectives and Directive Principles of State Policy" adopted in Nigeria's 1979 Constitution, it was stated that government should control the "commanding heights" of the economy. This became a justification for the establishment of more public enterprises. This policy orientation was reaffirmed in 1986 by the Political Bureau, charged with the task of preparing a blueprint for Nigeria's development in the 1990s. However, within the framework of its adjustment programme, the government eventually abandoned this policy direction and is now committed to privatisation and commercialisation.

Prior to the adoption of SAPs in the mid- to late-1980s, very little attention was paid to the improvement of performance in public enterprises. In a few countries where changes of government or other special factors led to the establishment of commissions of enquiry on the performance of public enterprises (e.g., Ghana and Nigeria), the monumental weaknesses that were exposed (poor management, conflicting objectives, political interference, financial mismanagement, and widespread corruption) were merely documented in reports, with little follow-up actions.

However, evidence from the early 1980s onwards on the contribution of public enterprises to budget deficits gradually led to a concern with their reform as part of stabilisation and adjustment measures adopted in a few countries, such as in Senegal. By the end of the decade, public enterprise reform had become an issue in virtually every African country. Public enterprise reform programmes typically have two main features: (1) reduction in the number of public enterprises through privatisation or divestiture, and (2) rehabilitation and restructuring of public enterprises that remain in governments' hands, with a view to achieving improved performance. It should also be mentioned that the privatisation option was adopted in African countries in line with the worldwide trend of rethinking the role of state intervention in markets and society.

Assessment of Public Enterprise Reform

Serious implementation of public enterprise reforms has lasted less than six years in most African countries. Perhaps the most significant change to date is that there has been a virtual end to the establishment of new public enterprises. Because actual implementation of privatisation is only a few years old, firm conclusions would be premature. However, a recent World Bank study cites Niger and Swaziland among countries that have derived considerable benefits from properly executed privatisation programmes.[4] By contrast, Guinea and Togo have proceeded with privatisation without adequate preparation, resulting in unsatisfactory outcomes. An ongoing review of privatisation in some African countries (including Benin, Ghana, Nigeria, and Senegal) in the Technical Department of the African Region of the World Bank will document both successes and failures.[5]

With regard to the enterprises that remain in the hands of governments, the concern with performance improvement has produced mixed results. To be sure, there is general agreement on the reform measures that should be implemented, including (1) redefinition and improvement of government-enterprise relations; (2) introduction and facilitation of a competitive business environment; (3) managerial autonomy respective of price, investment, and staffing policies; and (4) strengthening management capacity and improvement of management systems and procedures. Implementation, however, has been half-hearted, slow, or both. A good illustration is the experience with the adaptation of the French-inspired "contract plans" (also called performance contracts) in such countries as Nigeria, Senegal, and Uganda. The limited success recorded in these countries contrasts with the impressive results in France, and the major explanatory fact is the half-hearted application of the contracts by both governments and the enterprises. Efforts to improve government-enterprise relations have also faltered partly because of inadequate commitment and partly because of the phenomenon of relative political instability that has accompanied the ongoing democratisation process.

Local Government Reform

Under colonial rule, government institutions at the local level were essentially extensions of central government administrative systems. Although certain service-delivery and regulatory functions were entrusted to them, their primary role was to ensure effective control over local populations. The distinction between "indirect" and "direct" rule in British and French colonies respectively, was only significant in respect to the selection of traditional rulers. Although the British worked with established traditional rulers, the French generally imposed new ones. In both cases, the traditional rulers were obliged to support the local control system.

The idea of local democracy through the establishment of self-governing local governments was progressively introduced during the decolonisation years. This was strongly supported by nationalist leaders who invoked success in local elections as added justification for the granting of national independence. Although local governments were involved in varying degrees in economic and social development programmes of the 1950s, no serious attention was paid to the articulation of a developmental role for these institutions. In all, the emphasis was on *control*, with *local democracy* in second position and *socio-economic development* a distant third.

In the years immediately after independence, local government reform efforts continued to maintain the emphasis on viewing these institutions as instruments of control. Continuity with the colonial past was given a new justification: the imperative of nation building or national integration. The argument invariably invoked was that the newly independent governments had to ensure effective control over the entire territorial area of their respective countries (on this point see Chapter 6). In many cases, the practice of centralised administration was combined with a singleparty system. The organisational structures of both institutions tended to be fused at local district levels, especially in such countries as Ethiopia, Kenya, Tanzania, Zambia, and in the Maghreb countries of Algeria, Libya, Morocco, and Tunisia.

In the local government reform efforts that were launched in the 1980s, varying degrees of importance was attached to the issues of local empowerment and democracy and socio-economic development. Recent experiences in Botswana, Cameroon, Cote d'Ivoire, Kenya, Nigeria, Senegal, Tanzania, and Zambia illustrate the strong hesitations regarding the importance to attach to each orientation.[6] It is correct to argue that, against the background of central government embarrassment over the success of voluntary organisations at the local level, local government reforms of the past six years seek to combine the objectives of local empowerment and socio-economic development, with less emphasis on control. Ghana provides a good illustration of this trend. Here again, this trend is in line with worldwide movement towards democratisation and popular participation.

Assessment of Local Government Reform

The limited utility of local government institutions as instruments of control is now widely acknowledged, and the one-party systems with which this concept of local governance was associated is rapidly disappearing throughout Africa. Yet to emerge, however, is a sustained commitment to the design and implementation of local government reforms that simultaneously seek to promote local democracy and socio-economic development. Four possible exceptions are Botswana, Ghana, Nigeria, and Zimbabwe. Available evidence suggests that the results recorded in each country are mixed, with more tangible achievements in the mobilisation of local resources for development than in the promotion of local democracy.[7] In each case, it is not very clear whether the simultaneous approach is the preferred option or whether there is an implicit sequencing that puts socio-economic development ahead of local democracy. (It is arguable that the reversed order of sequencing would be more promising) An assessment of recent reform efforts in a wider range of countries is premature because implementation is also complicated by the phenomena of economic and political transitions.

Conclusion

The inevitable conclusion from this review of thirty years of reform efforts is that African public sectors have been resistant to change. Aside from inadequate commitment at the political level, reform strategies have been poorly designed. This in turn arises out of insufficient understanding of the issues. As such, implementation has been weak. This weakness has been reinforced by such factors as fragile political systems and recurring crises and lack of resources (both human and financial). Until recently, external actors have been largely disinterested in institutional reform issues. When and where they did get involved, this had very little impact. Resistance to change has been so entrenched that the relative success of the more recent reform efforts have been due to the paradigm shift in development thinking and practice, the harsh realities of a changing global economic order, the end of the Cold War and the breakdown of the post-war international order, and the leverage of "conditionalities" attached to stabilisation and adjustment programmes.

For current efforts to be sustained, it must be recognised that administrative reform is a continuous process. Management systems and organisational designs must continually be adapted to changing circumstances. Change always encounters resistance because of vested interests that want to maintain the status quo. For this reason, effective leadership at the highest level of government is required. It follows from this that the institutional base of administrative reform should be located in such a place as the office of the president or head of government. Such a base should also be wellresourced in terms of experience, expertise, and capacity. The analytical assumptions underlying intervention must not only take the micro-dynamics of organisational change into account but also key elements of political economy. Specifically, public sector reform programmes in the 1990s should emphasise the link between achieving efficiency and effectiveness to the promotion of good governance, focusing on the issues of accountability, rule of law, participation, openness, and transparency. In its analyses of these elements and in its emphasis on an inclusive concept of development management, it is to be hoped that this book will make a significant contribution to the understanding of the main issues in public sector reform in contemporary Africa.

Notes

1. On this point see Ladipo Adamolekun, *Politics and Administration in Nigeria* (London: Hutchinson, 1986), 169.

2. See, for example, P. Kellner and Lord Crowther-Hunt, *The Civil Servants: An Inquiry into Britain's Ruling Class* (London: Frank Cass, 1980).

3. See also, Mamadou Dia, "Improving Civil Service Efficiency in Sub-Saharan Africa" (Washington, DC: Capacity Building and Implementation Division, Africa Technical Department, World Bank, April 1993, processed paper).

4. World Bank, *Privatization: The Lessons of Experience* (Washington, DC: World Bank, 1992).

5. The study is based in the Capacity Building and Implementation Division of the department.

6. See Ladipo Adamolekun et al. (eds.), *Decentralisation Policies and Socio-Economic Development in Sub-Saharan Africa* (Washington, DC: World Bank, 1990).

7. Ibid.

Part Two

Challenges of Revitalisation

4

The Challenge of Productivity Improvement

Dele Olowu

Civil services generally operate outside the framework of market and profit considerations. Moreover, the far-reaching effects of public policy has sometimes made it difficult to apply narrow measurements of productivity to civil service operations. Nonetheless, widespread dissatisfaction with the efficiency and effectiveness of public sector bureaucracies has emerged as a distinct concern in the rethinking of the role of the state. In Africa, in particular, there is overwhelming evidence to suggest that such misgivings are fully warranted. As Chapters 2 and 3 have established, African civil services in post-independence years have been a drag on the development process and essentially parasitic on peasant producing economies. Yet, in the context of current economic reform and stabilisation initiatives, it is also recognised that the civil service has a crucial role to play in creating an "enabling environment" for improved economic performance. As this awareness gains ground, the question that arises is whether African civil services are up to this task. In particular, can the reform of African civil services to enhance their internal efficiency and effectiveness go hand-in-hand with their role in facilitating and supervising a fundamental improvement in productivity in the wider economy?

It is impossible to answer this question without understanding the nature of the crises facing African civil services. The argument of this chapter therefore is that African civil services have not given adequate attention to productivity improvement strategies because of the crises that have engulfed them. The nature of these crises must be understood so that effective strategies can be outlined for reversing the situation. Thus,

I examine the problem of productivity in African civil services and suggest what can be done about it. First, however, what is productivity?

The Concept of Productivity

The term productivity was introduced into the economics and related social science literature in the late nineteenth century by the English economist William Stanley Jevons, by way of his "marginal productivity" theory. The concept has since been analysed from a number of perspectives, and many new insights have emerged. Although there is no agreement over a precise definition of the term, the International Labour Organisation (ILO) is well placed, given its specialised concerns, to provide an authoritative characterisation. According to the ILO, productivity is the "effective and efficient utilisation of all resources, capital, land, materials, energy, information and time, in addition to labour."[1] Whatever perspective is brought to bear on the term, the ILO maintains that "the basic concept is always the relationship between the quality and quantity of goods produce and the quantity of resources used to produced them."[2]

In summary, productivity implies the addition of value to any factor of production and is often equated with the elimination or reduction of waste in the use of resources to produce goods and services. Conventionally, productivity is measured either in terms of efficiency or effectiveness, or both. However, as already noted above, in the non-profit-making setting of civil services, much less attention has been given to issues of quality, quantity, and costs. Moreover, the output of civil services is often difficult to quantify, given the service and process orientation of most functions. But current concerns that civil services must give value for money have led to growing interest in the efficiency and effectiveness of both operational activities and the content of substantive policy in most countries around the world.[3]

Unfortunately, in Africa, little or no attention has been accorded to productivity improvement strategies, even though the region's socio-economic conditions—declining growth, investment, and infrastructure—make these strategies even more compelling. I explain this paradox in terms of the crises in which African civil services are immersed. Nevertheless, part of Africa's managerial challenge is to overcome internal and external obstacles to productivity improvement.

Productivity in African Civil Services: The Record

Productivity in civil services can be analysed from several angles. One approach is to compare the growth in civil service employment with gross domestic product (GDP) over time. The assumption here is that if GDP grows faster than an input factor, such as employment, then productivity is improved. The limitation in making this comparison is that only civil service employment is taken into consideration (more usually, in fact, the data are for overall public sector employment) even though GDP measures overall domestic output. All the same, such a comparison can provide a suggestive—if not a definitive—trend. Comparisons for six African countries show that between 1975 and 1983 the rate of growth in public sector employment outstripped the rate of growth in GDP in the selected countries, except Sudan (see Table 4.1).

Table 4.1
Growth of Public Sector Employment in Selected African Countries, 1975-1983

Country	Public Sector Employment		Annual average growth 1975-83	
	1975	1983	of employment	of GDP
Ghana	75,000	200,000	15.0	1.3
Malawi	31,840	50,000	7.9	4.2
Mali	31,840	46,116	5.6	4.1
Nigeria	716,421*	1,732,519*	15.0	1.2
Sudan	231,621	261,893	2.6	6.3
Senegal	61,836	80,390	3.7	2.6
Zambia	240,000	280,000	3.3	0.2

* Includes both federal and state public sector employment.
Source: D. A. Lindauer et al., *Government Wage Policy in Africa: Some Findings and Policy Issues* (Washington, DC: World Bank, 1986), 20.

Further analyses of these figures confirm certain characteristics of public employment in post-colonial Africa as noted in Chapters 2 and 3. First, on one hand, most of the growth comes at the lower, or junior, cadre levels, where the recruitment process is less stringent and specialised skills are not required. On the other hand, a large number of vacancies remain for skilled staff at middle and senior levels. Indeed, some of the gains of localisation of skilled and professional staff during the 1960s and 1970s have been wiped out by the brain drain to the private sector and overseas. The brain drain in turn has been accelerated by poor practices of personnel management, including wage erosion.

Second, the growth of public employment has not been linked to any discernible expansion in operational and service activities. Hence a large number of these personnel are concentrated in the capital city and important service areas in the field are usually short-staffed.

This view that African civil services have declined in terms of productivity is supported by qualitative assessments by multilateral development institutions such as the World Bank and the Economic Commission for Africa (ECA). These assessments suggest that much could be done to improve the performance of African civil services, not only in terms of the operational modalities of policy formulation and implementation but also in terms of the efficacy of substantive policy. According to the World Bank, "Weak public sector management [in Africa] has resulted in loss-making public enterprises, poor investment choices, costly and unreliable infrastructure, price distortions . . . and inefficient resources allocation. . . . Even more fundamental in many countries is the deteriorating quality of government, epitomised by bureaucratic obstruction, pervasive rent seeking, weak judicial systems, and arbitrary decision-making."[4] According to the ECA, "The overall deterioration of socio-economic conditions was edged on by inefficiencies of public administration and management systems in Africa."[5]

The central question is why have productivity enhancement strategies been neglected in African civil services? It is crucial to understand the contextual factors inhibiting performance in African civil services. Perhaps the single most important issue has been the excessive centralisation of power and authority.[6] This situation has left civil service managers little scope for initiative and has encumbered them with bureaucratic rules that undermine their autonomy. In the same manner, the agencies that ought to ensure that the executive departments perform efficiently and effectively, such as the legislature, the judiciary, or the audit units were either legislated out of existence or effectively enervated.

Additionally, the politics of patronage and associated practices have the effect of undermining the sobriety of public management systems. The result of these problems for African civil services is generally well known:

- widespread political and bureaucratic corruption;
- defective systems of personnel management;
- inconsistency in upholding standards of performance;
- low levels of competence;

- absence of sound financial systems and practices;
- failure to exact accountability among officials;
- low investment in administrative technology;
- ineffective organisation systems;
- pay and compensation policies that fail to reflect market trends or staff performance;
- low morale among officials; and
- attitudes of inertia to public service work.

These contextual problems are real. Nevertheless, to the extent that productivity improvement is essentially an attitude of mind on the part of managers to make a "continual effort to apply new techniques and methods" and to have "faith in human capabilities," these problems represent challenges for Africa's public sector managers.[7] Overcoming internal and external obstacles to productivity improvement should thus be perceived as part of the managerial challenge. Sound management and organisational practices that are required to facilitate the multifaceted dimension of productivity improvement in the civil service include:

- effective personnel policies for recruitment, training, assignment, and promotion of persons on the basis of ability, merit, and performance;
- optimal location, capacity, and layout of offices;
- optimal scheduling of work;
- regular monitoring of operational processes and substantive policy for timely information about possibilities of innovation and new trends;
- upgrading of work skills of personnel through periodic programmes of creative training;
- involving of employees in the identification and solution of work problems through such devices as quality circles and productivity teams; and
- treating of employees as people with an interest in the success of the agency and providing them with opportunities for growth and higher earnings on the basis of their productive performance.[8]

As indicated in Chapter 3, a number of these issues have been addressed in post-colonial administrative reform efforts, but there has been little or no sustained follow-up to ensure that these actions have resulted in improved performance. In fact, as already highlighted, productivity improvement has hardly been an issue of concern in African civil services. Thus the challenge for Africa's civil service managers is thus not only to improve and enhance the competence of their respective agencies but, through these actions, to also provide an enabling environment for other managers outside the civil service.

Towards Improving Productivity
in African Civil Services

As the fulcrum of policy development and implementation, the civil service has a crucial role to play in national economic, fiscal, and financial management. To this extent, the civil service, like the proverbial physician, must not only be in a position to heal itself of its own diseases as and when they appear but must also facilitate the achievement of higher levels of productivity in the wider economy.

However, it should be clear from the foregoing that measures to improve civil service productivity initially requires political will to tackle simultaneously the underlying impediments on the better use of available resources. This, ultimately, is a question of the extent to which political authorities are willing, able, and sufficiently skillful to "insulate" civil service operations from the politics of patronage and associated practices. Dealing with the symptoms and not the underlying causes of poor civil service productivity is unlikely to lead to the desired results. Happily, responses to the current wave of populist clamour in several countries to make processes of governance more transparent, responsive, and accountable indicate that the required political will and skills may emerge in some countries. Dealing with the root causes is the route to take to ensure that the reform of civil services to enhance their internal efficiency and effectiveness go hand-in-hand with their role in facilitating and supervising a fundamental improvement in productivity in the wider economy. To the extent that the "insulation" of the civil service can be achieved, three critical measures are required to improve and sustain higher levels of productivity: better corporate management of the public service, rationalising civil service pay and benefits, and institutionalising a framework for promoting productivity.

Strengthening Corporate Management

There is need to streamline and rationalise civil service management by establishing an authoritative system of decision-making on civil service management issues. This will institutionalise the parameters of management procedures and actions but leave detailed implementation to the operational units. The challenge of productivity improvement lies primarily at the workplace. It is within the context of operational units that innovations leading to better performance can be generated. But there should be a well-established framework not only for the allocation of resources (and for providing accountability on the use of resources) but also for the flow of communications, including, of course, information on innovations. In personnel management, for example a corporate approach can ensure that personnel policies and practices in government are consistent. It can provide a mechanism for coordinating recruitment policies and training requirements for developing appropriate perform-ance appraisal instruments, and for ascertaining their systematic application. But such initiatives as the establishment of productivity teams and quality circles should be left to operational units.

In short, corporate management's concern with maintaining and upholding standards of competence throughout government can contri-bute significantly to the professionalism of the civil service. Higher levels of professionalism in the civil service will generate momentum to raise standards in such areas as financial management and policy analysis and development, as well as in other administrative functions. One way to bring this about is to encourage interaction between public and private sector management.[9]

Rationalising Pay and Benefits

As Adamolekun points out in Chapter 3, more attention has been given to the matter of pay and benefits than to any other issue in post-colonial attempts at administrative reform. Despite all this attention, wage erosion and compression of salary differentials was the main trend in civil service compensation during the 1980s. The variety of fringe benefits provided has also distorted compensation patterns in some countries.[10] Low, declining, non-market-related levels of compensation have been a major factor constraining productivity and efficiency in the public service, especially at a time when high levels of inflation and repeated currency devaluations had the effect of virtually wiping out the value of pay. Needless to say, this produced deleterious consequences, such as attitudes of indifference, laxity at work, moonlighting, indiscipline, lack of care for public property, pilferage, brain drain, and a host of other problems.

A large part of the problem is that pay in most African countries is not related to the market value of labour or to labour productivity. In some countries, this has resulted in inflated wages for the unskilled and semi-skilled cadres and depressed salaries for skilled and professional personnel. High-level staff have also been better placed which helps them to augment their income through corrupt practices. This undermines morale among staff who are not so well placed. As far as possible, civil service pay should be closely related to prevailing market rates. Wherever possible or feasible, civil service pay should also include a performance-related component. Pay and fringe benefits packages should be subjected to regular review, negotiation, and adjustment as conditions change. Those that manage public service employment must not lose sight of the fundamental relationship between pay, motivation, and performance.

Promoting Productivity

As African economies recover, there is need to support and reinforce productivity improvement efforts in the civil service and the wider economy. An institutional framework in the form of a national productivity centre can provide a mechanism for coordinating and monitoring policy measures that have an impact on productivity in the work place. Such a centre can also provide consulting and technical services, including research. The results of such research go a long way in educating public opinion, informing national policies, and influencing workplace practices. Indeed, knowledge is scanty on issues such as how specific African cultural settings influence management and workplace practices and as to what are the optimal organisational structures for intervention at the local level and for rural areas.[11] Beyond improving the knowledge base on management and organisational issues, productivity centres can also help facilitate the adoption, adaptation, and indigenisation of appropriate technologies and equipment. Productivity improvement requires the continual raising of awareness on all of these issues. For these reasons productivity organisations at national and subregional levels need support and strengthening. In the final analysis, it is only by increasing levels of productivity at the workplace in both the public and private sectors that Africans can expect to raise their standard of living on a sustainable basis and assure the transformation of African economies.

Conclusion

For the civil service to be capable of spearheading African economic recovery and transformation, its own productivity must be improved and sustained. To this end, I have advocated such measures as strengthening civil service corporate management, improving pay and compensation to acknowledge and strengthen the link between motivation and performance, and institutionalising a framework for promoting productivity. I have further argued that such reforms must be accompanied by efforts to deal with the underlying causes of low productivity in African civil services. In essence, this requires political will and skill to "insulate" civil service operations and processes from the politics of patronage and associated debilitating activities. As much as this kind of support is desired, productivity improvement is also a workplace challenge. It requires sound management and organisational practices to undertake the multifaceted dimensions of using available resources efficiently and effectively. In the non-profit-making setting of civil services, much less attention has been given to issues of quality, quantity and costs. But justified concerns have arisen over the parasitism of the civil service, it must give value for money. Productivity improvement is central to assuaging these concerns. To this extent, issues of productivity improvement constitute an important part of the new African development management paradigm.

Notes

1. See Joseph Propopenko, *Productivity Management: A Practical Handbook* (Geneva: International Labour Organisation [ILO], 1987), 4. Productivity in the public sector is also discussed extensively in the *World Labour Report*, vol. 4 (Geneva: ILO, 1989).

2. Ibid., 3.

3. Joseph Propopenko, *Improving Public Service Productivity: Problems and Challenges* (Geneva: ILO, 1989).

4. World Bank, *Sub-Saharan African: From Crisis to Sustainable Growth—A Long-Term Perspective Study* (Washington, DC: World Bank, 1989), 3.

5. Economic Commission for Africa (ECA), *Beyond Recovery: ECA Revised Perspectives on African Development—1988-2008* (Addis Ababa: ECA, 1988), 24.

6. See J. S. Wunsch and D. Olowu, *The Failure of the Centralised State: Institutions and Self-Governance* (Boulder, Co: Westview, 1990).

7. Proceedings of the 1985 Rome Conference on European Productivity, quoted in Constantino Rodas, "The Anatomy of a National Productivity Movement," *The Manager* (bi-annual journal of the Ethiopian Management Institute), July 1989, 10.

8. See P. N. Rastogi, *Productivity, Innovation, Management and Development* (London: Sage, 1988), 31.

9. See Milan Kubr and John Wallace, *Successes and Failures in Meeting the Management Challenge: Strategies and Their Implementation* (Washington, DC: World Bank Staff Working Papers No. 585, 1983).

10. See D. A. Lindauer et al., *Government Wage Policy in Africa: Some Findings and Policy Issues* (Washington, DC: World Bank, 1986).

11. Only fairly recently is attention being turned to such issues by researchers. See for example, M. J. Esman and N. T. Uphoff, *Local Organisations: Intermediaries in Rural Development* (Ithaca: Cornell University Press, 1984); Mamadu Dia,

Cultural Dimensions of Institutional Development in Sub-Saharan Africa (Washington, DC: World Bank Discussion Paper, 1991); and Dele Olowu et al., *Local Institutions and National Development in Nigeria* (Ile-Ife: Obafemi Awolowo Press, 1992).

5

Promoting Ethics and Accountability in African Civil Services

Sadig Rasheed

The civil service (taken here to mean ministries, departments and "core" agencies of central government) in African countries faces overwhelming and deep-rooted problems. The details are ably covered in other chapters in this book. To be sure, tracing and establishing cause and effect for the predicament of the civil service in Africa—and similar phenomena elsewhere—as in most endeavours of social science inquiry, is a decidedly complex venture. Nonetheless, many scholars and practitioners have over the past thirty years gone to great lengths to assess and reassess the issues. Indeed, a long list of literature with this focus bears testimony to their efforts.[1] Any diligent survey of this literature cannot fail to observe that, notwithstanding the diversity of theoretical perspectives and approaches, some concepts of a deficit of ethical norms and values as well as weak institutions and practices of accountability are iterative themes in the explanation of both cause and effect of the civil service predicament.

But what, precisely, is involved in promoting civil service ethics and accountability in contemporary Africa? To the extent that there is broad consensus that a deficit of ethical norms and values is a major contributory factor to the inefficiency of the civil services and the ability of the state to manage development, what are the main remedies and how can they be made to be more effective? In addressing these questions, I identify specific policy prescriptions and institutional practices that can be adopted to enhance ethical norms and strengthen accountability in African civil services. First, however, some conceptual clarifications are necessary.

Ethics and Accountability:
Conceptual Clarification

Theoretical and philosophical debate on the meaning of ethics can be eschewed here in favour of a more practical characterisation. Public officials and other individuals whose professions have codified what constitutes appropriate professional practice have no difficulty in understanding the practical meaning and application of the concept. From this perspective, professional ethics can be defined as the values attached to right or wrong, appropriate or inappropriate conduct, within a professional or occupational setting. Accordingly, the International Association of Schools and Institutes of Administration (IASIA) study group on ethics has suggested that a "problem of ethics in the civil service may be said to exist where public servants, individually or collectively, use positions, or give the appearance of doing so, in a way which compromises public confidence and trust because of conflict of loyalties or values or as a result of attempts to achieve some form of private gain at the expense of public welfare or common good."[2] To this extent, professional ethics is fundamentally a matter of value judgments on occupational morality. In civil service occupations, professional ethics are the values underpinning impartiality, objectivity, integrity, efficiency, effectiveness, and discipline of public servants when acting in the public interest in general and when exercising discretionary powers in particular. Hence one writer has suggested that professional ethics constitute part of the nonmaterial resource of society without which material progress becomes well nigh impossible.[3]

This line of reasoning suggests that ethics and accountability complement one another. That is to say, in any occupational group, professional ethics is the basis of accountability. Accountability itself refers to the obligation required of a subordinate to be answerable to the superordinate in carrying out assigned duties and in exercising discretionary powers. Indeed, the basic framework of organisational or institutional structure in most human activities—public or private—depicts a hierarchical chain of accountable relationships. In the civil service, the concept and practice of accountability is expected to make public officials responsible for their actions or inactions. Accountability is supposed to make government transparent, emphasise and enhance governmental responsiveness and legitimacy, and improve policy implementation. In terms of modern democratic theory and practice, the main principle at work here is that the civil service derives its authority from the population as a whole and its responsibilities and duties from the public interest. As such it must be answerable or accountable to the general public through the official—ideally, elected—representatives of the populace. Although the institutionalisation of ethical norms is the basis of accountable relationships, in the current African context in which public servants and their political masters operate, it has to be recognised that the links in this chain of authority-responsibility-accountability relationship are weak or even broken in some places. Poor civil service performance has been one of the consequences. This, in itself, is a commentary on the crisis of governance in contemporary Africa and the subject of a vast literature.[4]

It is a fundamental assumption of this chapter that the crisis of governance should not provide an alibi or constitute an apology for the difficulties faced by African civil services. Moreover, it is a matter of simple empirical observation that the extent and character of the crisis varies from place to place and country to country. But it has to be recognised that there is broad consensus that a deficit of ethical norms and values and weak institutions and practices of accountability are critical factors in the explanation of both cause and effect of the civil service predicament and the negative impact thereof on performance, efficiency, productivity, and on the efforts to bring about recovery and development. Accordingly, the position taken here is that a practical agenda of reform can and should be adumbrated to reduce the destructive impact of this deficit.

If public administrative history teaches any lessons, it is that bold and imaginative reforms in less-than-perfect political systems are the first milestones in the evolution overtime of a professional, efficient, effective, responsive, and flexible civil service. Administrative reforms have a way of generating their own momentum in reaching further milestones. For example, the Northcote-Trevelyan reforms of the British civil service in 1854, widely acknowledged to be the first milestone in the evolution of the professionalism that now characterises Whitehall, were made within a framework of governance that could have hardly been described as democratic. Similarly, the bureaucratic reforms in Japan following the Meiji Restoration in the 1870s provided the basis for the consolidation of a well-trained civil service of good standing and tradition, endowed with a strong sense of duty and an equally strong sense of esprit de corps. It is against the background of such lessons of history that a practical agenda for promoting ethics and accountability in contemporary African civil services can be outlined. Important to stress here is the need for the systematic, comprehensive, and dedicated implementation of this agenda.

This agenda is made up of six key areas of action, as follows:

- fostering and promoting enabling conditions of service to enhance professional and ethical standards;

- advancing and affirming sound policies on recruitment, training, and public personnel management;
- encouraging civil service occupational associations to play a leading role in institutionalising professional values and defending occupational interests;
  promoting a psychology of service in political and public life;
- upholding the integrity and effectiveness of public institutions of accountability; and
- fostering popular participation to sustain norms of accountability.

Fostering and Promoting Enabling Conditions of Service to Enhance Professional and Ethical Standards

It is widely acknowledged that poor working conditions, increasing levels of civil service employment, and unrealistically low salaries are key problems that have undermined the professional standing of African civil services. Indeed, these difficulties have been the focus of a number of interventions by the region's multilateral and bilateral development partners since the early 1980s. In regard to civil service working conditions, in many parts of Africa they were nothing short of dismal by the early 1980s. James Nti, for example, has noted that "shortages of stencils, duplicating paper, functioning typewriters, and photocopiers were rampant in many ministries and departments in a number of African countries. . . . The monitoring and supervision of subordinates in the field, visits to projects, and the performance of extension work have also been frustrated by the immobility of public servants, an immobility resulting either from the lack of serviceable vehicles or the shortage of fuel. In some cases, vehicles are declared unserviceable because of the lack of minor parts such as brake pads or tires!"[5] Poor working conditions were accompanied by significant increases in civil service employment during the post-colonial years. It is sometimes difficult, if not impossible, to be certain of precisely what is included in civil service employment data. Nonetheless, the evidence of a phenomenal increase in civil service employment is persuasive. This is discussed in Chapters 2, 3, and 4 in some detail. A recent United Nations Department of Technical Cooperation for Development (UNDTCD) study of ten African countries concluded on the basis of available data that civil service employment increased throughout the 1970s and early 1980s and only started to decline after 1986, in response mostly to the introduction of structural adjustment programmes. In Cameroon, for instance, civil service employment doubled in the six years between 1970 and 1976. It doubled again by 1984, peaked in 1987, and started to decline thereafter.[6] The

UNDTCD study further suggested that analysis of the structure and composition of the civil service revealed that the growth in its size has been uneven and concentrated in the lower grades made up of unskilled and semi-skilled labour. To this extent, the typical African civil service has been understaffed and overstaffed. It is significantly understaffed in professional and managerial areas and overstaffed in semi-skilled and unskilled areas. But the study also cautioned that it is extremely important to undertake a thorough analysis and diagnosis of the structure, composition, and institutional capacity of the civil service before making prescriptive statements about restructuring and redeployment.

Conditions in African civil services have also been undermined by unrealistic pay and compensation patterns. One of the prominent features of civil service pay in the region is that it has generally trailed private sector pay. In the industrialised countries that belong to the Organisation for Economic Cooperation and Development (OECD), by contrast, average public sector pay has broadly been in line with average private sector pay, in some cases has even been slightly better.[7]

More serious has been the dramatic fall in real wages that has occurred since the beginning of the 1980s in Africa. The International Labour Organisation/Jobs and Skills Programme for Africa (ILO/JASPA) estimates that, on average, real wages declined by 30 percent between 1980 and 1986 and that in several countries the average wage rate has declined by 10 percent or more every year since 1980. The same source concluded that "wage erosion seems to have been more pronounced in the public sector than in private enterprises."[8]

Another ILO survey of civil service pay in Africa has shown that real starting salaries have declined in all 14 countries that were surveyed. In some countries there has been virtual collapse of real wages. Only in one country, Zimbabwe, did starting salary increase in real terms. The study found that "on the average, the lowest starting salary dropped by about one-half between 1975—1985, while that for the highest grade plunged by nearly two thirds. Real wages continued to decline in the second half of the 1980s. By September 1980, the starting salary in the lowest and highest grades in Uganda stood at 70.0 and 22.4 per cent respectively of their purchasing power of 1985. In Sierra Leone, the respective indices were 68.8 and 42.7 at the end of 1989."[9] Other studies also point in the same direction. The UNDTCD study mentioned above found out that lower, middle, and top civil servants in Tanzania lost over 55 percent, 65 percent and 70 percent of their real wages, respectively, between 1982 and 1987; in Ghana real wages for these categories of public servants in 1989 were between 48 percent and 36 percent of their equivalents in 1977.

Wage freezes, inflation, and substantial currency devaluations, which have accompanied the introduction of structural adjustment programmes, have been mainly responsible for this phenomenon. No wonder then that it has not only become difficult to attract and retain the best and brightest but also that even among those who stay in the service, it has become unrealistic to expect reasonable, let alone optimum, job performance. Inevitably, such conditions have, furthermore, provided not only an excuse but virtually an incentive for graft, corruption, and related behaviour.

Against this background, the first step in promoting ethics and accountability in African civil services must be to foster enabling conditions of service, particularly adequate pay levels and economic incentives, that would encourage productivity and efficiency and enhance professional standards. To be sure, several economic and institutional reform initiatives have been introduced to improve performance and enforce ethical behaviour. But the evidence suggests that public sector adjustment policies have not only failed to address the problem, but also have actually worsened it through the enforcement of pay restraints in a context of rapidly declining real earnings. To the extent that adjustment policies have also tackled such problems as elimination of ghost workers from the civil service payroll and streamlining to reduce overstaffing, the total wage bill in many African civil services is being significantly reduced. Some of this saving should be channelled into improving pay and benefits.

Affirming Sound Policies on Recruitment, Training, and Public Personnel Management

It remains a fundamental requirement of civil service professionalism that recruitment should be carried out on the basis of ability, and also that advancement within the service must depend on merit. These are basic considerations that must underlie current efforts at institutional capacity-building in the region. It is recognised that ethnic, gender, and related factors have to be taken into account in recruitment and promotion opportunities. Nonetheless, the calibre of people recruited and the extent to which merit is the determining element in their subsequent prospects of promotion and career development is perhaps the most crucial factor in institutionalising professionalism in the civil service.

In this regard, the Northcote-Trevelyan Reforms in Britain are particularly instructive. It is useful to recall the overall concern of the Northcote-Trevelyan Report: "The government of the country could not be carried on without the aid of an efficient body of permanent officers, occupying a position duly subordinate to that of Ministers who are directly responsible to the Crown and to Parliament, yet possessing sufficient independence, character, ability and experience to be able to advise, assist, and to some extent, influence those who are from time to time set over them."[10] Fostering civil service professionalism through policies on recruitment, training, and public personnel management acts as an important safeguard for ensuring ethical and accountable behaviour. An associated requirement for professionalism in contemporary African civil services is a sound educational system—from primary to tertiary and university levels—to provide the skill levels that are required. In this regard, the rehabilitation and revitalisation of African educational systems is a necessary condition for increasing levels of professionalisation in the civil service and in other occupations as well.[11]

Encouraging Civil Service Professional Associations to Institutionalise Professional Values

Civil service occupational associations—like all combinations of workers—are organisations run by their members to promote their interests. But they can also be used as instruments of transmitting expectations of the public to their members. They further constitute vehicles through which the morale, feelings, and attitudes of public servants can be communicated and maintained. To this extent, "the informal support of public servants staff associations for the formal system helps to sustain professional values and ethics of civil service."[12] To be sure, many African countries have a tradition of effective trade unionism in the public and private sectors, and, indeed, trade unions were prominent in the struggle against colonial rule and, more recently, in articulating populist demands for democratic change. Typically, members of a trade union or staff association present their organisation and occupation as a socially responsible enterprise. Public administration in Africa has been so presented by some of its practitioners, complete with a regionwide association in the form of the African Association for Public Administration and Management (AAPAM) and a Code of Ethics to be imbibed by all practitioners. The AAPAM Code begins with this stirring declaration:

> To none will we deny Service
> To none will we delay Service
> To none will we pervert Service[13]

However, as O. M. Laleye has noted, although the role of professional organisations in promoting high professional and ethical standards cannot be overemphasised, these organisations still have a lot to do in this respect.[14] AAPAM itself has so far limited its efforts to research, training, and advocacy. As such, its most active members have primarily been individuals with an academic interest in African public administration rather than practitioners. The association needs to extend its role to establish or support effective national and branch chapters that are more directly responsive to the day-to-day needs of practitioners. It is only by building such a "grass-roots" base that its Code of Ethics will carry conviction. Moreover, strong and vibrant staff associations at branch levels will not only be more effective in promoting their members' interests in improving working conditions, salaries, and benefits, but—given the divisive tendencies of ethnicity and religion in contemporary Africa—will also help to foster a sense of solidarity and esprit de corps. Ultimately, the basis of civil service professional ethics is a strong sense of shared purpose in the duty to serve the public. In the Meiji Reforms in Japan in the 1870s, as was earlier noted, much emphasis was placed on socialising public servants to inculcate such a sense of duty. Such socialisation must, however, also extend beyond that to encompass the family, the education system, the media, etc., to extol and popularise ethical values.

Promoting a Psychology of Service in Public and Professional Life

It was suggested above that professional ethics are fundamentally a matter of value judgments on occupational morality. Eschewing the finer points of philosophical and theoretical debate on this matter throughout human history, value judgments on appropriate conduct of publicans—politicians and officials—have been quite consistent. That is to say, publicans have been expected to uphold some concept of the public good within the framework of the rule of law. Indeed, the notion of legitimacy in the modern state as a form of political organisation is tied to this expectation. For civil service officials, this expectation has been summed up as follows: "Working within a framework provided by law, being required even in the sphere of informal administrative practice to maintain certain standards of procedural fairness, acknowledging a political control and accountability, being subject to an obligation to use resources as economically as possible yet also efficiently and beneficially, being expected to contribute to policy development as well as to effective policy implementation, having some kind of duty, no matter how hard it is to formulate it, to serve the public."[15] Duty to serve the public requires a psychology or culture of service in national political and public life. Africa's political leaders bear a heavy responsibility to promote such a psychology through their own example and actions. Indeed, one shrewd observer of development problems in the region has put the issue as follows: "In my considered view, the answer to Africa's socio-economic crisis lies in visionary leadership and managerial excellence. Resources are no doubt a major constraint in development. Nonetheless, the capacity to create, manage and optimise the required resources is part of the challenge that faces leadership and management."[16] Senior civil service managers and their political masters must provide a healthy combination of vision, dynamism, common sense, and pragmatism. They must have the stature and ability to earn the respect and confidence of their colleagues, in the lower ranks of the service, in general, and in the people they serve, in particular. One study of four outstanding senior civil service officials in Kenya during the 1970s and early 1980s has demonstrated how such qualities of leadership helped to instill professionalism in their respective civil service organisations. The four men had an extraordinary drive and ability for hard work that was sometimes of legendary proportions. They worked exceedingly long hours and were extremely disciplined. They were careful to place the interests of the ministries and departments they served above their own pursuit of personal gain. They also demonstrated a willingness to take risks in advocating and pursuing policy innovations. In their relationships with their political masters "they were able to mobilise support at critical junctures not by building independent bases of support for themselves or their organisations, but from personal access to and the confidence of the President."[17] In their staffing of their organisations, they sought to maintain the highest professional standards, resorting to the use of non-Kenyans where this was justified. The professional reputations of the four senior public officials contributed significantly to donor confidence in Kenya during the period in question. There are many public officials and politicians with similar qualities in the region today who are effective role models in promoting a psychology of public service. It is the responsibility of political leadership at the highest levels to encourage such attributes of public duty.

Upholding the Integrity of Public
Institutions of Accountability

It was suggested above that professional ethics is the basis of accountability and, as such, ethics and accountability are complementary.

Within the framework of the modern state, accountability is supposed to make government transparent, emphasise and enhance governmental responsiveness and legitimacy, and improve civil service efficiency and policy implementation. Recent international attention on the question of "governance" has focused on these dimensions of public accountability. Indeed, in this volume Rasheed and Demeke, Landell-Mills and Serageld-in, and Hyden discuss some of the issues. According to the characterisation offered by Landell-Mills and Serageldin: "Good govern-ance depends on the extent to which a government is perceived and accepted as legitimate, committed to improving the public welfare and responsive to the needs of its citizens, competent to assure law and order and to deliver public services, able to create an enabling policy environ-ment for productive activities, and equitable in its conduct."[18] Whatever characterisation is adopted, it has become generally understood that accountable governance requires a political commitment to uphold the integrity and effectiveness of public institutions of accountability and the technical efficiency of the national public administrative system. Some African countries have fairly effective systems of accountability, and a number of others are beginning to strengthen public institutions of accountability. But it is clear that much remains to be done, as a recent survey by Olowu of legislature, judiciary, and executive-based institu-tions of accountability in eight African countries in 1991 revealed.[19] A summary of Olowu's findings follow.

Whatever practical limitations attend the principle of popular sovereignty, the legislature is the key institution through which the sovereignty of the people is exercised. Members of the legislature are representatives of the people and are empowered to initiate, debate, and pass bills into law, review and amend the budget prepared by the executive, as well as to exercise oversight over actual expenditures based on reports submitted by the authorities responsible for public auditing. In some countries, they are also required to approve important political appointments, investigate abuse of office, and generally provide opportunities for citizens to participate in the governing process.

Olowu's survey revealed that, with the exception of only three of the sample countries, the legislatures were hardly playing any significant role in any of the functions conventionally performed by legislatures. Of the eight countries in the sample, the worst were Nigeria, Cameroon, and Malawi. But even in the best performing countries (Tanzania and Uganda) the legislatures' roles were circumscribed by one-party constitutions. (See Table 5.1)

Table 5.1
The State of Africa's Legislative Assemblies (Selected Countries) 1991*

	Botswana	Cameroon	Kenya	Malawi	Nigeria	Tanzania	Uganda	Zimbabwe	Scoring
1 Role in law making	1	1	1	1	0	1	1	2	For Qns1 - 6
2 Role in budgetary process	1	0	1	0	0	3	1	3	3=Very High 2=High 1=Modest
3 Role in scrutinising the public account	2	0	2	1	1**	3	1	3	0=Non-Existent
4 Role in confirming top government officials	0	0	0	0	0	0	1	0	
5 Role in investigating corruption and other abuses	1	0	1	0	0	3	3	1	For Qns 7-8 2=Positive
6 Effectiveness of ombudsman	0	0	0	0	1	3	3	1	0=Negative
7 Remuneration of legislatures	2	2	2	2	0***	0	0	2	Max Score = 22
8 Separation of legislature from executive	0	0	0	0	0	2	2	2	
Total score	7	3	7	4	2	15	12	14	
% Score	32	14	32	18	9	68	55	64	

* All information provided is only indicative.

** Even though the scrutiny of public accounts is not carried out by a formal legislature, the military government successfully revived the Public Accounts Committee in 1990.

*** As proposed in the Third Republic Constitution.

Source: Sadig Rasheed and Dele Olowu (eds.), *Ethics and Accountability in African Public Services* (Nairobi: ICIPE Science Press, 1994).

The survey of judicial institutions revealed a similar pattern. Judicial and quasi-judicial institutions are charged with responsibilities of adjudication among institutions, organised groups, and individuals. But African judiciaries, like legislatures, tend to be poorly resourced, circumscribed, or managed as part of the executive branch. This also appears to be the fate of quasi-judicial institutions such as public service commissions. Most of the powers of public service commissions, especially in respect to top administrative appointments, have been severely circumscribed or taken away in almost every African country and have been treated as the prerogative of the head of state or president. Of the eight countries in the sample, only in Botswana did judicial and quasi-judicial institutions seem to enjoy relative institutional authority. See Table 5.2.

Table 5.2

The State of Africa's Judiciary Institutions (Selected Countries), 1991

	Botswana	Cameroon	Kenya	Malawi
1. Independence	3	0	2	2
2. Institutional separation from the executive	2	0	2	2
3. Partial or Limited Jurisdiction	2	0	2	2
4. Efficiency in terms of time used in processing cases	3	1	3	0
Total	10	1	9	6

	Nigeria	Tanzania	Uganda	Zimbabwe	
1. Independence	2	3	3	3	Scoring
2. Institutional separation from the executive	0	2	2	2	Qn 1 3 = Very High 2 = High 1 = Low 0 = Non-Exis-tent
3. Partial or Limited Jurisdiction	2	2	2	2	
4. Efficiency in terms of time used in proces-sing cases	2	1	1	1	Qns 2 & 3 2 = Positive 0 = Negative Qn 4 3 = Very Efficient 2 = Efficient 1 = Just Fair 0 = Inefficient
Total	6	8	8	8	Max Score=10

Source: Sadig Rasheed and Dele Olowu (eds.), *Ethics and Accountability in African Public Services* (Nairobi: ICIPE Science Press, 1994)

Thus, the general trend in most African countries is that the political executive has increased its powers at the expense of other branches of government. To this extent, external controls on the executive have generally been ineffective. The single-party system also had the effect of consolidating the dominant position of the executive branch and limiting the relative autonomy of the civil service as an instrument serving the general interest.

The parlous state of institutions of public accountability in most African countries provide much insight on the plight of the civil service in upholding ethical norms and values. Recent trends in political reform and in civil service capacity-building provide some hopeful signs, but the more sensitive matter of strengthening the institutional capacity of the legislature and judiciary also needs to be addressed. Further, there is a need to rebuild the capacity of such bodies as public service commissions, public complaints' commissions or ombudsman, auditors-general, etc. Voluntary or non-governmental organisations also have a special role to play as "watchdog" bodies. Indeed, the concept of development management advocated in this book assumes that NGOs will increasingly take such initiatives.

Fostering Popular Participation to Sustain the Accountability of Governance

The best safeguards and best practices of promoting ethics and accountability do give way to abuses. Accordingly, the ultimate safeguard of high standards of public ethics and accountability has to fall on the ability of average citizens not only to hold public officials accountable for their actions but also to ensure that public institutions fulfil their functions and responsibilities. In this regard, people's organisations have crucial roles to play as watchdogs and as supporters of the role of other watchdog organisations, such as the media and ombudsman, sensitising the public on blatant abuse of power and office, exposing corrupt and unethical behaviour, and demanding that such acts should be corrected and punished.[20] For these reasons, efforts to support and strengthen NGOs and people's organisations, as advocated in the *African Charter for Popular Participation in Development*, deserve to receive priority.[21] In view of the recent wave of popular demands for democratic reforms that has swept across the region, there is no reason to doubt the growing capacity of civil society in Africa to oppose structures of state domination and to direct political behaviour towards accountability and transparency. The challenge, however, is to channel such populist capacity and energy into institutionalised forms of popular association and participation, such as political parties, pressure groups, and the media.

Conclusion

Lack of accountability, unethical behaviour, and corrupt practices have become entrenched and even institutionalised norms of behaviour in civil services across Africa, to the extent that the issue has become a matter of major concern. The obvious implication of this is that concerted action, such as contained in the practical agenda for reform outlined in the preceding discussion, must be embarked upon and systematically implemented by all concerned. Although elements of this agenda are, to varying degrees of effectiveness, being pursued in several countries, the general trend has been a worsening of the problem. This leads to the conclusion that much remains to be done. Action must be taken on all fronts and must not be restricted to isolated elements of the agenda. Equally important is the conclusion that certain elements of the agenda that deal with central bottlenecks, particularly declining real earnings, require urgent attention. The serious deterioration of economic conditions and the impact of structural adjustment programmes have actually made a mockery of the concept of a "living wage." Public sector adjustment policies cannot continue to ignore the implications of this for efficiency and ethical behaviour.

It must also be recognised that even the best safeguards and practices can give way to abuses and such notorious cases as Watergate or the perennial occurrence of corruption at the highest levels of Japanese government readily illustrate this. For this reason, a crucial safeguard of high standards of public ethics and accountability in Africa has to fall on the ability of average citizens and their organisations and associations not only to hold public officials accountable for their actions but also to ensure that public institutions fulfil their functions and responsibilities properly and effectively.

Notes

1. See for example, Fred Riggs, *Administration in Developing Countries: The Theory of Prismatic Society* (Boston: Houghton Mifflin, 1964); A. L. Adu, *The Civil Service in New African States* (London: Allen & Unwin, 1964); B. B. Schaffer, "Deadlock in Development Administration," in Colin Leys (ed.), *Politics and Change in Developing Countries* (London: Cambridge University Press, 1969); A. H. M. Kirk-Greene, "The New African Administration," *Journal of Modern African*

Studies 10 (1), 1972; A. H. Ryeyemamu and G. Hyden (eds.), *A Decade of Public Administration in Africa* (Nairobi: East African Literature Bureau, 1975); David Hirschmann, "Development or Underdevelopment Administration? A Further Deadlock," *Development and Change* 12, 1981; Goran Hyden, *No Shortcuts to Progress: African Development Management in Perspective* (Berkeley: University of California Press, 1983); David F. Luke, "Trends in Development Administration: The Continuing Challenge to the Efficacy of the Post-Colonial State in the Third World," *Public Administration and Development* 6 (1), 1986; African Association for Public Administration and Management, *African Public Services: Challenges and a Profile for the Future* (New Delhi: Vikas, 1987); Adebayo Adedeji, "The Evolution of the African Public Service," *The Courier*, No. 109, 1988; David Abernathy, "Bureaucratic Growth and Economic Stagnation in Sub-Saharan Africa," in Stephen K. Commins (ed.), *Africa's Development Challenges and the World Bank: Hard Questions, Costly Choices* (Boulder, Colorado: Lynne Reinner, 1988); and M. Jide Balogun and Gelase Mutahaba (eds.), *Economic Restructuring and African Public Administration* (West Hartford, Connecticut: Kumarian, 1990).

2. See Kenneth Kernaghan and O. P. Dwivedi (eds.), *Ethics in the Public Service: Comparative Perspectives* (Brussels: International Association of Schools and Institutes of Administration [IASIA], 1983) 18; see also O. P. Dwivedi and J. G. Jabbra, "Public Service Responsibility and Accountability," in O. P. Dwivedi and J. G. Jabbra (eds.), *Public Service Accountability: A Comparative Perspective* (West Hartford, Connecticut: Kumarian, 1988).

3. See Sadig Rasheed and Dele Olowu (eds.), *Ethics and Accountability in African Public Services*, Nairobi: ICIPE Science Press, 1994), "Introduction."

4. See, for example, Peter Ekeh, "Colonialism and the two Publics," in *Comparative Studies in History and Society* 17 (1), 1975; Patrick Chabal (ed.), *Political Domination in Africa* (Cambridge: Cambridge University Press, 1986); Colin Legum, "The Coming of Africa's Second Independence," *Washington Quarterly* 13 (1), Winter 1990; J. S. Wunsch and Dele Olowu (eds.), *The Failure of the Centralised State: Institutions and Self-Government in Africa* (Boulder, Colorado: Westview, 1990); Carol Lancaster, "Democracy in Africa," *Foreign Policy*, No. 85, 1991-1992; and Stephen Riley, "The Democratic Transition in Africa," *Conflict Studies*, No. 245, 1992.

5. See James Nti, "The Impact of the Economic Crisis on the Effectiveness of Public Service Personnel," in Balogun and Mutahaba (eds.), *Economic Restructuring and African Public Administration*, 124.

6. See J. H. Oyugi, "Size, Cost and Effectiveness of the Civil Service Reform Programme in Africa," in Rasheed and Olowu (eds.), *Ethics and Accountability in African Public Services*; see also David Abernathy, "Bureaucratic Growth and Economic Stagnation in Sub-Saharan Africa," in Commins (ed.), *Africa's Development Challenges*.

7. For further reading see Peter Heller and Alan A. Tait, *Government Employment and Pay: Some International Comparisons* (Washington, DC: International Monetary Fund (IMF) Occasional Paper No. 24 [Revised Edition], 1984, 13; see also Selcuk Ozgediz, *Managing the Public Service in Developing Countries: Issues and Prospects* (Washington, DC: World Bank Staff Working Papers No. 583, 1983), 53;

and Derek Robinson, "Civil Service Remuneration in Africa," *International Labour Review* 129 (3), 1990.

8. International Labour Organisation/Jobs and Skills Programme for Africa (ILO/JASPA) *African Employment Report* 1990 (Addis Ababa: ILO/JASPA, 1991), 35.

9. Ibid., 36-37.

10. The Northcote-Trevelyan Report cited in Ladipo Adamolekun, *Public Administration: A Nigerian and Comparative Perspective* (London: Longman, 1983), 112. For a detailed discussion of public personnel management see the same source.

11. On this point, see Economic Commission for Africa (ECA), *Africa's Human Resources Agenda for the 1990s and Beyond* (Addis Ababa: ECA, 1991); and ECA, *Strengthening the Viability of the African University in the 1990s and Beyond* (Addis Ababa: ECA/Special Action Programme for Administration and Management [SAPAM] 1992).

12. See S. Agere, "Promotion of Good Ethical Standards and Behaviour in Public Services in Africa," in Rasheed and Olowu (eds.), *Ethics and Accountability in African Public Services*.

13. See African Association for Public Administration and Management (AAPAM), *African Public Services*, Appendix 2.

14. See O. M. Layele, "Mechanisms for Enhancing Ethics and Public Accountability in Francophone Africa," in Rasheed and Olowu (eds.), *Ethics and Accountability in African Public Services*.

15. Neville Johnson, cited in Adamolekun, *Public Administration*, 24.

16. Adebayo Adedeji, "'L' and 'M' Factors in the African Development Equation," *African Journal of Public Administration and Management* 1 (1), 1992, 3.

17. See David Leonard, "The Secrets of African Managerial Success," *Institute of Development Studies* (IDS, University of Sussex) *Bulletin* 19 (4), 1988, 39.

18. See Chapter 14.

19. See Dele Olowu, "Organisational and Institutional Mechanisms for Ensuring Accountability in Anglophone Africa: A Review," in Rasheed and Olowu (eds.), *Ethics and Accountability in African Public Services*.

20. These issues are discussed in more detail in Chapter 13.

21. ECA, *African Charter for Popular Participation in Development* (Addis Ababa: ECA, 1990).

6

Decentralisation for Sustainable Development

Peter H. Koehn

Over the course of the past thirty years, many academics, political leaders, military rulers, and public servants have advocated some form of decentralisation as a means of attaining development objectives. Today, most would agree that the results have not met the expectations. The decentralisation "movement" has not escaped the popular scepticism that currently envelopes the performance of the public sector in Africa.[1]

In this chapter I assess the extent to which scepticism is warranted with regard to decentralisation efforts in Africa. The goal of promoting sustainable development is the standard against which decentralisation is evaluated here. The first task is to determine whether genuine decentralisation measures actually have been implemented. The second exercise involves identifying the principal constraints on implementation, along with the results associated with the devolution of authority, in three widely heralded African cases. The focus of attention in terms of outcomes is on enhancing local capacity for sustainable development. In the final section I look toward the future. What changes would overcome the weaknesses that have impaired past decentralisation efforts in Africa and generate a more effective process for the transfer of authority to the community level? What are the implications for the future of development management in Africa?

Working Definitions

It is important to recognise and bear in mind that a tight perspective on decentralisation has been adopted for the purpose of the analysis

71

presented in this chapter. Fundamentally, genuine decentralisation involves the process of transferring power.[2] Whereas standard definitions encompass deconcentration, delegation, and devolution, the treatment presented here is limited to devolution, which has been described as "the most extreme form of decentralisation."[3] This is because this is the one aspect of the decentralisation process that requires the transfer of power from central institutions and actors to constitutionally distinct, community-based institutions and actors. Specifically, I am interested in the extent to which devolution has been practised in Africa and its results. This tight focus enables us to assess the degree and impact of efforts to decentralise authority and responsibility to units of government that are characterised by extensive constituency control over allocative decisions (including rural and urban local governments and village and neighbourhood councils). Thus, I avoid the possible confusion of including references to less substantial forms of decentralisation, which do not alter the essential dynamics of control and decision-making and are known to have failed to bring about fundamental performance improvements.[4] Privatisation also falls outside of this definition; it is treated here as an alternative to governmental decentralisation.

In contrast to the restrictive approach taken above, the working definition of sustainable development utilised here is an expansive one. The concept merges the interrelated goals of (1) expansion of the pool of goods and services available to members of the community and (2) increased equity in distribution, with the notion that both processes must be perpetuated over the long term—although not necessarily indefinitely. The desired outcomes are ecological sustainability, "sustainable livelihood security," and improvement in the quality of life for the poor.[5] The term is invoked most frequently to focus attention on protecting and enhancing the natural-resource base and on minimising environmental degradation resulting from human interventions, but sustainable development, as employed here, also encompasses the ongoing need for community maintenance of equipment, infrastructure, and projects. The realisation of sustainable development is dependent upon revenue mobilisation, empowerment of the poor for participation in decision-making, accountability to constituents, learning and adaptability, sociopolitical reform, and changes in the structure of the global economy.[6]

Three Cases of African Decentralisation

At the height of the independence era in Africa, Frantz Fanon set forth a forceful argument for "decentralisation in the extreme." Most fundamentally, according to Fanon, "the whole people [must] plan and decide even if it takes them twice or three times as long." Fanon believed that "the time taken up by explaining, the time lost in treating the worker as a human being, will be caught up in the execution of the plan. People must know where they are going and why."[7]

Across much of Africa, decentralisation constituted a major policy tool during the terminal colonial period. Through decentralisation, colonial authorities "sought to divert pressures for greater citizen participation in governance to local government and other lower level bodies, thus limiting access to the most senior decision making levels." In the immediate post-independence era, in contrast, "most African governments effectively reduced local autonomy in favour of centralised planning and direction."[8] Since the late 1960s, scholars and practitioners have extolled the virtues of decentralisation or found fault with "over" centralisation in relation to a wide array of development objectives. Dennis Rondinelli has set forth an enduring summary of the potential benefits of decentralisation in terms of local development.[9]

In post-colonial African practice, however, there are few examples of governmental "decentralisation in the extreme." The widely publicised official decentralisation endeavours during the 1970s in Sudan and Kenya, for instance, were not characterised by the devolution of substantial authority and responsibility to units of local government under community control.[10] Devolution is not encountered in most of francophone Africa, although "reforms during the 1980s have widened the responsibilities of local urban councils, loosened central controls, and created a measure of democratically elected government in Dakar and Abidjan."[11] In most cases, therefore, disappointing results relative to development expectations are associated with efforts that have been limited to deconcentration or delegation and have not been based upon a commitment to local control and empowerment.

In light of the focus on the most extreme form of decentralisation adopted for this chapter, those relatively rare attempts on the continent to promote development through devolution merit special scrutiny. I have selected three well-studied cases for review here: Tanzania, Ethiopia, and Nigeria.

Tanzania

Although Rondinelli maintained that "Tanzania's decentralisation policy fell somewhere between deconcentration and delegation," it clearly involved the transfer of substantial authority and responsibility to rural and urban units of local government.[12] The *ujamaa* village programme constituted an indigenous experiment with devolution. Village and ward development committees and local party cells played a central role in Tanzania's bottom-up planning process.

The results in Tanzanian are mixed. Promising steps toward sustained local development were negated by constraints on rural and urban community control and on the empowerment of key constituents at the subregional and subdistrict level, as well as by bureaucratic interference, inadequate resource transfers, and failure to provide vital services and infrastructure prior to relocation exercises. Moreover, whatever progress some villages made in embarking on development projects tended to be lost in the controversy over the increasingly coercive nature of the central government's extensive and unpopular villagisation exercise and as a result of lack of attention to basic principles of repair and maintenance. Nevertheless, local residents have managed to avoid certain central directives and to move in their own preferred directions.

Ethiopia

Ethiopia's post-revolution military leadership inherited a highly centralised political-administrative system.[13] During the initial post-revolution period, the Derg established local peasant associations and neighbourhood urban cooperatives and assigned major development responsibilities to these grassroots institutions and their elected leaders. John Markakis has noted that peasant associations "attained a remarkable degree of self-rule" during the "early and creative phase of the revolution."[14] Urban associations (*kebele*), led by an elected policy committee, assumed responsibility for a broad array of community self-help functions and for resolving local disputes over land and housing. Many Ethiopian peasant families experienced considerably improved living conditions in the first years following the overthrow of the imperial regime. However, the new regime often failed to provide peasant associations with the resources that their members needed to engage in sustainable development activity. Conservation measures imposed from above were neither linked to traditional practices nor integrated into local farming systems. In addition, high-level administrators subverted the Derg's official commitment to decentralisation by failing to delegate, but implementing bureaucratic strategies that concentrated authority, and by insisting on central intervention in local affairs in order to ensure that the devolution of authority would not be "abused." Despite professed support for the principles of self-government and regional autonomy, moreover, the Derg never implemented "a real measure of devolution, political or social, to major constituent communities within the Abyssinian heritage."[15]

Following the brief post-revolution period during which the new regime created grassroots rural and urban councils and expressed commitment to radical decentralisation, the military leadership pursued a consistent strategy of recentralising authority. Mengistu Haile Mariam's consolidation of power in 1977 resulted in an official return to centralising tendencies. The regime established co-opted "higher" institutions that undermined the local policy-making authority of peasant associations and *kebele*. By the early 1980s, "centralism" had become a key slogan both in the media and in official statements. Donald Rothchild concluded that "among the avowedly Marxist states, no regime is more bureaucratically centralist in formal orientation while being less able to control antagonistic elements in its midst than Lt. Col. Mengistu Haile Mariam's regime in Ethiopia."[16] The consequences of recentralisation included substantially diminished legitimacy at the peasant association level, loss of enthusiasm among constituents, and declining agricultural productivity. The central government's emphasis on physical-structure conservation measures and its concentration on complex externally designed schemes in surplus-producing areas also undermined local capacity to arrest environmental degradation and to minimise natural-resource depletion. Finally, as in Tanzania, a top-down villagisation programme (as well as extensive involuntary north-south resettlement) produced negative results from the perspective of sustainable development.

Upon gaining power after defeating Mengistu's forces in 1991, the transitional government of Ethiopia, under the leadership of Meles Zenawi, reversed many of the previous regime's centralising policies. In the *National/Regional Self Governments Establishment Proclamation No. 7 of 1992*, (Article 9, Section 1) the government embarked on a more radical devolution to the regional level of "legislative, executive and judicial powers in respect of *all matters within their geographical areas except* . . . defence, foreign affairs, economic policy, conferring of citizenship, declaration of a state of emergency, deployment of the army . . ., printing of currency, establishing and administering major development establishments, building and administering major communication networks and the like, which are specifically reserved for the central . . . government because of their nature." The transitional government's devolution experiment is unique in that it is deliberately patterned along nationality lines. At the time of this writing, Eritrea was bound for constitution as an independent country. With the exception of the capital, Addis Ababa, the fourteen "national/regional transitional self-governments" specifically parallel the geographical distribution of Ethiopia's population by nationality (Article 1). Moreover, the country's *Transitional Charter* affirms the right of nations, nationalities, and peoples to "determine their own affairs by themselves." These developments are likely to allow the various nationalities to exercise stewardship over their area's natural resources.[17]

Nigeria

Decentralisation in Nigeria can be characterised as a pendulum process. Periods of centralisation have been followed by devolution exercises that, in turn, are undone by recentralising regimes. In light of this chapter's focus on devolution, I concentrate on the immediate post-1976 local government reform period.

The 1976 reforms involved a substantial measure of devolution based on the conventional British local government model. Edicts promulgated by each state established local governments to serve populations of not less than 150,000 and not more than 800,000 constituents, created councils with at least three-fourths elected membership, and devolved to local governments exclusive responsibility for, and authority to enact, by-laws regarding an extensive list of functions. The Nigerian Constitution of 1978 recognised "democratically elected" local government councils as a third tier of governmental organisation and, in the Fourth Schedule, reaffirmed that most functions on the exclusive list must be conferred on them.[18]

By the end of 1979, 95 percent or more of the local governments in the ten northern states that I surveyed reported that they performed only three of the exclusive functions on the extensive list: provision and maintenance of markets and motor vehicle parks and of livestock slaughter houses and slabs, and sanitary inspection. Similar percentages participated in community development, in the provision of primary and adult education, and in the delivery of agricultural and medical services—delegated activities from the state government level.[19] In sum, most local governments in the northern states were involved in certain key local development functions but had not assumed responsibility for others (e.g., regulation of grazing grounds and forest estates, fire protection, housing, and the operation of commercial enterprises). In the southern states, the 1976 devolution exercise also resulted in a marked enhancement in the ability of local governments to execute development projects and to operate certain service functions.[20] It is interesting to note that in a 1980 survey of about 1,400 Gongola State residents from a variety of local government areas, 60 percent of the respondents indicated that the level of government that did something for them was the local level, and three-fourths of those interviewed felt that the local government had been the most responsive to the needs of ordinary citizens.[21]

Despite improvements, however, post-reform local government performance in Nigeria remained far from adequate to meet the vast and rapidly growing needs of rural and urban constituents. In fact, the national political bureau concluded that the contribution of local governments to Nigeria's development process "has been minimal." In addition, there is little evidence of progress toward sustainable local development in Nigeria. Among the most powerful explanations for the continued weaknesses in local government performance during this period are state government constraints and encroachments, lack of an adequate resource base, the absence of constituent participation in planning and decision-making and the attitudes toward community development held by many key local government administrators.[22]

Lessons for Sustainable Decentralisation

The three case studies examined here yield unimpressive results with regard to development in general and sustainable development in particular. What lessons can be learned in terms of building local capacity for sustainable development from the few instances in which devolution has been implemented as an official development strategy on the African continent?

The most compelling finding from these cases is that decentralisation has not been pursued far enough. The rhetoric of devolution has outstripped its practice. Efforts to devolve authority have been seriously constrained or subverted by central authorities, state government actors, and/or rural and urban elites. Within a few years, the promising devolution exercises adopted in Tanzania, Ethiopia, and Nigeria were officially reversed or undone by countervailing measures. In the absence of genuine devolution, conservation efforts fail to attain sustainable results for familiar reasons—including the persistence of external control, emphasis upon a technological solution, unmanageable size, and limiting projects to discontinuous tasks.

In the cases examined, moreover, the central government implemented devolution on a top-down basis without substantial constituent pressure. With the exception of recent developments in Ethiopia, when the impetus for local autonomy and self-help has arisen from below, it has been suppressed, discouraged, or ignored by governments. As a result, the most impressive development achievements have occurred largely or entirely outside of the formal structure of local government in Africa and have received little external support from major aid donors. For instance, the number and value of community self-help projects initiated in Nigeria's Kwara State during the late 1970s and early 1980s far outstripped the combined undertakings of local, state, and national governments. Furthermore, the benefits of governmental decentralisation often have been co-opted by powerful local elites in the absence of broad-based constituent mobilisation.

Conclusion: Towards Sustainable Decentralisation

The poor record of governmental performance in Africa lends ammunition to calls for "privatisation"—used in this sense to mean the transfer of authority to non-governmental institutions. In the context of the management of development projects, privatisation involves NGOs as well as business enterprises. Among the three forms of decentralisation, only devolution offers the potential to compete with privatisation as a strategy suited to promoting sustainable development.

Several changes are needed in past practice if devolution is to encourage sustainable development. First, as advocated by the *African Charter for Popular Participation in Development and Transformation,* governments must reward rather than discourage or ignore any impetus for self-reliance that is initiated from below. Appropriate rewards include inter-governmental budget transfers and the assignment of authority to tap potentially lucrative sources of local revenue that will be applied to sustainable development activities.

Second, devolution ("decentralisation in the extreme") must be implemented at the level that is closest to the people. Attention should be focused on *who participates, who benefits, and who controls.* Indeed, empowering poor villagers and urban dwellers will continue to present the principal challenge for development management in Africa. The process of empowerment includes building people's capacity to analyse alternative approaches and to formulate and implement local development initiatives.

Many of the successes recorded by NGOs are attributable to their fundamental recognition of the central importance of constituent participation in governance, planning, and decision-making, distribution of benefits, and sustaining development projects. Devolution offers the prospect that energised and dedicated public servants will find it in their interest to utilise their knowledge and skills in the service of active and committed local residents who are aware of the need to conserve natural resources and to maintain valuable infrastructure. Peter Oakley has maintained that if rural constituents participate in decisions about the "use of communal resources, e.g., grazing land or forests, then they would be more likely to protect these resources and indeed bring pressure to bear on others to do likewise."[23] Devolution to the village and neighbourhood level is also likely to enhance the willingness of popular NGOs to cooperate with governmental institutions.

Devolution by itself will not resolve the problems faced by the poor nor will it bring about sustainable development. Nevertheless, if decentralisation in the extreme is pursued consistently and with conviction, it remains a viable alternative to privatisation and offers an approach that promises to check the overconcentration of power, emphasise accountability for results as well as resource usage, promote ecological sustainability, uphold community interests, and enhance the ability of the rural and urban poor to articulate and address pressing needs.

Notes

1. See Herbert Werlin, "Linking Decentralisation and Centralisation: A Critique of the New Development Administration," *Public Administration and Development* 12 (2), 1992.

2. See Joel Samoff and Jonathan Jensen, "Decentralisation: Hope and Hype in African Government Reorganisation" (a paper presented at the annual meeting of the African Studies Association [U.S.], Atlanta, 1989).

3. Dennis A. Rondinelli, "Government Decentralisation in Comparative Perspective: Theory and Practice in Developing Countries," *International Review of Administrative Sciences* 47 (2), 1981, 37-39.

4. James S. Wunsch, "Sustaining Third World Infrastructure Investments: Decentralisation and Alternative Strategies," *Public Administration and Development* 11 (1), 1991; and Diana Conyers, "Decentralisation: The Latest Fashion in Development Administration?" *Public Administration and Development* 3 (1), 1983.

5. See Robert Chambers, "Sustainable Rural Livelihoods: A Key Strategy for People, Environment and Development," in C. Conroy and M. Litvinoff (eds.), *The Greening of Aid: Sustainable Livelihoods in Practice* (London: Earthscan, 1988); and Peter Oakley, *Projects with People: The Practice of Participation in Rural Development* (Geneva/International Labour Organisation [ILO], 1991).

6. On these issues see, for example, Dennis A. Rondinelli, "Decentralising Water Supply Services in Developing Countries: Factors Affecting the Success of Community Management," *Public Administration and Development* 11 (5) 1991; Douglas Hellinger et al., "Building Local Capacity for Sustainable Development" (Washington, DC: Development Group for Alternative Policies and Economic Development Programmes, 1983); and W. M. Adams, *Green Development* (London: Routledge, 1990).

7. Frantz Fanon, *Wretched of the Earth* (New York: Grove Press, 1963),193, 118; see also Peter H. Koehn, "Revolution and the Public Service in the Third World," in Ali Farazmand (ed.), *Handbook of Comparative and Development Public Administration* (New York: Marcel Dekker, 1991).

8. See Samoff and Jensen, "Decentralisation: Hope and Hype," 11; and Philip Mawhood, "General Themes: Decentralisation and the Third World in the 1980s," *Planning and Administration* 14 (1), 1987, 13.

9. Dennis A. Rondinelli, "Government Decentralisation," 133, 135-136.

10. Ibid., 134; and Dennis A. Rondinelli, "Decentralisation of Development Administration in East Africa," in G. Shabbir Cheema and Dennis A. Rondinelli (eds.), *Decentralisation and Development: Policy Implementation in Developing Countries* (Beverly Hills: Sage Publications, 1983), 79, 83, 92-93; see also John R. Nellis, "Decentralisation in North Africa: Problems of Policy Implementation," in Cheema and Rondinelli (eds.), *Decentralisation and Development*.

11. See Richard E. Stren, "Urban Services in Africa: Public Management or Privatisation?" in Paul Cook and Colin Kirkpatrick (eds.), *Privatisation in Less Developed Countries* (New York: St. Martin's Press, 1988); Richard Vengroff, "The Transition to Democracy in Senegal and the Role of Decentralisation" (unpublished paper, 1992); and Richard Vengroff and Ben Salem, "Assessing the Impact of Decentralisation on Governance: A Comparative Methodological Approach and Application to Tunisia," *Public Administration and Development* (forthcoming).

12. See Rondinelli, "Decentralisation of Development Administration in East Africa," 86; see also Joel Samoff, "The Bureaucracy and the Bourgeoisie: Decentralisation and Class Structure in Tanzania," *Comparative Studies in Society and History* 21, 1979; Frances Hill, "Administrative Decentralisation for Development, Participation, and Control in Tanzania," *Journal of Modern African Studies* 6, 1979/80; and Richard Stren, "Urban Local Government in Africa," in Richard Stren and Rodney White (eds.), *African Cities in Crisis: Managing Rapid Urban Growth* (Boulder, Colorado: Westview Press, 1991).

13. Asmelash Beyene, "Some Notes on the Evolution of Regional Administration in Ethiopia," *Ethiopian Journal of Development Research* 9 (1), 1987.

14. John Markakis, *National and Class Conflict in the Horn of Africa* (Cambridge: Cambridge University Press, 1987), 266.

15. Basil Davidson, "Thirty Years of Liberation Struggle," *Africa Today* 34, 1987, 11-12.

16. Donald Rothchild, "Hegemony and State Softness: Some Variations in Elite Responses," in Zaki Ergas (ed.), *The African State in Transition* (New York: St Martin's Press, 1987), 130-131.

17. For further reading on Ethiopian, see, for example, Alemneh Dejene, *Environment, Famine, and Politics in Ethiopia: A View from the Village* (Boulder, Colorado: Lynne Reinner, 1990); Peter H. Koehn, "Agricultural Policy and Environmental Destruction in Ethiopia and Nigeria," *Rural African* 25-26, 1986; John M. Cohen and Peter H. Koehn, "Rural and Urban Land Reform in Ethiopia," *African Law Studies* 14, 1977; Adrian P. Wood, "Natural Resource Management and Rural Development in Ethiopia," in Siegfried Pausewang et al. (eds.), *Ethiopia: Options for Rural Development* (London: Zed Books, 1990); and Paul H. Brietzke, *Law, Development, and the Ethiopian Revolution* (Lewisburg: Bucknell University Press, 1982).

18. See A. Y. Aliyu and P. H. Koehn, *Local Autonomy and Inter-Governmental Relations in Nigeria* (Zaria: Institute of Administration, Ahmadu Bello University, 1982).

19. See Peter H. Koehn, "Functional Performance and the Quest for Autonomy Among Post-Reform Local Governments," in Joseph O. Egwurube (ed.), *Public Administration and Local Government: A Book of Selected Readings from a Nigerian and Comparative Perspective* (Zaria: Institute of Administration, Ahmadu Bello University, forthcoming).

20. See John B. Idode, "Nigeria," in Donald C. Rowat (ed.), *International Handbook on Local Government Reorganisation: Contemporary Developments* (Westport, Connecticut: Greenwood Press, 1980), 400.

21. See Umar Toungo Ibraheem, "Political Participation and Development in Gongola State of Nigeria," unpublished Ph.D diss. Northwestern University, 1981.

22. On these issues, see Adebisi Adedayo, "The Implications of Community Leadership for Rural Development Planning in Nigeria," *Community Development Journal* 20 (1), 1985; Richard A. Hay et al., "Community Development in Nigeria: Prevailing Orientations Among Local Government Officials," *Community Development Journal* 25 (2), 1990; and Peter H. Koehn, *Public Policy and Administration in Africa: Lessons from Nigeria* (Boulder, Colorado: Westview Press, 1990).

23. See Peter Oakley, *Projects with People*, 37-39; 41.

7

Toward Effective Financial Resource Mobilisation and Utilisation

Hamadan Benaissa

Government intervention to mobilise domestic resources in the African region have in recent years encountered difficulties in reaching their objectives. Policy in this area has generally had little effect on the overall savings rate in the private sector and reforms of the financial system have been rather slow. In the public sector, resource mobilisation through reforms of the tax system, attempted in the past decade, have met only with varying degrees of success. I review these issues, focusing in particular on three critical aspects of resource mobilisation and utilisation strategies in the region: (1) an appraisal of the post-independence policy environment for financial sector development and review of trends in policy reform, (2) review of current issues in the reform of financial intermediaries, and (3) review of current issues in the reform of taxation policies and systems. The emphasis on reform is in keeping with this book's overall theme of a new development management paradigm: in this instance, the issues involved in fostering partnership between—and capacity in—the private and public sectors for financial resource mobilisation and utilisation.

Policy Environment for Financial Sector Development

The financial system inherited by most African countries at independence could not facilitate the post-independence development objectives of their governments, which were to develop industry and agriculture.

Many African governments, therefore, moved to gain control of the financial system through outright nationalisation or majority ownership in commercial banks. They also established a range of specialised development finance institutions, such as banks for housing and construction and agricultural and industrial development.

More importantly, the established central banks did not function merely as autonomous authorities that fulfilled the function of indirect control of money supply and the role of enforcers of prudential regulation. Not only did they create credit to meet government needs for bank finance but they enforced the channelling of bank credit to preferred sectors and activities, either through quantitative controls or provision of special rediscount facilities. The central banks also maintained interest rates at low, often negative, real levels in an attempt to limit the cost of borrowing by government and preferred sectors. In the discussion of these issues I begin with an appraisal of the post-independence policy environment for financial sector development before I examine the rationale underlying specific trends in policy reform.

The Policy Environment: An Overall Assessment

The policy environment in post-independence African countries can be examined from patterns in the behaviour of savings. Macroeconomic distortions, artificially low interest rates, and underdeveloped financial sectors have combined to depress the volume of savings in most African countries. Domestic savings were largely channelled into physical assets, but very little were held in the form of assets convenient for transactions in domestic financial markets. Some of the funds joined the outflow as capital flight in response to higher interest rates or more stable currency values. Therefore, the growth of financial savings, defined as the change in broad money, (known by the formula M2), did not show sustained increased in relation to the gross domestic product (GDP) in most African countries in the 1970s and 1980s.

The policy of maintaining low interest rates became a significant source of disincentive for financial savings, and it often led to narrow spreads between loan and deposit rates. Banks discriminated against small- and medium-sized enterprises in order to minimise transaction costs and lending risks. Ironically, such discriminatory tendencies were not reduced by qualitative credit controls. Instead, these controls channelled resources for the financing of government deficits or for large firms operating in the preferred, usually heavily protected, industries. The large excess demand for credit, coupled with binding interest rate ceilings, led to a situation in which projects financed by banks were selected on the basis of credit security, not necessarily on rates of return of projects.

The interest rate distortion was frequently complicated by the maintenance of overvalued exchange rates and restrictive exchange controls, which provided no incentives for banks to tap foreign sources of funds for on-lending to domestic financial markets. On the contrary, the risk of exchange rate devaluation and the difficulty of outward transfers of bank profits caused the financial institutions to hedge by limiting local financing to funds collected locally.

Competition and Efficiency

As a result of financing problems at the macro- and micro-levels the drying up of international sources of finance, and pressure from donors and creditors in the form of conditionalities, since the 1980s several African countries have adopted new approaches to the financial aspects of development management. These approaches involve disengagement of governments from direct participation and control of economic activities and more reliance on the private sector and market forces. Governments are therefore limiting themselves to the creation of an enabling environment to facilitate efficient mobilisation and allocation of resources. Attempts to improve the overall performance of African economies have also involved removal of subsidies and protective barriers and, in general, encouragement of open competition among economic agents.

To promote healthy competition, African governments have made the maintenance of stable economic systems an important development objective. Many governments now carefully coordinate implementation of monetary and fiscal policies in order to limit recourse to money creation, which results in adverse impact on inflationary pressures.

Efficient credit allocation is maximised in a financial system that responds to market signals. The promotion of solvency and efficiency in the financial system may not, however, always be mutually consistent. Appropriate intervention by government is a prerequisite for promotion of the delicate balance between solvency and competition in financial systems. Considerations for solvency may favour fewer and larger financial units, but this conflicts with the pressure for competition to improve market efficiency. Competition itself may lead to concentration through the absorption of weak and inefficient financial units by the larger ones. This calls for a balanced approach to policy formulation and to financial market development. In this regard, there is a need for strengthening competition in financial intermediation as a whole, not in the banking system alone.

Government Intervention

Not withstanding the current emphasis on market forces and competition, a case can be made for government intervention that creates a diversified financial system so that risky but socially necessary ventures are funded—for example, small-scale enterprises. This is because the main financial institutions have been hesitant in providing financing in priority areas, such as small businesses and food production, due to high risks. The question is what sort of interventions are required for creating an enabling environment to permit banks to respond to market signals?

The main policy instruments of economic adjustment programmes for the financial sector that are featured in most African countries include deregulation of foreign exchange market and interest rates, adoption of a market-based approach to the allocation of credit, restrictive monetary and credit policies, institutional development and legislative changes, and active use of prudential regulations and capital adequacy requirements.

Many countries of the region have embarked on the arduous task of reforming their financial systems. Progress, in this regard, however, has varied among countries, depending both on economic circumstances and on political expediency. The measures implemented have several thrusts. Apart from their continuation of flexible interest rate policies and regular adjustments of exchange rates that had been resorted to along with the conduct of monetary policy since the mid-1980s, several countries took steps towards diversification of financial instruments and application of indirect methods of monetary control. A few countries also put in place measures designed to reduce arrears on domestic debt servicing and improve domestic debt management. Other strands in the reform effort include the opening of the banking system to increased competition, the restructuring of existing banking institutions and procedures, the creation of new institutions to take over the management of ailing ones, and the adoption of measures to improve bank supervision and regulations.

Financing Fiscal Deficits

Data on central government deficits for a large sample of African countries in recent years indicate that about 50 percent of such deficits have been financed by credit from central banks. The resulting monetary expansion largely contributed to high inflation in many countries. Thus,

part of the reform efforts focuses on reducing the extent of financing by
the central banks. Although success in this direction has been limited,
governments in most countries of the region are increasingly conscious
of the dangers posed to monetary stability by undue reliance on central
bank financing. The federal government of Nigeria, for example, prepared
its 1991 budget with concern to fiscal viability and kept borrowing from
the central bank to the barest minimum. In Ghana, government has
refrained from borrowing from the central bank since 1988.

Interest Rate Policy and Credit Allocation

The growing recognition of the harm that administered interest rates
can cause has recently led many governments in Africa to deregulate
interest rates, especially since the late 1980s. Indeed, many countries,
including Ghana, Kenya, Madagascar, and Nigeria, have recently allowed
interest rates to reflect market conditions and have even begun to reduce
credit controls. Senegal and other countries in the Union Monétaire Ouest
Africaine (UMOA) group have undertaken comprehensive financial sector
reforms anchored on liberalisation. The empirical evidence on the effects
of such reforms indicates that, although the impact on savings was
generally small, the measures succeeded in channelling a larger proportion of savings through the domestic banking system toward productive
investment, including savings that had previously been invested abroad.
The experience of such countries as Gambia and Senegal suggests that
positive real interest rates encourage the transfer of remittances from
abroad. Most African governments have sought to remove obstacles to
implementing a market-based approach to credit control. In Ghana, for
example, part of the preparatory work for implementing the market-
based approach to credit control was the removal of excess liquidity in
the system and the recapitalising of insolvent banks. Although it
maintains credit ceilings, the Bank of Ghana already conducts open
market operations and seeks to control the banking system through its
net domestic assets. Soon the Bank of Ghana will be in a position to allow
market forces to allocate credit while dismantling credit ceilings. Nigeria
is also planning to dismantle credit ceilings in the near future. Nevertheless, many governments are unwilling to eliminate directed credits
entirely, but they are, however, increasing the flow of credit to the
private sector and reducing their own role in credit allocation.

Institutional Restructuring

In most countries of the region, the financial sector is afflicted with the
problem of insolvent banks. Efforts are being made in those countries to

recapitalise the insolvent banks and review the entire financial system, but progress along these lines has been slow. In many countries, banks must comply with prudential regulations and be supervised. Prudential regulation is accomplished through prescriptions on capital adequacy, liquidity, provisioning for non-performing assets, restrictions on banking business, and licensing requirements. Prudential supervision is carried out through off-site surveillance and on-site examination, in accordance with central bank guidelines. The scope of monitoring by the central bank is often quite wide, including the extent of adequacy of a bank's capital, the standards, as well as the level of provisions, for non-performing assets, the quality and performance of management, staff development, standards of bookkeeping, and the effectiveness of internal control arrangements. New institutions are also being created. In Ghana, for example, the government has established the Non-Performing Assets Trust, and the Bank of Ghana has encouraged a consortium of banks and insurance companies to establish a discount house. In Nigeria, the possibility of having a discount house appears great, and efforts are being made to solve the problem of insolvent banks. The Central Bank of Nigeria and the federal government have jointly established the Nigerian Deposit Insurance Corporation as part of the reform efforts, designed, among other reasons, to assist with the problem of bank restructuring and recapitalisation.

An important trend in institutional restructuring has been the growing computerisation of functions in the financial sector in several countries of the region. Data processing, as a result, is being done more speedily and with greater efficiency than was possible in the pre-computerisation era, when most transactions were done manually with desk calculators.

An institutional development worthy of note has been some countries' establishment of foreign currency deposit schemes. Such schemes were designed to induce a greater flow of remittances into the country and to discourage capital flight. However, success in this area depends, among other things, on achieving macroeconomic stability, with positive real rates of interest and realistic exchange rates.

Although most African governments have recognised the advantages of indirect control of credit, their implementation of the scheme seems lacking. Many central banks are unable to introduce such a policy measure because the successful operation of the policy requires the completion of a number of banking reforms: Commitment by government to fiscal responsibility; disciplined control of monetary and credit required for macroeconomic stability; a market-oriented financial system; and working relationships between the central banks and the ministries of finance, which allow the central bank day-to-day operational control without political interference.[1] The governments' commitments must be matched by changes in the operation of the financial markets discussed earlier.

The experience with institutional reforms in African countries provides a number of important lessons. First, stable macroeconomic conditions, cautious financial policies, and a competitive real exchange rate have proven to be essential for sustained structural reforms, particularly in the external and financial sectors. Second, when rigidities and distortions are pervasive, insolated measures in a few sectors are unlikely to yield significant benefits and may actually reinforce distortions in other areas. Third, a careful sequencing of reforms is called, for given the different speeds of adjustment in goods and financial markets and the limited administrative capacity of most countries of the region. Fourth, movement to indirect control of credit should not be undertaken unless preceded by financial sector reforms and other steps that ensure a smooth functioning of markets.

Reforming Financial Intermediaries

The policy reform trends that have been reviewed above and the new approach to development management that recognises the need to strengthen private sector capacity for both mobilisation and utilisation of funds have exposed the fragility and inadequacies of existing financial institutions. Many of these have been adversely affected by economic crises and gradual withdrawal of government intervention. These trends require, therefore, that, in the 1990s, the whole range of African financial institutions should be made efficient, competitive, and solvent. The following discussion of the issues in the reform of commercial banks, development finance institutions, non-bank financial institutions, security markets, and central banks, makes this clear.

Commercial Banks

The current structure of commercial banks makes them essentially urban institutions. With few exceptions, they have failed to develop an appropriate network to serve the bulk of African households and businesses in the rural areas. This is explained by short-run economic factors, but the long-run benefit of helping to improve rural savings habits tends to be ignored. On one hand, where commercial banks have been persuaded to extend their networks into rural areas, they have not been able to achieve the highest efficiency in credit mobilisation or in meeting rural credit needs because of their rigid procedures, high operation costs, red tape, and consequent delays in decision-making. On the other hand, the rural population has not been easily attracted to the banks as lending or savings institutions because of the inability of the banks to adapt their facilities, procedures, initial deposit requirements, instruments, and other services to the character of the rural and small savers, most of whom also lack formal education.

The commercial banks have also failed to meet the credit demands of small and rural borrowers, preferring instead to accumulate large excess reserves.[2] In reflection of the short-term maturity structure of their deposits, the commercial banks have typically maintained preference for liquid assets and short-term loans, which are not suitable for the borrowing requirements of African economies. Although loans may be renewed for some clients, the short-term approach creates uncertainties for clients with long-term projects. The banks have also been risk-averse, causing them to attach much significance to conventional guarantees such as deeds, mortgages, and other marketable assets.

Successful extension of the services of the commercial banks to small-scale enterprises and rural sectors will require the banks' adoption of features that are attractive to clients operating on a small scale. These features, according to empirical evidence, include: (1) convenience of the place of deposit and withdrawal; (2) flexibility of procedure; (3) liquidity and security of deposit; (4) low service charges; (5) personal relationship with the depository or borrower; and (6) professional secrecy.[3] (Some of these issues concerning entrepreneurship are examined in Chapter 11).

Commercial banks have to become more competitive and have to strengthen the management of their portfolios to better serve African economies. Government intervention to create an enabling environment should also involve the promotion of the establishment of rural-based financial intermediaries, postal savings banks, and credit associations, which would compel the commercial banks to behave competitively. Rural-based institutions could undertake joint venture activities with the commercial banks, to their mutual advantage.

There are also compelling reasons for commercial banks to establish specialised departments to compete with development banks. Though the specialised finance institutions have certain advantages in development banking, the potential for commercial banks to engage in development projects should not be underrated. Commercial banks have a greater familiarity with enterprises that maintain accounts with them; they are able to pool risks much more than development banks because of the diversity of their portfolios; and they are in a position to mobilise resources at a lower cost than are development banks. But these reasons also underscore the need for development banks to diversify into commercial banking.

Commercial banks, however, still have to address the core problem associated with financial transactions in developing countries: high transaction and intermediation costs and poor and costly information in economies that have large informal sectors. Given the positive role the informal financial sector plays many of them today recognise that integration through simple formalisation of informal activities may not be appropriate. Other ways to achieve the integration include: (1) infusing into the formal institutions some of the flexibility of informal operations; (2) strengthening the structure and performance of the informal market operations; and (3) developing links between the formal and informal financial sectors. (Again, Chapter 11 on entrepreneurship, examines these issues in more detail).

This line of thinking has been echoed in a recent study by P. Wellons et al. They have recommended the integration of the informal sector into the formal system, to reduce financial dualism through in-depth institutional and operational reforms of the formal system, as well as an interlink between the informal and formal sectors by maximising the positive and minimising the negative aspects of each. The objective is to "reduce the gap between the two sectors by promoting closer links between formal and informal operators on a more systematic scale."[4] The informal sector is seen as "a means of retailing formal financial services to areas, sectors or population groups that are difficult to reach."[5] They further proposed that integration and interlinks should be undertaken not only concurrently but also somewhat sequentially, arguing that links in the short term would bring integration in the long term.

Certain existing rural and informal finance institutions easily lend themselves to the implementation of such measures. One example is the rural bank that has been promoted in Ghana by the Bank of Ghana in partnership with entrepreneurs from smaller towns and villages. The rural banks are structured as independent commercial banks, operating only in towns or villages in which they are located. The staff of the bank are locally recruited and trained; the directors are local people selected for integrity rather than for education; and the management and operating procedures emphasise the cultural characteristics and needs of the community served. Thus not only are the operating costs of the rural bank lower than that of a branch of an urban-type commercial bank but also the rural bank is better adapted to serve the rural sector. Indeed, empirical evidence presented in one study indicates that the rural banks in Ghana tend to serve the rural sector better than do the rural branches of commercial banks that were set up in Nigeria under government directives.[6]

Other informal financial "institutions" that deserve assistance are the savings and credit associations, which pool savings of their members and tie their loans to the deposits. They usually solve the problem of collateral by enrolling only members who have mutual confidence in each other. These institutions can be given added capacity if they are encouraged to develop working relationships with the formal financial institutions. For example, they can be useful in collecting savings, which can be kept in a formal financial institution, earning interest rather than being left idle in the safekeeping of a treasurer. Beyond this, savings and credit institutions can become channels for lending by the formal financial institutions to small enterprises in the rural areas through such schemes as group lending and cooperative finance.[7]

Development Finance Institutions

Development banks and other finance institutions (such as agricultural development corporations, industrial development corporations, or district or area development corporations) are expected to provide adequate financing services for economic growth. However, the record of their performance has been disappointing. First, as promoters of development, these institutions have generally failed to play the expected catalytic role in assisting new entrepreneurs and new enterprises. Second, they have at times misallocated financial resources by lending to the large and entrenched entrepreneurs at interest rates lower than those charged by commercial banks. This was not as much due to lower transaction costs as it was to the funds made available to them at subsidised rates by governments and international donor agencies.

Development banks cannot depend on handouts from donors and governments if they continue to misallocate resources. They should be encouraged to make real commercial judgments and to compete on an equal basis with other financial institutions, without government support and political pressures. Such reorientation of the development finance institutions requires that they be allowed to apply market interest rates in project selection and financing and in attracting savings. These institutions have acquired skills and expertise in project evaluation, appraisal, and supervision, but they should also develop managerial and professional skills similar to those of commercial banks and leasing companies with which they compete.

In terms of their operations, making development banks competitive and viable involves extending the range of their services to include commercial banking activities. More appropriately, however, such extension should begin with consulting and leasing, areas in which their experience, skills, and expertise could be readily applied. Moreover, if they undertake cofinancing and joint ventures with other financial institutions, development finance institutions could apply their expertise while benefiting from the experience of their partners.

Non-Bank Financial Institutions

The question that naturally arises in the consideration of non-bank financial institutions is whether their limited presence does not indeed suggest that they may be less useful in meeting the development challenges of Africa. The relevant issues raised are: (1) improvement in the allocation of resources; (2) improvement in the pricing of financial resources; and (3) "additionality" in the mobilisation of domestic resources.[8] These depend on specific requirements, characteristics, and alternative facilities of each country.

Despite their potential benefits, the leasing companies and venture capital companies may not be suitable for every African country. The most limiting constraint relates to the need for an environment of risk taking. Risk averse individuals will not be attracted to high risk and high expected return investments, whether physical or portfolio in nature, whereas high risk-taking attitudes are societal and cannot be created easily by governments. Besides, venture capital companies require a source of long-term investment resources and an active secondary market, which does not exist in all African countries. For these reasons alone, it appears logical that full-fledged, independent leasing and venture capital companies, on one hand, cannot be developed to help meet some of the development finance needs of Africa in the 1990s. On the other hand, they can be promoted as part of the effort to extend the range of services provided by commercial banks and the development finance institutions.

Security Markets

The development of security markets is a difficult and delicate process. Hence despite their relevance to current development challenges in Africa, only a few countries are making progress towards their development. African governments can assist in creating a suitable environment, such as stable macroeconomic conditions, provision of fiscal incentives, removal of legal obstacles, and establishment of a regulatory and supervisory framework to protect investor rights. Successful establishment of a market for securities requires an active and competitive private enterprise sector. As Chapter 12 indicates, there is a beneficial link between current efforts towards financial market development and privatisation in African countries.

Central Bank

The central bank usually stands at the apex of all financial institutions. In the present conjuncture of reform in African countries, central banks are at the centre of current efforts to liberalise and restructure the financial system. Success in these efforts assumes a parallel reform of the central bank itself. Such reform should remove from the central banks the task of directly financing government deficits and should provide mechanisms through which they can manage liquidity in the economy, without too much involvement in directing the allocation of credit for specific purposes and functions.

Another important consideration is to strengthen the central banks, so that they can meet the development challenges of the decade. Central bank reform should fulfil the overriding need to maintain or, where necessary, restore public confidence. In this regard, a strong, autonomous, and effective central bank should have such characteristics as a clear sense of its primary role and responsibility; a medium-term perspective; a solid professional base; and public understanding.[9]

Reforming Taxation Policies and Systems

Reform of taxation policies is proposed to promote mobilisation and efficient utilisation of domestic resources. The ultimate purpose is to increase the rate of growth and to resolve the problem of poverty and unemployment, which threatens economic and political stability.

The tax revenue component of fiscal policy is expected to support rather than interfere with the private resource mobilisation normally carried out through personal and business savings. The goal of the expenditure component of fiscal policy emphasises the need for efficient utilisation of scarce resources necessary in the various items of public spending, such as building up an efficient body of infrastructure or providing lending facilities for purposes of productive investment in the private sector.

African countries have had a variety of problems in the past decade. Severe droughts or civil disorders have brought about a difficult environment for economic growth in certain countries of the region. Adverse consequences of cyclical slowdown, prolonged recessions, and anaemic recovery in industrial countries have also taken their toll. These factors have created a pattern of weak demand for primary commodities, inducing shortfalls in the region's export earnings. Output growth has continued to fall short of expectations, constraining revenue growth from existing tax structure.

The quest for policy changes in the tax system emanates from the conviction that reforms in its structure would facilitate mobilisation of domestic resources, thereby enabling countries to realise their economic objectives in a manner consistent with equity considerations. As in several industrial and developing countries outside the region, tax reform has increasingly attracted the attention of policy-makers in African governments in recent years. Important changes to existing tax systems have been enacted by the governments of several countries notably Congo, Ghana, Kenya, Uganda, Sierra Leone, and Madagascar. Other countries have proposed major changes in their tax systems or have introduced limited tax measures, pending the adoption of more comprehensive tax reform.

The growing interest in reform reflects concern that the existing system has major weaknesses that need to be removed and distortions that should be rectified. In many cases, such deficiencies as unfairness, complexity, and vulnerability to tax avoidance and evasion are cited.

Raising the tax effort may be an important objective in some African countries. Taking the African region as a whole, the tax effort as measured by the ratio to GDP of tax revenue raised by general government, which includes both central and local government, has reached 23.8 percent in 1987, compared to 19 percent for developing countries as a group. The ratio is ten percentage points lower than the average for industrial countries. This seems to be in line with the direct relationship between per capita income and tax ratio proposed by various authors.

The structure of taxation in Africa, as in other developing regions, remains biased towards indirect taxes, which are, in effect, regressive. Direct taxes, including taxes on income, profits, and capital gains are of the order of 6 percent of GDP, or only half of the share of these taxes in a typical industrial country. The bulk of Africa's tax revenue comes from indirect taxes levied on domestic products and on imports. The tax system of African countries, therefore, remains relatively inelastic. Moreover, tax revenue tends to be vulnerable to exogenous factors associated with changes in the terms of trade and to domestic cyclical fluctuations.

During the period from 1977 to 1987, Africa's tax effort has shown a mildly rising trend of approximately three percentage points, which compared favourably with the trend in industrial countries. Again, this development seems to be in agreement with the supply-side view that the tax base expands more than proportionately to the growth of income. Although theoretical arguments exist in support of a causal relationship between these variables, a more comprehensive explanation goes beyond purely economic links and recognises that historical and social factors play a role.

During the past decade, there have been significant fiscal changes in African countries following the external debt crises early in the decade, when access to foreign sources of finance was restricted, followed by painful structural adjustment. In Africa, as in other developing regions, the brunt of fiscal adjustment was borne by government expenditure, particularly capital expenditure, rather than revenue. Revenue had shown a slight decline around the middle of the decade, but it recovered quickly and rose somewhat towards the end of the decade because of revised tax rates, improved collection practices, and some revival in economic activity. Under the impact of a sharp decline in capital expenditure and steady revenue trends African fiscal deficits dropped from 8 percent of GDP in the period from 1986 to 1988 to 3 percent from 1989 to 1991.

The changes introduced into existing tax systems in African countries vary from limited statutory changes in selected tax rates to far-reaching reforms, which are likely to have a significant impact on the level and structure of taxation. The reform proposals are directed towards issues concerned with elasticity, efficiency, and equity. The long-term strategy for reforming the system is aimed at increasing the ratio of tax revenue to GDP. This is partly met by increasing taxes on products consumed by higher-income groups and partly by closing loopholes and punishing tax evasion.

Tax-induced distortions often lead to efficiency losses, because output responds to changes in relative prices both in the product and the factor markets. Some tax-induced distortions may be deliberate if the activity that is taxed is meant to carry the full social cost. Polluting industries fall under this category. Differential taxation of factors and the variation in tax rates on final goods and services affect the choice of production methods, the combination of factor inputs, and the pattern of consumption. Distortion affecting returns to capital are of particular concern to low-income countries in the region, since any action that discourages saving in a country with shortage of capital disturbs intertemporal resource allocation and stifles growth.

Measures to improve the efficiency of existing tax systems concentrate on removing distortions in production and investment. Investment incentives are offered in some countries to offset the overstatement of income under inflationary conditions. At the same time, a cautionary note is in order, since investment incentives, may err at the other extreme by supporting production technologies that are labour replacing rather than labour absorbing. Put differently, explicit investment incentives, such as selectively applied investment credits and accelerated depreciation, should take the employment situation into account as well as changes in inflation rates and variations in financing patterns.

In Africa, the persistence of inflationary pressures on the domestic economy of several countries throughout the 1980s has compounded other economic problems. Wherever the tax system was left unindexed, taxpayers found themselves subject to rapidly rising tax rates as they moved up the brackets. In some instances, inappropriate treatment of inventories that used historical instead of replacement cost tended to inflate the amount of profit and the related tax liability of firms.

The tax treatment of income earned or cost incurred in the use of borrowed funds has a significant influence on investment behaviour. The practice of defining interest on principal in terms of taxable interest income and deductible interest cost continued to favour consumption over saving. Whenever investment decisions were made, such practices often led to the choice of debt financed short-term outlay instead of equity-financed capital assets of long duration. The need for encouraging the expansion of production capacity using funds raised through capital stock issues and retained earnings should be emphasised.

In several countries, taxation of imported raw materials and capital goods discriminated against domestic manufactures that use these inputs. Introduction of value-added tax (VAT) to replace other indirect taxes, both on domestic manufactures and on imports, may be necessary to eliminate certain production distortions. Ultimately, tax reform efforts should give enough attention to expansion of savings, investment, exports, and production, irrespective of the source of such development.

In countries in which the existing tax system is perceived as being inequitable, reforms can be directed to remove a number of exemptions that currently erode the base of personal income taxation. By way of example, governments may consider introduction of new direct taxation of agricultural income earned by wealthy landowners. In many developing countries, there is still room for raising indirect taxes on luxuries.

The extent of distortion varies directly with changes in tax rates, the size of elasticities of product demand and of factor substitution. Empirical studies in several industrial countries show that the tax-induced sensitivities of labour supply in recent years have been greater than the results of earlier studies, which were considered relatively unimportant. Similarly, the response of saving volume to tax-induced changes in the rate of return net of tax can be considerable.

Tax distortions result in welfare cost, to the extent that it creates excess burden. This cost is measured by the reduction of income resulting from behavioural response to tax, which exceeds the actual transfer of resources to the government. Among the tax reform measures recently implemented or envisaged in Africa, many were conducted on a piecemeal basis, taking into account only selected parts of the tax system. Particular problems were considered sequentially, and at times in isolation, from changes that were likely to arise in other areas. By contrast, a few reforms undertaken in industrial countries, notably the United States, Japan, Canada, and Australia have taken a more comprehensive approach, with base-broadening and rate-cutting as a major theme. Measures have been taken to reduce the amount of exemption allowed and to eliminate deductions in calculating taxable income. A few other countries, among them, the United Kingdom and New Zealand, have given careful thought to more fundamental changes, such as shifting their tax base towards consumption.

A good tax system, as suggested earlier, is expected to be based on the principles of efficiency, simplicity, and equity. If the tax system departs from these principles, a reform is called to correct it. Those making any attempt to redesign the tax system encounter conflicts among multiple objectives. There is a trade-off between efficiency and equity. An efficient tax structure that minimises distortion cannot at the same time provide horizontal and vertical equity. If distributional considerations are deemed important, governments should be required to use a combination of instruments, such as taxes, transfers, and direct expenditure. An equitable tax system usually levies tax not only from consumption but also from savings, hence adversely affecting its supply. In countries in which income tax is a major source of revenue, savings are subject to double taxation. This may lead to savings-consumption distortion. Efforts to eliminate this distortion through a move to a consumption or expenditure tax results in the problem of regressiveness.

A differential consumption tax or a progressive expenditure tax could be proposed to overcome the conflict of objectives. Thus, taxing necessities lightly and luxuries heavily would be the right approach. Yet the principle of simplicity would be violated amidst the administrative complexity of a multiple-rate system of taxation. This shortcoming may be overcome, however, by the introduction of a more uniform and broad-based consumption taxation, preferably a VAT. An increasing number of developing countries have recently adopted some form of a value-added tax.

At the present stage of development, there seems to be limited scope for new types of taxation in many countries of the region, apart perhaps from a gradual move towards a VAT to replace other domestic indirect taxes. Governments should concentrate their efforts on improving revenue collection from existing taxes. If the tax system were simplified, the tax authorities would be able to administer it with relatively little strain.

A few specific measures can go a long way to broaden the tax base. An example is the establishment of action programmes to improve the assessment and collection of income and property tax. Converting specific taxes into value-added rates and widening the coverage may also raise the elasticity of indirect taxes with respect to output growth. Equally important is the need to design the tax system so as to make tax evasion and avoidance difficult.

Conclusion

In this chapter I have been concerned to identify previous and current weaknesses in financial resource mobilisation and utilisation strategies in Africa as a basis of reviewing current reform trends. It is clear from the review that a fundamental shift toward releasing resources for private initiatives and investment is the overall trend. Ongoing efforts at policy reform at the macro level, as well as the reform of financial institutions, taxation policies, and systems, have been designed to enhance allocative efficiency as much as to "crowd in" non-governmental actors. This underscores the concept of development management advanced in this book: Past strategies that have emphasised only one set of actors must be replaced by one that emphasises the role that everybody has and potentially can play and the interdependence of these roles. The business of mobilising savings and revenue, using the instruments of mobilisation as stimuli and incentives to generate certain responses, and channelling mobilised resources to different actors operating at different levels of economy and society, as well as to finance public policy, requires such an encompassing view of the development process. The challenge to financial managers and policy-makers in African governments is to make their policies and actions consistent with this view.

Notes

1. See J. S. Duesenbery and M. F. Mcpherson, "Monetary Management in Sub-Saharan Africa" (paper prepared under the auspices of a United States Agency for International Development [USAID] project, Harvard Institute for International Development, Cambridge, MA, September 1990), 31.

2. It is estimated that per capita bank credit in the private sector amounts to $48 per annum in Sub-Saharan Africa, but 90 percent of economic operators have no access to it. (On this issue, see M. Nowak, "Financing the Traditional Economy in Africa," *The Courier*, No. 117, September-October, 1989).

3. On these issues, see I. P. Akaah et al., "Formal Financial Institutions as Savings Mobilisation Conduits in Rural LDCs: An Empirical Assessment Based

on Bank Savings Behaviour of Ghanaian Farm Households," *Savings and Development*, 11 (2) 1987.

4. See P. Wellons et al. *Banks and Specialised Financial Intermediaries in Development* (Paris: Organisation for Economic Cooperation and Development [OECD], 1986), 214.

5. Ibid.

6. See J. H. Frimpong-Ansah, "Domestic Resource Mobilisation in Africa" (Abidjan: African Development Bank, unpublished consultant's working file, 1987).

7. For details of such schemes, see World Bank, *World Development Report* 1989 (Washington, DC: World Bank/Oxford University Press, 1989).

8. On this issue, see Wellons et al., *Banks and Specialised Financial Intermediaries in Development*.

9. See Richard D. Erb, "The Role of Central Banks," *Finance and Development*, December 1989.

8

Challenges and Opportunities of Information Technology

Herbert Girkes

Management has become unthinkable without the use of information technology. Last minute information from data bases all over the world has crucial impact on decision-making in any setting—the private, public, or voluntary sector. Negotiations are faster and more efficiently executed by using fax machines. Government offices search worldwide data bases by keywords in order to receive vital information for their policies and relations to other countries. Institutions dedicated to regional integration, such as the European Community (EC) now European Union (EU), interconnect the public sectors of their member countries, with the aim of facilitating integrated approaches. Political leaders and administrators have fully embraced the idea of the value of information. Africa has not yet come that far. The reasons for this can be quickly identified. The base of human resources in the field of information technology in Africa has been small. Information-technology personnel employed by government services vanish all too often into the private sector because government wages are not tailored to keep these "technocrats" on board. Some African leaders were not prepared to encourage information flows within their countries, and alternative information sources were generally not available on the continent. The only source of information considered to be useful was statistical data, received mainly from outside the country; textual or graphical information was seldom used in planning.

Some information technology used in developed countries has been prohibitively expensive until fairly recently. The introduction of micro-computer-based technology and the combined efforts of national and international institutions since the early 1980s have changed this dark prospectus for Africa. The establishment of the Pan African Development

Information System (PADIS) in 1980 (then called Pan African Documentation and Information System) within the Economic Commission for Africa (ECA) and the combined efforts of the United Nations Educational, Scientific, and Cultural Organisation (UNESCO), the International Development Research Centre (IDRC) of Canada, the German Foundation of International Development (DSE), and the Commonwealth Secretariat, to name just a few major donors, to implement national information policies in Africa have slightly changed the attitude of public sector institutions towards the value of all kinds of information.

Information technology is now available at a fraction of the cost of ten years ago. Micro-computer-based systems can manage a myriad of information and put it at the ready disposal of public management. Improvements in telecommunications in Africa, though not yet in all countries, allow access to data bases around the world. With small technical investment, satellite pictures can be received to be used for agricultural forecasting. Graphical Information Systems (GIS) allow analysis of drought and desertification problems on the continent. Compact disks with read-only memories (CD-ROMs) allow desktop access to data bases where earlier expensive dedicated lines had to be established in order to use mainframe-based information sources. North African countries have introduced up-to-date data transmission facilities. In the case of PADIS, thirty-nine countries have signed up to enhance the information flow among African countries, at least as far as bibliographical and referral information are concerned.

These efforts are not yet sufficient. One can observe a widening gap between the "information-rich" in the north and the "information-poor" in the south. In particular, Sub-Saharan Africa is still lacking far behind even other developing countries as far as the use of information technology is concerned. Road authorities still keep manual card files on vehicles in some countries; customs departments are using outdated mini-computer technology from the early 1980s to produce otherwise not accessible trade statistics; and regulations and laws are kept in printed format and are not electronically searchable. Even in those countries where micro-computers are in use, they are mainly isolated from each other, without being networked. Countries are using incompatible data formats that are home-bred instead of adopting international standards and this hampers the exchange of data. All too often projects collapse when foreign financing ceases or foreign experts end their services. Replacement policies for equipment are either not established or are lacking resource allocations, which require precious foreign currency.

Africa as a whole, and its public sector management in particular, have to catch up with available and emerging information technology. Personnel has to be trained and equipment has to be installed not only to tackle today's problems but also to plan a better future. The challenges are formidable but the opportunities can generate higher levels of efficiency and effectiveness. In keeping with this book's overall theme of a new development management paradigm encompassing the public, private, and voluntary sectors, I examine the issues constituting both the challenges and the opportunities. The chapter is divided into four parts and begins with a survey of the importance of information technology in public sector management and the significance of enhancing the flow of information between the public and the other sectors. The second part looks beyond the public sector to examine how widely these facilities have been used in African countries. The third part examines some major constraints in the wider use of information technology, and the fourth offers possible solutions.

The Importance of Information Technology in Public Sector Management

Any decision, whether in the private, voluntary, or public sector, has to be based on sound information. This might be raw statistical data, processed data such as the gross domestic product (GDP), information on laws and regulations governing the subject in question, or forecasts based on economic theory. Considering the basic tasks of public sector management, one could identify at least three areas of particular importance for information technology: within government agencies, between government agencies, and in the external relations and activities of government agencies.

Information Technology Within Government Agencies

It is a matter of simple observation that many government agencies in Africa lack efficient procedures that could be greatly improved by the use of appropriate information technology. The following examples illustrate the point.

Messages sometimes take one day or more to reach the addressee in the same town because the messenger has no transportation, or they cannot be delivered because a secretary was absent. This problem could be solved by a simple electronic mail (e-mail) message system. E-mail facilitates the sending and receiving of messages by using a computer. Usually the computer is connected to a direct telephone line, and thus messages can be sent or received at any given time to and from all over the world.

Sometimes data cannot be used because personnel cannot access them; for example, when an employee has locked his or her desk before leaving on a business trip. Data on a simple Local Area Network (LAN), however, would be available at any given time. The LAN is a direct connection of computers by cables. A special operating system allows access to all data stored in other computers connected to the LAN. Very often, one computer has an additional connection to a telephone line, allowing all users in the LAN to send data to other users and to receive data from elsewhere.

Important messages that cannot be sent from Ethiopia to Nigeria, for instance, because the normal telephone lines are busy can be sent by fax within minutes. Perhaps the payroll of the government service cannot be finalised because the huge central government computer has a breakdown and spare parts are not available. In this case a decentralised system, interconnected by modem, could finish the job without delay. Secretaries are typing the same or similar letters over and over again, including the avoidable errors, but a word processing system can free them for other duties.

All these are examples of events happening on a day-to-day basis in government offices all over Africa. The introduction of the information technology systems mentioned above, i.e., e-mail systems, local area networks, micro-computers, and fax machines, could help enormously to improve the internal efficiency of Africa's government agencies when used as intermediate measures to precede the introduction of full-fledged management-information systems such as those used in the developed world. Moreover, these examples of information technology are still within reach in Africa, even considering the meagre base of specialists in information technology.

Information Technology Between Government Agencies

What has been said about the internal working of government offices is equally true for the relations between offices of different government agencies. Flow of information could be enhanced by the use of e-mail systems connected by normal telephone lines and accessibility of data throughout the public sector could be guaranteed by local area networks. The enormous amount of time that is spent on meetings, sometimes just for the sake of exchanging information, can be reduced by teleconferencing using micro-computers or a LAN system.

Modern information technology can also be used between government agencies to coordinate the exercise of development planning. Planners in such different sectors as agriculture or urban development sometimes formulate their respective plans independently. Optimally, both officers should have each other's data in order to avoid duplication of efforts. The reality shows that the consolidation process starts only at a very late stage, thus perhaps forcing a rethinking of concepts or strategies after a lot of work based on wrong or inadequate data has been done. Access to data of different agencies and exchange of information at an early stage of the planning process could avoid such a situation. The proper use of information technology could help significantly.

It is understood that the state of the infrastructure in African countries seldom meets the high standards needed to allow for the smooth operation of an electronically based system: For example, internal telephone lines are sometimes worse than international telephone lines, thus limiting the usefulness of electronic interconnection. But modern micro-computer technology could help even here: The exchange of large data sets by using tape-streamers or CD-ROMs would allow access to all existing data in government agencies. It would free government from the necessity of creating huge centralised computer centres, which often become a burden in terms of costly maintenance. The consumption of computer paper, an imported item in most African countries, could be dramatically reduced if such centres did not have to distribute information in printed form: A considerable amount of the printed paper goes straight into the wastebasket after a short glance. The same information on a micro-computer screen wastes no paper.

Such high-technology equipment as CD-ROMs are not oversophisticated in the African context. Production equipment for this type of data storage facility is available today for less than US$10,000, which makes the use of such centres an affordable means of information distribution within and between government agencies. The advantages are clear: Large amounts of information could be made available on a regular updated basis at the individual officer's level.

Information Technology in the External Relations of Government Agencies

Public administration produces a great amount of data of all kinds. It is clear that not all data can be distributed to the public because measures have to be taken to safeguard confidentiality. There are data, however, that are not confidential or sensitive and are of high value to agents in the voluntary and private sectors. One example is that of regulations and laws: Chambers of commerce could greatly benefit from electronically searchable textual data bases on these subjects. An even greater impact could be reached through sharing with private businesses and NGOs information that government receives on a regular basis from international organisations such as the United Nations or the European Community. For example, international information on trade could give business persons indicators of trends and export opportunities. Information on the prevention of particular diseases could be useful to NGOs working on health related projects at the village level.

Such information is available in almost all African countries, but usually one has to visit a dozen or so ministries to get it. The number of printed copies available is normally small forcing one to photocopy pages of interest, if a photocopier is available or is working at all. References to other publications may urge the user to seek information in a different department or ministry further delaying the use of existing information. Most data from international sources are available today in one of the electronical storage mediums, such as disks, tapes or CD-ROMs. Repackaging useful information focusing on national priorities from such sources and distributing it would greatly enhance the relationship between the public, private, and voluntary sectors. It would not only improve the effectiveness of the public sector in facilitating an enabling environment but would also strengthen the common search for a better future. In the context of the external relations of government agencies, one should extend the saying "knowledge is power" to the strategy that "shared knowledge and information is the path towards development," an idea obviously needed on the African continent. Indeed, this kind of cooperation underscores the concept of development management advanced in this book.

The Status and Use of Information Technology in Africa

Most of the surveys concerning the use of information technology in the public sector focus on developed countries or developing countries, which are more advanced than the average African country. Because of rapidly changing technology, particularly micro-computer technology, surveys carried out two or more years ago might give false information on the actual situation of information technology in Africa, particularly because recent advances have created new possibilities of providing up-to-date equipment at all levels and in all settings—public, private, or voluntary—even with small budgets.

A further constraint on the assessment of the actual status and use of information technology in Africa stems from the diversity of donors supporting its introduction. Bi-lateral donors often insist on using equipment produced in the donor country or at least in their own economic regions. International organisations are often influenced by their respective headquarters to advise using particular equipment. This leads to an inconsistent, highly diverse equipment base in African government agencies. In addition, there is little or no coordination between different government agencies: The ministry of agriculture might work with Food and Agricultural Organisation (FAO) data bases tailored to FAO standards, and the planning ministry, is supported by the European Union (EU), may use European equipment and follow EU standards, but the ministry of health may have a bi-lateral project with the United States Agency for International Development (USAID) and follow US government rules. Moreover, the acquisition of additional equipment or even the setup of LANs may be handled at the ministerial or divisional level and may not be recorded anywhere so that sometimes even the permanent secretaries may not be aware of technology introduced in their respective ministries.

Given the issue of rapidly changing technology and problems ascertaining who is using what equipment or technology in Africa, this assessment of the status and use of information technology is based on my observations during missions to African countries rather than on data based on a representative sample. This does not mean that the value of sample surveys should be taken lightly but that time lags between data collection and publication of the findings might render the results only of historical interest.

There are two possible approaches to the use of information technology in Africa: the centralised storage of and access to mainly statistical data on a mini-computer or a mainframe-equipped government computer centre or the decentralised storage of data in stand-alone fashion, available only at a single department, ministry, private, or voluntary sector agency. Both approaches have their advantages and disadvantages for development management.

The Centralised Approach

Some countries in Africa have a long history of computerisation, with the earliest installations going back to the 1960s. The choice of computers generally followed the preferences of the former colonial powers; in Kenya, for example, the majority of computers installed were International Computers Limited (ICL) and made in Britain. A slight shift in this pattern came with external support during the 1970s as part of computerisation for census purposes. At that time, mini-computer systems were installed in many African countries, particularly from Hewlett Packard, Honeywell, Bull, and Wang. Most of these systems were based on common business oriented language (COBOL), a programming language developed in the United States in the 1950s. The focus of training of African programmers at that time was directed towards these requirements.

These systems were also used for public administration applications beyond the production of census statistics, such as government payroll and trade statistics. Mini-computers had the advantage of being much cheaper than mainframe technology, used at that time in developed countries: Mini-computers cost about US$100,000, compared to several hundred thousand US dollars for mainframe technology, and mini-computer disks could easily handle the amount of data to be processed. Basic programmes for census statistics production were distributed by a number of international organisations, however, including the United Nations. The main disadvantage of this technology was that almost all applications had to be written in-house by COBOL programmers. But the turnaround time from start of programming to finalised product was long because most programmers were not very experienced; few standard programme packages were available. Furthermore, these machines were relatively expensive to maintain: Yearly maintenance costs of US$40,000 were usual and spare parts were available only from abroad. Governments sometimes faced serious problems in budgeting these costs and allocating the necessary foreign currency once external support for these systems ceased, particulary since the value of nationally generated statistics had not been fully recognised. For some governments, it seemed easier to apply for a new donor-supported project that included new equipment and a maintenance budget than to cover maintenance costs from the regular government budget.

Mini-computers are multi-tasking, multi-user systems, meaning that several computing tasks can run concurrently on the machines and a defined number of users can use the machine simultaneously. The latter is particularly important because data input, apart from data cleaning, is the main bottleneck in processing government data or statistics, and numerous data input clerks are needed to feed the data into the computer. The multi-tasking facility did not play a large role in African computer installations since the capacity of the mini-computers would slow down too much if the demand grew beyond a certain level, and computer managers allowed only one task at a time.

The human component for the operation of the computers also emerged as a major problem. In the civil service, electronic data processing was considered to be just like any other government service, like accounting, and thus the same salary structure applied. Although a "generalist" civil servant theoretically had the chance to reach the rank of permanent secretary, in the data processing or computer field, the highest available post was usually far below that level. Technical positions at senior levels were rare, and thus there were few promotion incentives for computer personnel. But the private and parastatal sectors also had their own demand for computer personnel. Given the few people in developing countries trained in computing, competition soon began: The salary structure for data processing personnel, even in public enterprises, was usually higher than that offered in the civil service, not to speak of the private sector. This led to a situation in which personnel, trained under bi-lateral or international financing for government computing, sought out higher-paying jobs outside the civil service. Thus the need for new training arose. To keep the necessary personnel, some administrations created artificially higher-level posts, only to see technical personnel become more engaged in meetings than at the computer.

In Europe and North America, meanwhile, more and more attention was given to comprehensive storage and retrieval of data, i.e., the development of data bases. In Africa, there was more concern with the production of statistical tables and government payrolls. Dedicated lines to connect computers within the government were too expensive, and local telecommunication authorities were mainly occupied with more pressing needs, such as the buildup of a working telephone infrastructure. Almost every programmer or foreign expert seemed to create his or her own format for data storage; and even today there is almost no compatibility between government entities of the same country or between countries, particularly for statistical data bases. As mentioned before, there was, and is, only a limited number of standard software packages available for mini-computers, partly due to the proprietary operating systems used by the different computer producers. Organisations such as the International Monetary Fund (IMF), the World Bank, the EU or the OECD have more African data stored in data bases than are found in any African country or even on the continent as a whole. This situation is absurd, and only lately are some African countries recognising and addressing the problem.

Data base development in Africa using mini-computers was not encouraged by mini-computer-oriented software development. Proprietary data base systems, such as the Image 3000 data base system for Hewlett Packard 3000 systems, written in a computer language available only on this machine, required heavy COBOL programming to make it a useful tool. Data entry and data correction were still mainly based on line editing, the most rudimentary method of entering and updating data. Searches in these data bases required a specialised language, more of a computer language than a natural language, and thus required the expertise of data processing personnel. A simple request from a planning ministry officer for some basic data might require several days to receive because the data had to go through different stages of processing until they are returned to the officer's desk.

In the world of mainframes, which are also represented in government computer centres, the situation was slightly different. International Business Machines (IBM), the main supplier of mainframe computer power throughout the world, was in a position to set the standards accepted by other producers. Their Structure Query Language (SQL) data base system became the de facto standard for mainframe data bases. This meant that the use of data bases required less programming and was more oriented towards the use of natural language than was the case for mini-computer-oriented systems. Admittedly, more and more mini-computer data base systems are emerging that use this standard as well, particularly with the UNIX operating system. This development facilitates a better exchange of data between different computers and reduces the training needed by an individual in order to use the data base system. Nevertheless, African countries have not made much of an effort to use these new data base systems.

There is no clear definition of user needs for data bases in Africa, although data bases have been accepted as a solution to the problems of standardisation and harmonisation of data and their concepts. It is true that, at first sight, it looks rather exotic to put emphasis on the creation of data bases in the midst of drought, desertification, and a hungry population. But it is equally true that proper analysis, executed by a computer using up-to-date software, might indicate the best place to build a health centre so that the access time is minimal for the population. This would use the continent's scarce financial resources most efficiently and thus reduce the health threats to the population.

One aspect of computing seems never to have reached African government agencies: Text-oriented data processing. The main emphasis in African countries is on statistical data. They have been slow to recognise text-oriented processing as an important contributor to development. Beginning with the military use of computers for deciphering encrypted messages in World War II, European and North American countries have gained experience with this type of data processing. Universities have also experimented with all types of text-oriented systems, leading to hypertext and artificial intelligence (AI), which more and more are coming into practical use. Major efforts by organisations such as UNESCO have only recently led to computerised bibliographic data bases to be installed in the computer centres of African governments. But there has been a reluctance to use this kind of information in an appropriate way: Statistical data still dominate the information realm in African countries.

The case of mini-computers or mainframe technology poses the greatest challenge to Africans in terms of the commitment on financial resources this technology entails. This is as true for the purchase and maintenance of the equipment as it is for the human resource expertise that is required to install and use it. Some African countries with a huge population, such as Nigeria, have no other choice than to use computer technology. But decision-makers should be aware of trends in the developed countries. Such large systems are being phased out in favour of smaller ones.

The Micro-Computer Approach

Since the mid-1980s, more and more micro- or personal, computers have been flooding into Africa. Regarded first as useful toys, posing no threat to the supremacy of mainframe technology, today micro-computers represent the major computer power in most organisational settings. This does not mean that personnel in government agencies are executing the tasks considered to be the most important on micro-computer systems but that they and people in the private and voluntary sectors are working with these systems more than they are on mainframe or mini-computers.

The use of lower-tech, lower-cost systems in Africa was dictated partly by the recognition that follow-up costs for the installed computer base was too high to be supported by national budgets, as well as by donor funding. Micro-computers, even though extremely expensive at their introduction as compared with today's prices, are still a cost-efficient alternative for most applications that require computer power. The promotion of micro-computer based programmes for census processing by the United Nations census system and the US Department of Commerce, the migration to micro-computers of popular standard statistical software, and the relatively low cost of personal computers, maintenance underscores their value.

Today there is almost no major department in any African government without such a computer. This does not mean necessarily that computers are used to their full capacity: All too often one finds micro-computers on display in directors' offices while their secretaries still use mechanical typewriters! Micro-computers were once considered to be just word processing machines, but micro-computer technology has advanced to the point where it rivals not only mini-computer technology but even that of mainframes.

Despite the fact that micro-computers are relatively widespread, there are still too few of them in African government agencies, private businesses, and the voluntary sector: It has been observed that up to twelve professionals have to share one or two machines, even in statistical offices where calculation is one of the basic tasks, forcing personnel to do a great number of calculations on table calculators, even tasks as complex as the calculation of the GDP. Often, many secretaries must share one printer, if they have micro-computers at all, thus delaying correspondence.

The use of micro-computers in Africa like everywhere in the world, is concentrated on word processing, preparing spreadsheets, and working with simple data bases. Interestingly, there seems to be a language-based distinction in the software used: Francophone African countries tend to use the programmes Word (for text processing) and Supercalc (for spreadsheets), but anglophone countries seem to prefer WordPerfect and Lotus. In addition, all kinds of graphic software are used, basically to produce simple business graphics such as bar- or pie-charts. Only very recently can one find a few LANs for in-house use, most often introduced under a foreign-financed project. In most national participating centres of PADIS, which are mainly libraries or documentation centres, one finds a text-oriented data base system created and distributed by UNESCO. Its main use is for bibliographic information processing.

As already mentioned above, most of these micro-computers are used on a stand-alone basis. This means that data can only be transferred by means of diskettes, and tools such as e-mail or bulletin boards are generally not available. In addition, this separation has the effect of "data hiding": There is no overview of what is stored on a particular computer. It must also be noted that quite a number of the installed micro-computers are already obsolete. Most of the machines are still based on 286 micro-processors, a relatively slow processor, have hard disks with small memory capacities, about twenty to forty megabytes, and monochrome screens. These machines cannot handle new software, especially in the graphics area, and their storage capacity is too limited to be effective. Because hardware prices have dropped dramatically there no longer seems to be necessity to limit hard disk space or memory.

Additional problems stem from the old or nonexistent micro-computer peripherals. Printers in African countries are usually matrix printers, producing only low-quality output. Plotters and laser printers are still a rarity. Scanners, graphic tablets, or CD-ROM drives are very seldom found. The only modern peripheral generally found is the tape-streamer used to store statistical census data.

Probably the most serious problem with the use of micro-computers in most African countries is the computer illiteracy of staff. In Europe and North America, basic computer training is already part of the elementary school curriculum, thus necessitating training only for particular applications in the workplace. This is not the case in Africa. Efforts have been made to broaden the base of personnel that is computer literate, but it seems that there are never enough properly trained in-house instructors to do so.

Indeed, there are many problems with the training of computer personnel. In many African countries today, one can find private firms offering micro-computer training of all kinds. Unfortunately, most of these "training centres" are of low quality: There seems to be the understanding that any person having attended a training course elsewhere is thus qualified to be a trainer. Innovative teaching techniques are usually unknown to the instructors in training centres. Their experience is usually limited, and they tend to have problems adapting to the work actually done in their students' offices. Often these training courses" produce an impressive certificate but no well-trained staff. Managers thus have to be very careful in selecting computer training for their staffs.

In-house instruction may have the same flaws. Those trained abroad might have no teaching ability at all. Teaching is more than the transfer of knowledge: In-house computer instructors should at least have successfully followed train-the-trainer courses before they are chosen for their tasks. In addition, they should have the opportunity to gain practical experience before being assigned to teach colleagues. Most existing in-house trainers do not fulfil these requirements.

A final obstacle to a wider and more efficient use of micro-computers is caused by a certain ideology-especially in government agencies. A considerable number of computer staff in government, in particular, higher level officers, have reservations against the wide use of micro-computers. They have been trained on mini- or mainframe-computers and strongly believe that this type of machine is the only "real" way of computing. Decentralisation of computers, which might reduce the power of high-level officer, is frequently opposed.

Major Constraints in the Wider Use of Information Technology

A number of problems concerning information technology have already been enumerated and discussed. Here, three key issues are singled out for emphasis. First, the biggest constraint on the wider use of information technology in Africa is the region's dependency on imports of information technology. All equipment has to be imported, maintenance engineers have to be trained abroad, and spare parts have to be paid for in foreign currency. Compared to some Asian countries, such as India, Africa has not yet produced a skilled workforce for the development of its own hardware and software, although some progress has been made in a few countries, such as in Nigeria and Zimbabwe. This dependency means that foreign exchange has to be set aside not only for software but also for the replacement of old equipment. This perennial shortage of foreign exchange often leads to a situation in which consumables for computing are not available and spare parts are missing, thus reducing the value of the equipment.

A second major problem is the availability of human resources. In most African countries, the status of technical education is low. This means that fewer students are interested in informatics. The same pattern has been observed in the salary structure for technical personnel within government agencies. These two components—limited number of trained people and relatively low salaries in the civil service—put additional constraints on the development of a computer workforce in the civil service.

A third problem is the indifference to computer use at senior levels of management. As observed in the early days of the introduction of computers in Europe and North America, high-ranking managers, whether in the public or private sector, very often refuse to use these tools. Typing their own memos is considered to be secretarial work not suited to their rank. Some of them are more inclined to receive information in printed form than on their computer monitors. Studies in developed countries have shown that it is a psychological problem: Using a machine that slightly resembles a typewriter reduces status; a subordinate who reports to his or her superior in person demonstrates more personal power. Unfortunately, this attitude is also found in African public sectors.

These problems are not insurmountable. In the following discussion I examine some possible solutions.

Towards a Wider Use of Information Technology

There is no single way to facilitate a wider use of information technology in Africa given the diversity of existing equipment, human resources, and financial possibilities. Solutions have to be tailored to meet country needs. What might be the best for Botswana might be wrong for Benin. But some basic ideas can be spelled out here.

Creating the Basic Environment

As mentioned above, an important issue is computer literacy. This could best be gained by including the basics of computing in the curriculum of elementary or high schools. It is recognised that this is not an easy task: School equipment in Africa is poor or nonexistent, and electricity is not always available.

The introduction of attractive salaries and conditions for computer personnel in the civil service and the creation of special career paths could help enhance the use of information technology. Well-trained personnel could grow into experienced staff, thus improving the quality of services and support they can offer in developing and implementing government policy.

Inside and outside the civil service, senior managers should reconcile their attitudes towards information technology. What-if analyses are more than necessary in development management, particularly in poor countries. Management should encourage the use of information technology by using it themselves, to be better prepared for the challenges of their positions.

Careful Planning

The introduction or extension of information-technology systems can be both a relief and a threat. Thinking too big or too small can offset any benefit from these tools. Using integrated management-information systems sounds fantastic. Advocates of these systems promise the world, or at least the whole ministry, at your fingertips. The introduction of these systems has to be approached carefully because systems analysis, design, and implementation might incur years of development and an unforeseeable amount of money. Thinking too small is equally bad. In order to save a few hundred U.S. dollars one might be tempted to buy machinery that is no longer adequate after a few weeks of day-to-day work. The golden middle, as it is with most other decisions, is the path to follow.

Some advisers in information technology use technical language that is hard to follow. If a computer layperson cannot understand what a proposal means, it is better to postpone its implementation until it has been explained enough for the person to understand it.

It is crucial that countries consider diversity when setting up computer systems. Using only one supplier might lead to disaster. High-tech firms in Africa come and go at a pace unknown in other parts of the world. Decision-makers should carefully consider all possibilities and problems including maintenance and servicing assistance, before making a commitment.

Good Training

As discussed earlier, there are differences in the quality of trainers. In-house instruction is usually less expensive. But countries must be sure that in-house trainers are not only knowledgable in their field but also have the necessary teaching skills. External training by private firms should be based more on the practical applications of information technology and less on theory. This means that the type and quantity of work in the agency or organisation has to be analysed and the instruction has to focus on defined and agreed priorities.

Proper Budgeting

Once information technology is introduced, managers have to ensure that there are funds available for maintenance and other requirements. Donors are less likely to provide funding for ongoing maintenance. It has to be recognised that most components of information technology have to be bought from abroad, thus requiring foreign exchange. Thus the budgetary implications of introducing and maintaining information technology have to be foreseen.

National Policies

Ideally, each African country should have a national policy on information technology. Some countries in Africa already have a policy framework in place. But all too often these policies are ignored: In negotiations with bi-lateral development partners, all rules are left behind. This has led to the diversity of equipment and concepts of information technology frequently found in Africa. Nonetheless, as useful as an overall policy framework is, it is not advisable to postpone all activities concerning the adoption and use of information technology until all the policies are defined and implemented. Improvisation is one of Africa's strengths and necessities; it should also be applied in the case of information technology.

The issue of the adoption of information technology in Africa was presented to the thirteenth meeting of the Technical Preparatory Committee of the Whole (TEPCOW) of the Economic Commission for Africa (ECA) in April 1992. The committee observed that although information technology, particularly in the form of computers, was fairly well disseminated in Africa, its potential for information access and exchange had yet to be exploited. It found that the impact of computers and telecommunication facilities on the quality of socio-economic information in the region had been negligible.

As with the position argued in this chapter, the committee agreed that the "appropriate technology" issue was a false one in information technology and that it prevented Africa from being competitive. It concluded that Africa could bypass technology generations and acquire the most up-to-date tools. This is particularly true because prices of information technology are constantly falling, in contrast to that of other technologies. One of the specific recommendations of TEPCOW was the promotion of human resource development in order to facilitate self-reliance in the use of information technology and to correct the shortfall in technological skills.

Following the recommendations by TEPCOW, in May 1992 the ECA Conference of Ministers adopted resolution 732 XXVII, which called upon African countries to adopt policies related to the acquisition and utilisation of appropriate information technology.

Sub-Regional and Regional Cooperation

There is much scope for regional cooperation in matters relating to the use of information technology because African countries face common problems. Within ECA, there is capacity to provide information and advice on information technology issues within the framework of PADIS. Unfortunately, PADIS has been used mainly for bibliographic purposes, despite that fact that other types of services could be made available. Efforts such as PADIS should be recognised and used as a source of information and advice. Subregional organisations such as the Preferential Trade Area (PTA) or the Economic Community of West African States (ECOWAS) should also be encouraged to make matters relating to the acquisition and use of information technology a priority area of cooperation.

Conclusion

In this chapter I have assessed the challenges and opportunities of information technology in development management in contemporary Africa. Of course, information technology cannot solve all of Africa's problems, but it may increase the efficiency of information flows within and between the public, private, and voluntary sectors on a mid- to long-term basis. Shared knowledge and information is the path towards development. Failure to take concrete steps to promote the use of information technology in African countries is a failure to use the many opportunities this medium offers. Information technology is indispensable, and its introduction has already begun. The challenge for Africans is to put it to work practically and effectively.

Further Reading

Bhatagar, C. Subhash and Niels Bjorn-Andersen (eds.), *Information Technology in Developing Countries* (Amsterdam: North-Holland Publishers, 1990).

Commonwealth Secretariat, *Information Technology in Government: The African Experiences* (London: Commonwealth Secretariat, 1988).

Economic Commission for Africa, *Impact of Automation and Modern Technology on Efficiency and Effectiveness of Financial Management in Public Enterprises in Africa* (Addis Ababa: Economic Commission for Africa, Public Administration, Human Resources and Social Development Division, Development Management Series No. 2, 1992).

Hanna, K. Nagy, *The Information Technology Revolution and Economic Development* (Washington, DC: World Bank Discussion Papers No. 120, 1991).

Heeks, Richard, "Impact of Information Systems in Developing Countries," *Information Technology for Development* 4 (3), 1989.

Mann, K. Charles and Stephen R. Ruth, *Expert Systems in Developing Countries: Practice and Promise* (Boulder, Colorado: Westview Press, 1992).

Peterson, B. Stephen, "From Processing to Analysing: The Use of Microcomputers in Development Bureaucracies," *Public Administration and Development* 11 (4), 1991.

United Nations, *Management and Government Information Systems* (New York: United Nations Department of Technical Cooperation for Development, 1989).

United Nations, *Computerisation of Government Accounting in Developing Countries* (New York: Department of Technical Cooperation for Development, 1991).

Part Three

Managerial and Economic Empowerment of Women

9

African Women in the Public Sector: Status and Strategies for Advancement

Maria Nzomo

The principle of equality of men and women, as enshrined in the *United Nations Charter*, in the majority of national constitutions, and in numerous international instruments—such as the *Universal Declaration on Human Rights* (1948), the *Covenant on Human Rights* (1976), the *Convention on the Elimination of All Forms of Discrimination Against Women* (1979), and the *Nairobi Forward-Looking Strategies* (1985)—provide generally accepted standards of legal equality. The awareness of these standards among women worldwide was significantly raised during the United Nations Decade for Women (1975-1985), albeit to varying degrees depending on the cultural and educational background of women and the sociopolitical climate in their country. However, with or without UN's conventions and declarations on behalf of women, it goes without saying that full and effective participation is a responsibility of all citizens. Indeed, the inclusive concept of development management advanced in this book recognises the importance of women's participation in decision-making at all levels in all three sectors: public, private, and voluntary. Effective solutions to international, national, and local problems can best be achieved only when citizens can exercise their equal rights to participate fully in public life and in decision-making at the highest levels. Furthermore, it is now generally accepted that women constitute a key national resource, whose ideas, creative solutions, and concern for cohesiveness of the social fabric can help change the quality of life and society at large. To accomplish these changes their participation in public decision-making roles is essential. The reality, however, is that, despite the enactment of national and international instruments affirming the legal rights of women, they remain severely deprived of their right to influence decisions determining the present and future of society. Even in the Scandinavian countries, which have the highest percentages of women in decision-making positions in legislative and executive bodies, the participation of women in the top echelons of private boards, companies, and other influential institutions is extremely low.

Complementing Chapter 10 in this book, which discusses women in the private sector, this chapter focuses on the public sector and is divided into three parts. The first assesses the status of women in the public sector via case studies of Zimbabwe, Nigeria, Zambia, Senegal, and Kenya. The second examines the factors constraining women's access and advancement in the public sector and the third outlines some strategies for women's advancement in the public sector.

Status of African Women
in the Public Sector

Comprehensive data on the status of women in the public sector are not available for most African countries. However, the picture that emerges from available evidence suggests that women in public sector employment occupy low-paying positions, with little decision-making power or influence. Almost all the top positions, whether in the political system, government bureaucracy, parastatal bodies, etc., are invariably occupied by men. Examples from a number of African countries illustrate this point.

Zimbabwe

In Zimbabwe, which is one of the few countries in Africa where major legal amendments and reforms have been made in favour of women's advancement since independence in 1980, the situation of women in the public sector has improved quantitatively but not qualitatively. One study has noted that although in 1980 there were 3,242 established posts occupied by women out of 10,470 positions, by 1983 the number had increased to 10,228 out of 24,278 posts. This was an increase of about 14.2 percent. However, most of this expansion took place in those "soft" ministries traditionally associated with women's domestic roles, namely: health, education, community development, and women's affairs. Furthermore, even in these ministries, very few women actually fill the high-status jobs. In other words, most of the women in formal government employment were in the teaching and nursing professions. Indeed, women account for only 9 percent of the high-status categories of jobs in the public sector in Zimbabwe during the mid-1980s.[1]

Additionally, there were other discriminations in the Zimbabwean civil service. Irrespective of the positions they hold, women tend to earn less than men for the same work because of the dubious "breadwinner concept." Married women were virtually considered as temporary staff. Moreover, in the recent past, a pregnant woman had to resign a civil service post and reapply after delivery. It was not unusual for such a person to start at the bottom of the pay scale on rejoining the civil service. As if this was not enough, a married woman's earnings were heavily taxed because they were considered additional income of the husband. The legal situation has changed but the attitudes behind these practices die hard.

J. L. Kazembe's study noted similar disparities between men and women in the political arena. At the local government level, women constitute about 10 percent of councillors in local governing bodies that range from district councils to municipalities. At the national level, the study noted that the paucity of women is even more acute. Despite the fact that Zimbabwean women fought alongside men for the country's political liberation, six years after independence in 1986 there were only twenty-four women in the Central Committee of the ruling party, out of ninety members. In the highest decision-making party organ—the Politburo—there was only one woman out of fifteen members. And in the legislature, there were eleven women out 140 members, nine of whom were in the House of Assembly. Of the nine, two were ministers and one was a deputy minister. But by 1989, the number of women in the Cabinet increased to four and the number of deputy ministers to three, however, the number of women in Parliament remained the same.[2]

Nigeria

The information that is available for Nigeria suggests that the situation of women in terms of their representation in the public sector is remarkably similar to that of other African countries. In terms of political structures, Nigeria has a federal system, and government has alternated between civilian and military regimes, with more of the latter than the former. However, as one study has demonstrated, structures of opportunities and access for women under both civilian and military governments have remained virtually the same. "Both political systems operated a bureaucratic centralism in which women were either not represented or only marginally so."[3]

The situation of Nigerian women has been further complicated by the influence of Islam, which has affected the ability of women in northern Nigeria to participate in public life. One study noted in this respect that "In spite of the right to an education and the right to vote, Islam as practised in Kano, presents a major constraint upon any [federal] effort towards dramatic change in the public role of women, limiting freedom of choice and movement by gender and according privileges to men while defining restrictions for women. . . . Muslim women in Kano must present their husband's written consent to work. . . . Muslim women are not afforded the protection of the Nigerian Constitution of 1979, which relegates to the states matters covered by Islamic personal law."[4] Thus, despite the 1976 electoral decree that enfranchised all women in Nigeria, during the local government elections of that year, women from northern states could vote only in separate booths from men and could do so only at night in order to meet the Islamic requirement for women's seclusion from public view.

The women in the non-Islamic states of Nigeria, though in a relatively better position than their northern sisters, have not fared well either in their participation in public life. In the first republic (1960-1966) for example, women's political participation was marginal. Very few women contested the elections and none won a seat in the House of Representatives. Therefore, there were no women in the federal Cabinet. Three women were, however, appointed to the Senate, and three others were elected to the eastern House of Assembly. Several women were elected to local government councils in the south, however. There were no women ministers and no women in the top positions in the major parties.

The military government of Yakubu Gowon that took over power in 1966 had no women at any level of government. Indeed, the military was very remote from women. But during the civil war, women were recruited into the civil militia and promoted to officer cadres; they were also recruited into the Intelligence and Propaganda Directorates and held responsible positions for the duration of the war. After the war, the Gowon regime initiated the policy of appointing civilian commissioners at the federal and state levels. These consisted mostly of professional and technical experts. None of them was female, although there were many women professionals and academics who qualified. Moreover, in its preparations to return the country to civilian rule in 1979, the male-dominated military government ignored women in its fifty-man Constitution drafting committee, although the main criteria for selection were professional competence and equal representation from the nineteen states. Nevertheless, in the government of the second republic that took office in 1979, there were three women federal ministers and one woman commissioner in just about each state. Thus, in terms of the number of women holding formal political office in Nigeria, the second civilian government was evidently more successful than the first republic and the military regimes, but it was still assessed as "very poor" on women's issues. Moreover, Islamic and customary laws continued to discriminate against women.

In the military government that seized power in 1983, the civil service was relegated to the background, and the government relied far more on a greatly expanded national security organization, which had no women in the higher ranks. The top policy-making body was the Supreme Military Council, which was a military-police body. By 1984 the highest ranking women in the armed forces were a colonel in the army, one wing commander in the air force, and a commander in the navy. In the police force, there was an assistant inspector general of the police force.

Following the change in the leadership of the military that brought the Ibrahim Babangida regime to power in 1985, a more liberal climate favouring the participation of women in public life emerged. For example, it became the policy of the new regime that one in every four nominated local government councillors should be women and that one woman should be on every government board or panel. The regime also appointed the first woman vice-chancellor of a university—the University of Benin—in 1986, as well as two women members of a seventeen member political bureau that was set up in 1986 to coordinate a national political debate on the return to civilian rule. Thus there has been some improvements in the participation of women in public life in Nigeria in recent years, but the evidence also suggests that this has been marginal. Some reasons for their exclusion, in addition to the sociocultural barriers Nigerian women face, are related to state policies, which in practice tend to override federal standards, and to the weak and divided women's movement, which is unclear in its objectives and strategies.

Zambia

As in other African countries, women's participation in the state and party structures of public life since independence in Zambia has been far from impressive. Even at the lowest political level, the party leadership is largely a male leadership. The occasional woman holding political office finds herself in the same position as the female bureaucrat: in a male environment, judged by men's standards, and unable or unwilling to speak on behalf of women on particular issues. Few Zambian women have served at Cabinet level. Under the one-party regime (1964-1991), there were also few women in the Central Committee, the key decision-making body of the ruling party. A quick glance at the distribution of top party and government posts by sex, between 1974 and 1983, as shown in Table 9.1, clearly illustrates this position.

Table 9.1
Distribution of Top Party and
Government Posts by Sex: Zambia

Position	1974		1975		1976		1977		1978	
	F	M	F	M	F	M	F	M	F	M
Member of Central Committee	3	22	2	20	3	21	3	22	3	21
Cabinet Minister	1	22	1	20	0	23	0	25	0	26
Minister of State	2	11	2	11	1	14	1	13	1	14
Member of Parliament	6	129	4	129	3	128	4	128	7	128
Provincial Political Secretary	0	0	1	9	2	9	1	10	2	9
District Governor	2	65	2	61	1	58	2	60	2	66
District Political Secretary (Regional Officials)	52	202	49	108	46	105	54	102	53	88
Ambassador*	1	20	2	24	2	22	-	-	-	-

Position	1979		1980		1981		1982		1983	
	F	M	F	M	F	M	F	M	F	M
Member of Central Committee	2	20	2	22	2	23	2	23	2	23
Cabinet Minister	0	16	0	17	0	18	0	20	0	20
Minister of State	3	13	3	20	3	19	5	17	5	17
Member of Parliament	8	111	6	127	8	120	6	103	6	109
Provincial Political Secretary	3	14	4	14	4	14	4	18	4	18
District Governor	2	68	2	67	2	67	1	67	1	92
District Political Secretary (Regional Officials)	51	86	59	103	57	98	52	94	58	98
Ambassador*	-	-	1	9	0	28	-	-	0	24

* Statistics of 1977, 1978, 1979, and 1982 could not be obtained.
Source: Jane Parpart and Kathleen Staudt (eds.), *Women and the State in Africa* (Boulder, Colorado: Lynee Reinner, 1989), 134.

Even the 1991 multiparty elections in Zambia did not, as many women had hoped, bring about greater political representation of women. Indeed, women lost the only Cabinet position they had gained under Kenneth Kaunda's government. Table 9.2 illustrates the point.

Table 9.2
Positions Held by Women Before and After 1991 Election: Zambia

Category of Position	Before Election (UNIP)			After Election (MMD)		
	Proportion		Percentage	Proportion		Percentage
	F	M		F	M	
Cabinet Ministers	1	20	5.0%	0	23	0%
Deputy Ministers (Minister of State)	1	23	4.3%	5	36	13.9%
Executive Committee (Central Committee)	8	58	11.8%	4	38	10.5%
Members of Parliament	5	135	3.7%	6	125	4.8%

Source: Sara Longwe and Roy Clarke, *A Gender Perspective on the Zambian General Election of October, 1991* (Lusaka: Zambian Association for Research and Development, 1991), 15.

The literature on the status of women in Zambia concurs on the paucity and low-status positions women occupy not only in the public sector but in public life in general. In this regard, B. B. Keller has noted that "[although] a handful of professional women have risen through the ranks to become directors and general managers in government, parastatals and private companies, the result is that women are largely outside the board rooms, conference chambers and other arenas where male government leaders and senior bureaucrats take decisions."[5] In the same vein, M. L. Munachonga has noted that "despite pressure from women's organisations both inside and outside the party, legislative changes to improve the status of women have been slow or nonexistent . . . this suggests that women in Zambia still have less political power and influence in decision-making compared with men. They also have limited economic power, both in society at large and within the family."[6]

In the same study assessing the impact of Zambia's development policies on women since independence, Munachonga further observed:

> While some Zambian women have been able to attain high levels of education and hold responsible positions in the economy, most women either work in the informal economy or perform the least-skilled, worst-paid jobs. Even those women lucky enough to have wage employment (less than 15 percent), suffer from discriminatory practices by employers. Salaries tend to be lower for work of equal value. Employers often refuse to provide housing for female employees, especially if they are married. Tax policies penalize working married women—some women do not get holiday allowances and women are forced to retire five years before men. The employment act prohibits women from most night work. The only benefit women have achieved is a ninety-day paid maternity leave, and this often deters employers from hiring women.[7]

This assessment not only suggests that women's participation in wage employment is very low but also that women perform low-status work and face many discriminations.

Senegal

Senegal has been cited as a country that is more progressive on women's rights. By 1985, it had already ratified the UN conventions guaranteeing women equal political rights with men, equality in education, equal pay for work of value, and equal access to employment. However, Senegal signed but did not ratify the 1979 *UN Convention on the Elimination of All Forms of Discrimination Against Women*.[8]

Despite this "impressive" list of ratifications, the reality of women's status in Senegal was and is quite a different story. As one provocative study of women in Senegal has pointed out, these ratifications of UN conventions are but "a signature based on the intent of the government rather than one founded on the actual legal rights of women as they are observed in Senegalese society."[9] The reality is that customary and Islamic laws and beliefs, which generally place women in a subordinate status to men, largely shape gender roles and statuses, more so than do secular laws. Thus legally, women have full political rights, including the right to vote and to hold appointive and elective office at all levels, but their participation has been constrained by extra-legal factors.

For example, in 1978 there were only two women holding ministerial positions in government and a total of eight women members of Parliament (MPs) in a 100-member Parliament. By 1983, political representation had improved slightly to thirteen women out of 120 parliamentarians, with three women holding cabinet-level posts. But significantly, these women ministers occupied "soft" ministries associated with women's traditional and domestic roles—health, culture, and social affairs. No woman has ever been appointed to head any of the powerful ministries, such as economic planning, finance, justice, or foreign affairs. The first woman mayor was elected in 1984. But, on one hand, the majority of women in the labour force hold low-status posts, as typists, clerks, secretaries, and unskilled factory workers. On the other hand, men head the government, own most of the businesses, and are most of the university professors. Furthermore, it is men who act for the family in negotiations with the government or banks and who generally get title to family land. This has been underlined by F. Sow: "In white collar jobs, women occupy the lower levels of the professional hierarchies in spite of their professional competence. In blue-collar jobs, laws govern the length of the work day, possibilities for working at night, and exclude women from lines of work deemed to be too dangerous for them (mining, railroads, industrial machinery, etc.)."[10]

Kenya

Although representation of women in public sector employment has been rising gradually since independence, women still constitute a minority of Kenyans employed in this sector. Moreover, the majority of these women are employed in the lower ranks—a situation that does not reflect the significant strides in education women have made since independence.

As elsewhere in Africa, women in Kenya constitute the majority of the unemployed poor and those working in the informal sector of the economy. Women's absence in key decision-making positions in Kenya has been more glaring than in other African countries, though for many years Kenya has been lauded, especially among Western governments and international agencies, as a showpiece of democratic practice in Africa. Kenya has also signed and ratified many of the UN's conventions on human rights and equality of the sexes, including the 1979 *Convention on the Elimination of All Forms of Discrimination Against Women*. Kenya hosted the 1985 world conference to close the UN's Decade for Women and was among the 157 countries that adopted the *Nairobi Forward-Looking Strategies for the Advancement of Women*. Kenya's Constitution guarantees equal rights for men and women, including the right to vote, to be eligible for election or appointment to public office, and to exercise public functions at the local, national, and international levels. But Kenya's Constitution, as of 1993, contains one important omission namely an explicit statement that there will be no discrimination on the basis of sex. Perhaps because of this and other factors discussed below, the women of Kenya endure many forms of discrimination in all spheres of life. And their participation in high levels of public decision-making, whether in the public or private sectors, remains marginal.

Although there has been some expansion in women's public sector employment in Kenya since independence in 1963, this expansion has largely provided more stereotypical jobs for women, such as teaching, nursing, and other low-status jobs. For example, by 1982, on one hand, women held 93 percent of secretarial positions and 70 percent of nursing and paramedical posts. On the other hand, women were grossly underrepresented in highly technical and managerial positions. For example, by 1982, only 0.3 percent of architects, engineers, and surveyors were women, and 2.7 percent of general managers and salaried directors were women.[11]

Women's membership in Kenya's trade unions has always been low. In at least four of the thirty-three registered unions, there was no female membership up to 1985. Even in the few unions in which women's membership was relatively high (up to 30 percent of total membership), women did not hold leadership or decision-making positions. From 1985-1986 women took a mere 3.1 percent of trade union positions, up from 2.1 percent in 1970. Of the thirty-three unions on the register in 1985, seventeen had never had a woman on their executive board, at least since 1970.[12]

In the public sector, examples of this marginalisation of women in top decision-making positions are numerous. In the judiciary, the first woman judge of the high court was appointed in 1982, almost twenty years after independence; the second was appointed in 1986, the third in 1991, and the fourth in 1993. There are still no women who are members of the highest court in Kenya—the Court of Appeals despite some vacant positions. For the first time, in 1983, two women were appointed to head two of the many public enterprises in the country; fifteen others were appointed in 1986, seven as heads and eight as members of boards of parastatal bodies.[13] During the same year, two women were appointed to senior diplomatic positions: One became the first female high commissioner to Britain, but she was recalled in early 1992 and redeployed as permanent secretary in the Ministry of Foreign Affairs and International Cooperation; another woman was appointed Kenya's representative to the Nairobi-based United Nations Environmental Programme (UNEP), replacing a woman who had earlier resigned from this post. In 1987, a woman was appointed to be permanent secretary in the key economic Ministry of Commerce and Industry.[14]

It was only in November 1969, five years after Kenya's independence, that the first woman was elected to the National Assembly and another was nominated to sit in the legislative body, along with eleven male nominated members. Between 1969 and 1974, of the total elected members of Parliament, women accounted for 0.5 percent, but only 8 percent of the nominated members. Except for the period from 1974 to 1979, when women's representation improved slightly, the general trend has been one of women's marginalisation in political decision-making at the national level. Indeed by 1991, out of 200 elected and nominated members of Parliament, there were only two women MPs. Of the two, one sat on the front bench as an assistant minister for the Ministry of Culture and Social Services, along with sixty-nine male assistant-ministers. In the 1993 multiparty Parliament, there were six elected women MPs out of 200 members. Of the six, one was an assistant minister in the Ministry of Works.

Since 1974, when the first woman was appointed to the front bench, the position of assistant minister is the highest position a woman had ever held in Kenya's government. Furthermore, there has never been more than one woman holding this post at any one time. More significantly, the lone woman assistant minister has consistently been appointed to serve in the "soft" Ministry of Culture and Social Services. The current woman assistant minister was first posted to the Ministry of Culture and Social Services but was transferred to the Ministry of Works after an outcry from women activists. Table 9.3 gives a breakdown of gender representation in Kenya's Parliament between 1969 and the general election of 1992.

Table 9.3
Membership of the Kenya National Assembly
by Gender, 1969-1992

Year of Election	Elected Members		Nominated Members	
	Male	Female	Male	Female
1969	154	1	10	1
1974	152	5	10	1
1979	155	3	1	1
1983	157	1	9	2
1988	188	2	11	0

Sources: Supervisors of Elections: Attorney General's Chambers 1985; also cited in Republic of Kenya, *Women of Kenya* (Nairobi: Republic of Kenya, 1985), 42; and in M. Nzomo, *Women in Politics and Public Decision Making* (Association of African Women for Research and Development [AAWORD] Working Paper No. 2, Nairobi, 1992); also in U. Himmelstrand et al. (eds.), *In Search of New Paradigms for the Study of African Development* (London: James Currey, 1993).

Within the ruling Kenya African National Union (KANU) party hierarchy, women have had even more difficulty participating at the national executive level, save for the lone woman who has since 1989 held the position of director of Women and Youth Affairs and one woman party branch chairperson elected in early 1992. Indeed, women's status in the party hierarchy has consistently been relegated to that of mere rank-and-file members of the powerless Women's Wing.

Factors Constraining Women's Access and Advancement in the Public Sector

The paucity of African women in the public sector and their almost total absence in top management and decision-making positions suggests that there are serious obstacles to women's advancement in public life. Some of the factors constraining women's participation are discussed below.

Socio-Cultural Factors

Perhaps the most critical constraints identified in virtually all the literature are the socio-cultural beliefs and myths that inform the socialisation process and the kind of education and training to which most men and women are exposed from childhood. Sex stereotypes and gender segregation in employment and allocation of roles in private and public life are primarily a product of the early socialisation process and indoctrination of the social environment. Thus, for example, many women's lack of confidence in their ability to execute public leadership roles competently arises from this early socialization process.

In all the case studies included in this chapter, the socio cultural factor is thus highlighted in various forms as the most stubborn barrier to women's advancement in the public sector and public life in general. In Zimbabwe, for example, among the major obstacles cited as acting as barriers to women's advancement in formal employment include: (1) negative parental attitudes and actions towards their female children, which largely reflect on the parent's own socialisation, and (2) negative attitudes towards women by employers who refrain from hiring women, let alone promoting them to positions of influence in a managerial capacity or other high-status job. For women to be promoted, they have to prove themselves well beyond normal standards or expectations.

In Senegal, the combination of the myths and beliefs associated both with customary and Islamic tradition acts as a major barrier to women's advancement. In this regard, such beliefs that a man has the public wage-earning role and authority as the family head but a woman's duty is only to be a good mother, chaste, modest, and obedient to her husband, does not augur well for women's advancement. Worse still, the seclusion practice, such as occurs in northern Nigeria, restricts even women's ability to participate in electoral politics as voters. As pointed out earlier in this chapter, in the 1976 local government elections, for example, women from the north voted at night, because the seclusion practice did not permit women to come out during the day. In Zambia, customary practices that trample on women's economic rights, whether in regard to access to credit facilities and loans or to decision-making and ownership of domestic and other properties, were cited as major constraints to women's economic advancement. This was related to the belief that men are, by tradition and by nature, the heads of their households and that this confers on them ultimate authority. Anything that challenges this arrangement is not Zambian and should therefore be thwarted.[15]

Another aspect of sociocultural constraints takes the form of the multiple roles women are expected to fulfil. African sociocultural traditions perceive a woman's career as just an additional activity to her "primary" (domestic) roles. The literature on women is replete with the woes of the "double day" that working career women have to bear, especially since support services in Africa are few or absent.[16] And even where support services exist, they do not alter the existing unequal gender division of labour. In other words, sociocultural attitudes die hard. Hence, "most working women juggle harried schedules but there are few solutions except the drastic ones of having fewer children or becoming single, separated or divorced, in order to reduce time spent on husband-care."[17] Having analysed Zambian women's experience, Keller arrived at a similar conclusion, which summarised the general situation in most African countries: "Most working women must juggle marriage and career, and the supportive husband who facilitates his wife's job advancement is a rarity. Many women are discouraged from even trying."[18]

Educational Constraint

In addition to the attitudinal dimensions arising from society and culture, lack of access to formal education in Africa in itself acts as a major barrier to a woman's advancement in public life. Research has shown that the more education a woman has, the more likely she is to be employed.[19] Moreover, women's occupational advancement is more closely linked to their educational attainment than it is for men. Men use their educational credentials for entry to jobs and then rely on job-related experience for advancement. For women, however, formal credentials remain critical throughout their working lives.[20]

For all African countries, the major problem for women seems to be that many of them do not attain an adequate quantity and quality of education to compete effectively for job opportunities with men. A combination of high dropout rates (mainly due to pregnancies), parental attitudes, and sexist curricula that encourage female students towards stereotyped careers, such as nursing, and away from careers requiring knowledge of disciplines, such as management, science, and technology, marginalises women in an increasingly technical job market.

It follows from this that the opportunity structure in education to some extent accounts for the paucity of women in the public sector of African countries and their virtual absence in many top decision-making positions.

Legislative and Policy Framework

In theory, the legislative and policy framework in most African countries provides for equality between women and men, but in some countries, such as Kenya, the constitutions do not explicitly outlaw discrimination on the basis of sex. Furthermore, in some cases, even when the law provides for desirable benefits to women and girls, traditional attitudes and social practices continue to perpetuate discrimination and subordination. Further still, the simultaneous existence and application of customary, religious, and statutory laws leads to confusion, especially within the framework of family law: marriage, separation, and divorce custody and maintenance of children, etc. This confusion often results in the manipulation of the legal framework to create barriers to women's advancement in public and professional life. Earlier in this chapter, I noted that in Senegal, for example, despite the government's adoption of secular laws that protect women's rights, in practice there is considerable ambivalence due to the influence of Islam and the dependence of government leaders on the support of conservative religious leaders, who are opposed to secularisation of women's status.

There is progressive labour legislation, such as the Zimbabwean *Labour Relations Act* (1984), which, among other provisions, makes it an offense for an employer to discriminate against any employee or prospective employee on grounds of race, tribe, place of origin, political opinion, colour, creed, or *sex* in job advertisements, recruitment, creation or abolition of jobs, determination of wages and benefits, choice of persons for jobs, training, advancement, transfer, promotion, or retrenchment, and enables women to take ninety days maternity leave with up to 75 percent of salary. Even so, such laws can still be cleverly manipulated or otherwise used to deny women the protection of the law. Without providing reason, employers can subtly refrain from hiring women of childbearing age to avoid granting maternity benefits. Employers can also take advantage of the fact that it is very difficult to prove discrimination in hiring and promotions. In this regard, in relation to another piece of Zimbabwean legislation—the *Sex Disqualification Removal Act* (1983)—Kazembe has observed that there is still a lot of tacit sex discrimination in selections, appointments, and promotions.[21]

Indeed, in Zimbabwe the main problem since the passing of progressive legislation in favour of women has been one of implementation, both at the level of the administration of justice as well as at the level of obtaining the cooperation of the parties affected by the changes. Kazembe noted that in dealing with cases arising out of these reforms, administrators of justice have allowed their own prejudices to colour their judgments. At the level of the parties affected, she further noted that most women have continued to act as if legislative change has not taken place. On one hand, they cannot contemplate that they could ever be equal to men. The internalisation of inferiority complexes is such that they have little hope of living differently. Men, on the other hand, question the need for gender equity. They argue that no one should tell them how to run their homes or how to behave towards a wife for whom large amounts of dowry has been paid.[22]

Similarly, in Senegal, where some progressive changes in family law have been made in recent years, the provision for the legal choice between monogamy and polygamy leaves adequate room for men to exploit this option unfairly: In practice, a man may take a second wife despite his earlier choice of a monogamous marriage. In such cases men are rarely prosecuted for breaking the law.[23]

It has also been demonstrated that in some countries, such as Kenya, both employer preferences and prejudices and patterns of female socialisation have contributed more than has the legal structure to the sex-stereotyping of jobs and the slow advancement of women in the public sector. One study argued in this respect that "Although many existing laws that discriminated against women in employment were gradually amended, discrimination against women in the labour market continued, for the latter was not isolated from cultural practices and social processes that not only made sexual inequality normative but also reproduced it on a daily basis and in all walks of life. This is to suggest that, while changes in the legal regime are important in removing discrimination against women, transformation of cultural values, processes of socialisation and modes of economic production are even more fundamental."[24] Besides the discrepancy that exists between legal provisions and practice, there are some laws that clearly discriminate against women in employment and hence limit their possibilities of career advancement. In Kenya, for example, there is still on the statute books the now-outdated *Employment Act* (1975), which denies married women housing allowances on the assumption that they are dependants and housed by their husbands. The act also restricts the majority of women from working at night and from working in construction or in other professions considered "dangerous" for women. There is also the *Vagrancy Act*, which restricts the movement of women at night, and this law is frequently used to harass unaccompanied women. Although these women may be moving to or from a night job, it is often assumed that they are loitering for the purpose of prostitution.

Finally, the paucity of women legislators in Kenya and elsewhere in Africa remains a major obstacle to the enactment of progressive legislation on gender issues. In Kenya, again, the repeal of the *Affiliation Act* in 1969, which had required men to support all children they have fathered, and the repeated defeat of the *Marriage Bill* each time it has come for debate are clear cases of the dangers inherent in having a male-dominated legislative body.

Strategies for Women's Advancement
in the Public Sector

The foregoing assessment of the status of women in the public sector in contemporary African countries and appraisal of the factors constraining women's access and advancement in public sector employment suggests that action is required on several fronts. What follows is a listing of the key issues that need to be addressed.

- Governments must recognise the existing gender disparities in public sector employment in most African countries and should institute measures to deliberately promote and increase the number of women in this sector, especially in executive, managerial, and other key decision-making positions.
- African governments should employ and promote measures to guarantee equity and fairness in women's access to employment opportunities, including the adoption of quotas as appropriate. In addition, governments should regularly review the terms of service for women in the public sector to ensure that women enjoy such rights as promotions, equal pay for equal work, maternity leave with pay, housing, and medical benefits.

- Given the heavy responsibilities and workload accompanying the multiple roles of women in their reproductive and career roles, African governments should promote support systems for female employees, such as day care centres and maternal and child health services, conveniently placed and operated. Part-time employment and flexible working hours supportive of these roles should also be included.

- Given the biases against the participation of women and girls in scientific and technical disciplines, African governments should institute measures to increase the participation of females in these subjects to enhance their employment prospects. Executive-level training programmes are also required to provide women with appropriate managerial skills and experience.

- Governments should recognise the constraints on women's ability to pursue higher education because of multiple roles and family responsibilities and should employ appropriate incentives, including the provision of scholarships, flexible higher-education programmes, and family support structures to encourage women to pursue higher education.

- Given the inadequacy of data on women's status in most African countries, governments should support research and data collection to generate the required information.

- All African countries that have not already done so should review their Constitutions, with the objective of explicitly outlawing all forms of discrimination on the basis of gender. Governments should also review all legislation and enforcement systems, with the view of making them gender-sensitive in intention and practice. In particular, governments should adopt political, legislative, and development policies aimed at eliminating gender disparity and discrimination in all sectors and at all levels.

- Given the confusion and manipulation occasioned by the simultaneous existence of customary, religious, and statutory laws, African governments should review overlapping areas, with the view of harmonising laws that affect the status of women.

- Given that the influence and power of social and cultural practices and customary norms is a major barrier to African women's advancement, governments and non-governmental organisations should promote measures to overcome this. In particular, gender sensitisation and awareness-raising programmes should be included in school curricula. Key non-governmental organisations, such as the media, religious organisations, and women's organisations, should play an active role in transmitting information and images to change societal attitudes towards women and sensitise women to their rights.

- Women themselves should also play a leading role in pushing for changes in discriminatory laws and practices that obstruct their advancement. However, given that the women's movement is weak in most African countries, women should, as a matter of strategy, take the initiative to strengthen these movements to ensure that they are effective as viable pressure groups for gender-based issues.

Conclusion

In this chapter I have reviewed the status of women in the public sector in Africa, with specific reference to Zimbabwe, Nigeria, Senegal, Zambia, and Kenya. It should be clear from the cases examined that there is striking similarity in the status of women and in the uniformity of constraints that act as barriers to women's advancement in the public sector. Although I have focused on the status of women in the public sector of African countries, the same conditions and constraints apply to women in the private sector, as Chapter 10 also demonstrates. Moreover, the situation of women in the private sector may be even more desperate because agents operating in this sector often evade government control. It is also important to point out that the majority of women in Africa do not work in the modern public or private sector. Most African women support themselves and their families through activities in the so-called informal sector. Since this sector generally falls outside the formal machinery of government control and regulation, it tends to be neglected and marginalised. Therefore, in the search for strategies and solutions for the economic empowerment of women, the informal sector should be given due attention, alongside the modern public and private sectors.

Notes

1. See J. L. Kazembe, "The Women Issue," in Ibbo Mandaza (ed.), *Zimbabwe: The Political Economy of Transition, 1980-1986* (Dakar: CODESRIA, 1986), 397-398.

2. See P. Made and N. Whande, "Women in Southern Africa: A Note on the Zimbabwean Success Story," *Issue* 27 (2), 1989, 27.

3. N. Mba, "Kaba and Khaki: Women and the Militarized State in Nigeria," in Jane Parpart and Kathleen Staudt (eds.), *Women and the State in Africa* (Boulder, Colorado: Lynne Reinner, 1989), 27. Much of the discussion of Nigeria is derived from this source.

4. B. Callaway and L. Creevey, "Women and the State in Islamic West Africa," in S.E.M. Charlton and K. Staudt (eds.), *Women, the State and Development* (New York: State University of New York Press, 1989), 106.

5. B. B. Keller, "Struggling in Hard Times: The Zambian Workers Movement?" *Issue* 17 (2), 1989, 22-23.

6. M. L. Munachonga, "Women and the State: Zambia's Development Policies and Their Impact on Women," in Parpart and Staudt (eds.), *Women and the State in Africa*, 137-138.

7. Ibid., 132.

8. R. L. Sivard, *Women: A World Survey, World Priorities* (Washington, DC: 1985), 30.

9. Callaway and Creevey, "Women and the State in Islamic West Africa," 98.

10. F. Sow, "Senegal: The Decade and Its Consequences," *Issue* 27 (2), 1989, 32-36.

11. T. Zeleza, *Labour Unionisation and Women's Participation in Kenya* (Nairobi: Friedrich Ebert Foundation, 1988), 60.

12. Ibid., 129, 131.

13. See *Daily Nation* (Nairobi), 17 January 1986, 1.

14. See *Daily Nation* (Nairobi), 2 June 1987, 1.

15. See Keller, "Struggling in Hard Times," 23.

16. See, for example, E. Boserup, *Women in Economic Development* (London: Allen and Unwin, 1970); B. J. Dorsey et al., *Factors Affecting Academic Careers for Women at the University of Zimbabwe* (Harare: Human Resource Research Centre, 1989); A. Imam et al. (eds.), *Women and the Family* (Dakar: CODESRIA, 1985); and S. Stitcher and J. L. Parpart (eds.), *Women, Employment and the Family in the International Division of Labour* (London: Macmillan, 1990).

17. Stitcher and Parpart, *Women, Employment and the Family*, 6.

18. Keller, "Struggling in Hard Times," 23.

19. A. C. Smock, *Women's Education and Roles in Kenya* (Nairobi: Institute for Development Studies, University of Nairobi Working Paper No. 316, 1977).

20. J. Freeman (ed.), *A Feminist Perspective* (Palo Alto, California: Mayfield Publishing Co., 1984), 238.

21. Kazembe, "The Women Issue," 395.

22. Ibid, 395.

23. Sow, "Senegal", 34.

24. Zeleza, *Labour Unionisation and Women's Participation in Kenya*.

10

Enhancing the Capacity of the African Woman Entrepreneur

Zeinab B. El-Bakry

For many centuries African women have nurtured a long-standing tradition of entrepreneurship. They are primarily traders in local markets and have held a prominent place in international and intercontinental trade for specific items and commodities. Trading continues to be second only to agriculture among women's major activities. In the context of ongoing reforms and rethinking of development strategies in the region, a greater contribution to the region's development is expected from African entrepreneurs. To this extent, African women entrepreneurs occupy a pivotal position in relation to this expectation. Yet, as Chapter 9 has shown, the constraints on access and advancement that African women face in the public sector also applies to African women operating in the private sector. Additionally, there are further constraints on the growth and development of entrepreneurial capacity in the region that apply to all entrepreneurs irrespective of gender. Chapter 11 deals with these general issues.

The special problems of African women entrepreneurs are the main focus of this chapter. I provide an overview of the role of women as entrepreneurs in the region, examine the constraints they face, and assess the main policy trends that have emerged to overcome these constraints. Some recommendations then follow on how these policy interventions can better enhance the role and capacity of African women entrepreneurs.

Women as Entrepreneurs in Africa

As entrepreneurs, women operate at different levels of African economies. The impetus for undertaking trading, farming, and related activities arises because in the context of extended familial arrangements, African women have always been expected in some way to contribute to the provision of food for the family and, more generally, to provide some support for themselves, their children, and other relatives. The role of women as economic agents pre-dates colonial rule, and, indeed, colonial authorities imposed changes that generally undermined this role. In particular, colonial practices promoted the idea of the nuclear family as the norm. This generally changed the legal status of women within the context of the family. Women's customary role as economic agents were at best ignored, or at worst denied, by the new legal systems that were modelled on nineteenth-century European conventions. In nineteenth-century England and France, it was unusual for married women to have finances in their own names or to undertake business ventures without the consent of their husbands. This contrasted with the situation in many societies in Africa.

Despite colonial preferences, the entrepreneurial activities of African women continued and survived colonial rule. However, the pattern of economic differentiation that emerged during colonialism relegated women to the margins of entrepreneurial ventures. In post-colonial Africa, this pattern has hardly changed. Essentially, large-scale enterprises were mostly foreign-owned or controlled and were male-dominated. The promotion of public enterprise after independence reduced foreign control and ownership but not male domination. Entrepreneurial activity at the medium- and small-enterprise level has been largely the preserve of males, under colonial rule and also after independence. Nonetheless, a significant number of African women operate at this level. But it is at the level of informal sector micro-enterprises, basic income-generating and subsistence activities, that women have been prevalent. In recent years, informal sector ventures in urban centres have expanded as a result of the pressures of population growth, rural-urban migration, decreasing agricultural output, and the spillover effects of structural adjustment programmes, such as the contraction of public sector employment. Yet business policies and regulations in many African countries tend to suppress or discourage informal sector entrepreneurial activities. These and other constraints on the entrepreneurial capacity of women are discussed in the next section.

Constraints on African Women Entrepreneurs

As a first step, it is necessary to distinguish between different categories of women entrepreneurs. This facilitates the identification of different constraints that apply at different levels and to different categories. It further enhances the identification of intervention measures that are appropriate to the different situations in which women entrepreneurs find themselves. Three categories of activities in which African women entrepreneurs are prevalent can be differentiated as follows:

Subsistence activities. These activities include subsistence farming, street vending, and other operations that are on the borderline between household responsibilities and economic ventures.

Micro-enterprises. These businesses, which may employ less than ten full-time workers, are usually located in the home, use traditional technology, and typically serve local markets.

Small-scale enterprises. These may employ up to fifty workers, are usually located away from the owner's home, and use some modern technology as well as more complex procurement and marketing systems. Examples include dress-making, running restaurants, and bakeries, and making and selling crafts.

Subsistence and micro-enterprise activities are usually situated in the informal sector. Small-scale enterprises may be found in both the formal and informal sectors. The informal sector possesses several characteristics that facilitate and encourage the participation of women at the lowest level. Its loose structure and flexibility enables women to attend to responsibilities at home and at the same time engage in income-generating ventures. However, informal sector entrepreneurs face stiff competition because easy entry into the sector means that many people compete for the same market.

Furthermore, there is evidence that the informal sector in many African countries has expanded in recent years. The reduction in public sector employment that generally accompanies structural adjustment programmes has led to a situation in which redundant staff are turning to the informal sector to make a livelihood. Many of these new entrants in informal sector activities are males who are sometimes more educated and skilled and have better access to resources, and this has intensified the competition, thereby squeezing out women-owned ventures.

Other constraints faced by female entrepreneurs include the following:

Education and training. Female entrepreneurs in the informal sector very often learn their skills from other women, sometimes within their own households. However, as traditional production and marketing techniques decrease in importance as compared to modern business techniques and management, women tend to lag more and more behind male entrepreneurs. More specifically, the low literacy rate among women entrepreneurs hinders their ability to do the paperwork and to comply with administrative procedures such as loan applications for obtaining credit.

Credit. The main issues here include the problem of having collateral for loans, the cost of administering small loans, the lack of outreach of formal banks in rural areas, and the lack of gender-sensitivity among bank staff and loan officers. Moreover, banking practice is such that only the head of household, defined dejure as male, is eligible for a loan. Although many African households are headed by women, many countries' legal systems do not recognise women as household heads. Contrary to widespread customs and practices that require women to support themselves and their children through income-generating activities, there remains the official assumption that all economic resources are in the husband's control. This is despite the fact that in a large number of African households men and women keep their finances separate.

Low productivity. The productivity of informal sector businesses is often low because of such factors as low levels of technology. For women entrepreneurs, productivity is lowered even further because of pregnancies and lack of services and facilities to assist them with child care.

The Policy Environment. The policy environment in most African countries provides few incentives or strategic support for the growth and "graduation" of informal sector enterprises. Indeed, the informal sector has traditionally been deemed unimportant in the development process. No large-scale programme comparable to those found in Asia and Latin America for micro-enterprise development has emerged in Africa. Moreover, as a marginalised group, informal sector entrepreneurs themselves have been wary of interference and becoming involved with governments that tolerate but do not encourage or promote their activities. Hence micro-entrepreneurs, including the women among them, have been remote from the policy-making circles of government.

Even in the formal sector, women suffer from a weak business-support infrastructure and a policy environment that has not been consistent or strategic in its promotion of private sector development. Furthermore, women have not been active members of local chambers of commerce or among the major borrowers of banks. They remain practically unknown to investment promotion boards, export promotion associations, and other business-development agencies. Consequently, they are far less likely to benefit from these services, therefore they lose valuable business opportunities.

It should be clear from the foregoing that female entrepreneurs are important economic agents who operate in difficult circumstances. In the next section, I show that the constraints they face are being recognised in support programmes that have emerged in recent years.

Current Actions in Favour of Women
Entrepreneurs

The main initiatives to provide assistance to female entrepreneurs have come from donors and development partners operating in the region, such as the African Development Bank (AfDB) and the African Project Development Facility (APDF) as well as from subregional organisations, such as the Preferential Trade Area (PTA) of eastern and southern Africa. It is an open question how much impact and influence these initiatives have at the national and local level. However, a review of the issues provides some indication of both the types and the shortcomings of actions currently being undertaken to meet the needs of African women entrepreneurs.

African Development Bank

As a regional development bank, the African Development Bank (AfDB) mobilises financial resources at the international level for investment in the region, along the lines of normal banking principles. Essentially, the bank supports private entrepreneurs through two main mechanisms, as follows:

- The Bank extends lines of credit to a number of financial institutions in the region for on-lending to entrepreneurs operating small- and medium-sized enterprises. These businesses are normally too small for the (AfDB) to reach directly. However, loans on-lent by financial institutions still tend to be fairly large and are consequently beyond the reach of many women in small- and medium-scale enterprises. Accordingly, the AfDB's Women In Development (WID) Unit has emphasised the necessity of increasing the number of female beneficiaries from on-lending by financial intermediaries.
- The Private Sector Development Unit (PSDU) of the bank provides direct financial assistance to medium- and large-scale ventures. Here, again, female owned or managed businesses are not among the usual beneficiaries of PSDU activities.

Because of the difficulty of reaching African women entrepreneurs both directly and through the usual financial intermediaries, policy at AfDB on providing support to female entrepreneurs has been evolving. In particular, the bank's WID Unit has identified the provision of credit to women entrepreneurs as a priority. Several WID projects are specifically concerned with providing and channelling financing for female entrepreneurial ventures.

African Project Development Facility

The African Project Development Facility (APDF) is a joint initiative of the African Development Bank, the International Finance Corporation (IFC) of the World Bank Group, and the United Nations Development Programme (UNDP). APDF was established in 1986 to promote small- and medium-sized formal sector entrepreneurial ventures. It is primarily concerned with establishing a strong local consulting capacity to help entrepreneurs develop viable business projects for funding and other assistance.

Since its inception, APDF has helped prepare and raise financing for over 101 entrepreneurial projects in Sub-Saharan Africa. But only in fifteen of these projects were women the principal contributors or beneficiaries. This is partly because the investment ceiling for APDF supported projects is beyond the reach of many female entrepreneurs. In addition, the institutional and structural impediments women encounter make it difficult for them to take advantage of APDF services. APDF, however, is responding to these constraints through such measures as encouraging greater flexibility in the range of projects it sponsors; sensitising local banks and financial institutions to the situation of women entrepreneurs and their specific needs; increasing the number of women consultants that are available for project development; and developing and putting in place mechanisms for cooperation between various multilateral and bilateral sponsors in providing support to female entrepreneurs.

Preferential Trade Area

The Preferential Trade Area (PTA) of eastern and southern Africa provides an example of subregional initiatives. The PTA is a subregional effort aimed at promoting inter-African trade. The development and promotion of female entrepreneurial capacity has been a leading priority of the PTA secretariat. It's policies are designed to achieve the following objectives:

- to improve economic conditions of women in PTA countries;
- to increase awareness of women's issues at the policy level among member governments; and

• to integrate women into PTA trade and development programmes.

In particular, a Women in Business (WIB) programme has been developed at PTA. One of the activities of this programme is the establishment of a revolving fund to offer credit to women on concessionary terms and to provide assistance in identifying investment opportunities, undertaking market research, and related activities. PTA is also promoting the establishment of National Associations for Women in Business. At the continental level, this complements an initiative at the Economic Commission for Africa (ECA) to establish a Federation of African Women Entrepreneurs.

Assessment

The three initiatives described above as examples of policy trends that have emerged to overcome the constraints African women entrepreneurs face, tend to miss the majority of female entrepreneurs, especially those operating in the informal sector or undertaking subsistence activities. Instead, these enterprises are designed to fill the gaps left by the usual financial intermediaries and business development agencies in providing support for women entrepreneurs operating in the formal sector. Efforts to promote national or regional associations of women in business are similarly directed primarily at formal sector entrepreneurs. Indeed, a major bottleneck in providing support to all groups of female entrepreneurs is the lack of systematic and comprehensive data about their activities at the national level to enable proper targeting of assistance. These issues are taken up again below.

Conclusion and Recommendations: Towards Enhancing the Role and Capacity of African Women Entrepreneurs

The point that African women entrepreneurs are not a uniform group is one that deserves special emphasis. Hence their divergent needs cannot be addressed in a uniform fashion and neither can their opinions, needs, and specific requirements be assumed. The women themselves should participate in actions that are being undertaken to enhance their capacity.

In relation to this, the goal of "empowerment" should be borne in mind. The empowerment of female entrepreneurs through increased self-sufficiency should remain a central goal of all interventions. In this, the positive relationship between improving the means by which women can make a livelihood and bringing about more fundamental changes in their lives should not be forgotten.

The range of interventions that can be undertaken to enhance the role and capacity of African women entrepreneurs should be broad, encompassing not only the micro-project level and the national-policy level, but the regional level as well. Recommendations on the priority areas of action follow.

Policy Framework

The best-conceived measures of enterprise-level support can be completely counteracted by an inappropriate or inconsistent policy framework. Hence it is necessary for policy-makers not only to provide a supportive policy environment for women entrepreneurs at different levels but also to maintain regular channels of communication to facilitate responses to new or changing needs. This is by no means a simple process, but promoting gender-equitable opportunities requires ongoing policy dialogue. Donors and subregional organisations should also contribute to this dialogue if their initiatives are to be relevant to the actual needs of women entrepreneurs at different levels.

Information and Data

The lack of specific information and data concerning women entrepreneurs has already been identified as a gap hindering the targeting of appropriate intervention measures. Besides obtaining basic data, research processes should be broad enough to obtain qualitative information about the needs of women that is useful to both policy-makers and practitioners in entrepreneurial development agencies and donor organisations. In this context, two specific recommendations follow.

- The ECA should create a data bank on female entrepreneurs at the regional level. This should include all currently available relevant data and should be updated on a regular basis. Such data can be used not only to guide policy interventions but also to facilitate further research, including sample surveys.
- At the national level, all projects assisting female entrepreneurs should be documented, not only to avoid possible duplication but also to provide information on the lessons from both success and failure.

Organisation and Networking

Strong women's organisations and networks are an important part of a strategy of empowerment and advocacy. This is important for women entrepreneurs operating at all levels, including the most marginalised. Women entrepreneurs should also play an active role in mainstream organisations such as chambers of commerce. Governments and donors should encourage such participation through the appointment of women to the boards of commercial banks and business-development agencies. Efforts should also be made to support and strengthen women's organisations, including the subregional and regional initiatives of the PTA and ECA that were mentioned earlier.

Access to Credit

This issue of credit access has received considerable attention. It has also been identified as the area in which women entrepreneurs require most assistance. It is a complex issue that encompasses questions of policy on interest rates, the appropriateness of subsidies, the graduation of borrowers from subsidised to commercial sources of credit, the role of training and technical assistance and other institutional aspects of identifying viable projects for financing, and the sustainability of entrepreneurial ventures for which credit has been provided. These are some of the concerns that credit programmes for women entrepreneurs must address. Moreover, although several credit schemes for women entrepreneurs have been established in various countries of the region as a short- to medium-term measure, the structural aspects of the problem should also be looked at in the long term.

Training

Like credit, lack of management skills on the part of female entrepreneurs has often been identified as a major constraint in fulfilling their full potential. The response to this problem by governments, donors, and non-governmental organisations has been far-reaching and wide-ranging. A number of training materials, modules, and methodologies have been developed. These can be collated and assessed for their potential replication. Beyond this, a continuing challenge is to enhance the incorporation of management, business, and allied training in the curriculum of educational and vocational programmes of women and girls inside and outside the school system.

This chapter has been concerned with the special needs of African women entrepreneurs. African women have for long engaged in entrepreneurial activities, but recent economic crises, coupled with alarming population pressures, have accelerated the feminisation of poverty in the region. This has led millions of African women into entrepreneurial activities as an income-generating strategy at various levels of the economy but more so in the informal sector. The challenge is to use this outburst of entrepreneurial energy creatively. The recommendations that I have outlined provide indications of the kinds of problems that have to be addressed. Most importantly, policy dialogue with the potential beneficiaries of entrepreneurial development schemes remains the crucial catalyst in enhancing the capacity of the African woman entrepreneur.

Further Reading

African Project Development Facility, *Documents presented to the Conference on Entrepreneurship Development in Sub-Saharan Africa* (Accra: African Project Development Facility [APDF], 1992).

Marsden, Keith, *African Entrepreneurs: Pioneers of Development* (Washington, DC: International Finance Corporation Technical Paper No. 9, 1990).

Preferential Trade Area, *Report on the First Roundtable on Women in Business in Eastern and Southern African States, 1992* (Lusaka: Preferential Trade Area [PTA], 1992).

Van Hoeflaken, Maaike, "Women in the Private Sector in Africa," (draft technical note prepared for the African Development Bank (AfdB), Abidjan: AfDB, 1993).

11

Building Indigenous Entrepreneurial Capacity: Trends and Issues

David Fasholé Luke

This chapter is being written against a background of reforms since the early 1980s to liberalise African economies, restructure public sectors, and facilitate environments in which market forces can influence allocative efficiency. These reforms also reflect the rethinking of the role of the state in society and economy.[1] The consensus that is emerging suggests that development is no longer a public sector responsibility alone. The new development management paradigm advanced in this book underlines this point.

It should be acknowledged at the outset that in the African context, the ubiquitous informal sector is a fact of entrepreneurial life. Entrepreneurship remains the main vehicle of facilitating the "graduation" of informal sector ventures with realistic business prospects to better- established and better-endowed enterprises as well as the principal means of promoting economic diversification, export to niche markets, future growth, and higher living standards. To that extent, this chapter represents a timely contribution to the discussion of the issues on what amounts to a subject of utmost contemporary relevance. Indigenous entrepreneurship is the focus. It is taken as axiomatic that an increasing level of foreign entrepreneurial activity and investment is desirable in Africa. This chapter complements the assessment in Chapter 10 of the special problems of African women entrepreneurs and the review in Chapter 12 of privatisation and public enterprise reform.

In the discussion that follows I have three objectives. First, I tour the labyrinth of concepts characterising African entrepreneurship to distinguish between levels of entrepreneurial activity. Second, I examine the constraints on the effectiveness of entrepreneurs operating at each level.

And third, I distill from the discussion in the first two sections a number of practical insights and policy measures for overcoming the constraints. Before I turn to this prospectus, it is necessary to define the concept of entrepreneurship.

Joseph Schumpeter's classical characterisation emphasised that entrepreneurship means creativity and innovation (including—but not only—technological invention and adaptation) as well as competent management in a business setting to meet specific business objectives.[2] Alexander Gershenkron applied this to a development context suggesting that entrepreneurship also means the application of these attributes and practices to meet a nation's set objectives concerning economic development.[3] On both counts, entrepreneurial characteristics are relevant to various levels of private sector operations and public sector responsibilities. In short, an entrepreneur is a person who is able to perceive opportunities, is creative, innovative, and capable of marshalling the resources to bring the perceived opportunities to fruition. Accordingly, the term can be used in a very broad sense to include persons engaged in business ventures of any size or scope, as well as those in non-governmental organisations (NGOs) or government or, indeed, any other work situation.

Situating Concepts of African Entrepreneurship

Conceptualising business ventures operating on different scales has given rise to several concepts of size. The various characterisations point to a simple problem: Any concept of size is relative. The metaphor of an "iceberg" has been used by one author to describe the range of contemporary African entrepreneurial experiences.[4] It is a useful metaphor, modified here to make sense of the conceptual labyrinth of African entrepreneurship.

Deep below the waterline of the iceberg is a mass of very small, often one-person enterprises that typically operate outside any legal or fiscal framework. Such businesses are referred to as *microenterprises* in this chapter. A profile is presented in Box 11.1 to exemplify the reality of an African microenterprise. Excluding the subsistence agricultural sector, these entrepreneurs are engaged in selling assorted merchandise, providing a range of basic services, such as repairs, and producing goods, such as farm implements, indigenous craftware and consumer products, including clothing and furniture. It is well known that the 1972 International Labour Organisation (ILO) Employment Mission to Kenya introduced the term "informal sector" to describe such activities. The ILO went on to suggest that the proliferation of these activities is fundamen-

Part Four

Promoting Entrepreneurship and Private Sector Development

Box 11.1

Profile of an African microenterprise
The story of Gilbert Sarre who repairs
refrigerators and air conditioners

At 14 years of age Gilbert Sarre found himself out in the streets of Abidjan. He tried various jobs. That was in 1978. His father, a Burkinabe migrant, had moved to Abidjan from another city in the Cote d'Ivoire four years earlier as a houseboy/cook, earning no more than a minimum income or in any case, not enough to see his six children through school. Because of moving from place to place, Gilbert had no more than a few years of primary education.

Today he owns a small, but well-equipped workshop where he repairs refrigerators and air conditioners. Here is his story:

By chance, really. I had this friend who knew this priest in Port Bouet who, on a day when I was there, told us about a plan to set up a centre where young people could meet and also learn certain things. I thought that this was a good idea and I volunteered with other kids to help construct it. When the Pilot Centre as it is called opened in 1983, the 20 volunteers could enrol without being charged—subsequent apprentices paid 5,000 CFA to enter.

I decided to go for the repairs of refrigerators and air conditioners because a relative whom I admire is in this business. Unfortunately, he couldn't help me because he doesn't have his own workshop; he is employed by someone else. For our training, the Centre found a first-rate refrigerator repair man. He didn't have his own workshop—he worked in the open air. He agreed to the Centre's proposal: he would train apprentices while pursuing his business and they would provide him with a suitable work place free of charge. It is like that for all six trainers in the Centre.

I spent three years there. At the end the Centre gave me a certificate. Because it is difficult to find a wage-job and because I didn't have the means to set up my own workshop, I then became a mobile repair man. I went door-to-door on my little motorbike to repair refrigerators and air conditioners. Slowly I accumulated savings, I bought myself the necessary tools and, finally, I opened my own workshop. It is now my turn to train. I have six apprentices. I am a happy man. I earn enough and every month I give my mother some money to help her feed my little brothers. I don't live with them any longer. I am independent. I am thinking of marriage.

Source: Fred Fluitman (ed.), *Training for Work in the Informal Sector* (Geneva: International Labour Organisation (ILO), 1989), 114.

tally a consequence of un- (and under-) employment in a context of rapid population growth in rural and urban settings. Informal sector enterprises usually employ no more than five to ten persons including the owner and family and some apprentices. These enterprises normally require less than the equivalent of US$100 in starting capital and rarely up to the equivalent of US$5,000. (The figures on employment and capital are illustrative: Rigid adherence to them is not necessary.)

In the area around the waterline of the iceberg are those businesses that rarely operate according to the requirements of existing national legislation. They may or may not occupy known premises and may or may not own bank accounts. Such businesses straddle the informal and formal sectors and, like microenterprises, can be found in virtually all kinds of economic activities—financial services (such as savings clubs), agriculture, fishery, cottage industries, craftware, manufacture, mining, trade, construction, transportation, etc. They may employ as many as ten to fifty persons or more and their start-up capital could range from as little as the equivalent of US$100 to as much as US$10,000 or more. These businesses are referred to as here as *small-sized enterprises*. The following extract presents a profile of an African small enterprise in a less-abstract light.

"Irene Dufu, a Ghanaian nurse turned business woman, shows what access to resources in a more and more competitive economy can do to spark the entrepreneurial spirit. She registered her fishing company—Cactus Enterprise Ltd. in Tema, Ghana, in 1978, having started operations informally two years earlier. She began with a small wooden vessel and a crew of twelve. Today she employs sixty-five fishermen on three boats. Her turnover in 1989 was more than $1.2 million.

What was Mrs. Dufu's route to success? While serving as a nursing officer at the Accra military hospital, she was approached by a group of artisan fishermen from a village where her father had served as regent. These fishermen were seeking a loan to buy new canoes. They were illiterate and lacked collateral, so the banks had turned them down. Mrs. Dufu received a loan on their behalf, using her house as security. The fishermen repaid it in six months. This started Mrs. Dufu thinking about a career switch. Salaries in the army and public enterprises were not keeping pace with the rapidly rising cost of living, and she had three children to educate. Many successful trading businesses and bus transport companies in Ghana are owned by women. Why not go into fishing and marketing on her own? With an end-of-service gratuity from the army, she bought a truck, which she then used as collateral for a loan to purchase a secondhand wooden fishing boat. Then she recruited a captain with a nose for tracking down shoal movements and a crew willing to spend weeks at sea.

She found she could compete with the state-owned fishing company, selling cheaper yet still enjoying good margins. She then bought and repaired an inexpensive tuna ship which allowed her to break into the market for canned tuna, supplying a U.S. company."[5]

Above the waterline, where the iceberg becomes visible, but still well below the tip, can be found formal, known, registered companies established and operating according to legal standards defined in relevant national legislation. Such enterprises operate within the banking and fiscal framework and can be found in virtually all sectors of the economy. They may employ as many as 100 persons or more, including perhaps expatriate experts. Start-up capital could range from the equivalent of US$1,000 to as much as US$1 million or more. In this chapter, businesses operating on this scale are referred to as *intermediate-sized enterprises*. Again, a profile is presented in Box 11.2 to illustrate the reality of an intermediate-sized enterprise.

Box 11.2

Profile of an African intermediate-sized enterprise
The story of the Patels of Tanzania, automobile
radiator manufacturers

Tanzanian firm, Afro-Cooling is majority-owned by local Asians with a government minority equity holding. It started operations in 1979 to make radiators for automobiles by importing a dozen technicians from an Indian firm with considerable experience in radiator manufacture based originally on German technology. The experts designed a small two-shed plant and procured equipment from Germany and cheap, simple tools from India. Local employees working with the Indian technicians on the shop floor were trained intensively. Although the scale of operation was about one-tenth of international levels, the use of simple labour-intensive techniques enabled Afro-Cooling to keep costs down and produce an enormous variety of radiators efficiently. Its products were exported to other African countries and the Middle East, and it won a contract to supply radiators as 'original equipment' to the local Saab-Scania truck assembler after rigorous testing of its products in Sweden.

Source: S. Lall, "Structural Problems of Industry in Sub-Saharan Africa," in World Bank, *Long-Term Perspective Study of Sub-Saharan Africa*, vol. 2, *Economic and Sectoral Policy Issues* (Washington, DC: World Bank, 1990), 100-101.

At the tip of the iceberg can be found *large-scale-enterprises*—typically establishments with well over the equivalent of US$1 million in start-up capital and usually employing well over 100 persons. Large-scale enterprises operating in the region are engaged in all sectors: trade, agriculture, industry, mining, utilities, transport and communications, finance, insurance, utilities, and other services. Examples of indigenous privately owned enterprises of this size range from shipping companies and air travel and trading or manufacturing conglomerates in Nigeria to substantial industrial establishments in Egypt, Mauritius, or Tunisia. Although public enterprises are prominent in large-scale operations, there is evidence to suggest that the recent wave of privatisation is altering prevailing ownership patterns. Box 11.3 provides a profile of a large-scale enterprise at the tip of the indigenous entrepreneurial iceberg.

Box 11.3

Profile of an African large-scale enterprise
The story of Morogoro Shoe Company of Tanzania

Tanzania's state-owned Morogoro Shoe Company (MSC) is a case of wasted resources. Financed by the World Bank, MSC was based on Tanzania's large supply of hides and skins and seemed economically sensible. It was a relatively low-technology activity in which several developing countries have established export markets. It was supposed to have high local value added and economies of scale (it was apparently designed as the world's second largest shoe factory). Its products were aimed at the quality end of the market, with 80 percent of output to be exported to Europe. An Italian consultant designed the plant and installed state-of-the art equipment, highly automated, and technically capable of producing quality shoes. MSC came on stream in the early 1980s, with ample supply of imported raw materials to operate for two years. Because of a disagreement, the Italian consultant backed out before the plant became operational and the Tanzanians independently undertook the final phases of commissioning and training, with disastrous results. MSC achieved just over 5 percent capacity utilization at its peak; by 1986 the figure was below 3 percent. Most of the machines were never used, quality and design were abysmal, and unit costs were very high. MSC could not compete with long-established local shoe manufacturers, like Bata, which had much older technology but a well-trained work force, and exports were clearly out of the question.

· *Source:* Lall, *Structural Problems of Industry in Sub-Saharan Africa*, 100.

The metaphor of an iceberg, somewhat awkward in Africa's tropical context, nonetheless provides a useful means of pinpointing and illustrating various concepts of post-colonial African entrepreneurship. It facilitates a distinction between entrepreneurial activities in terms of level, size, and scope. With this outline as a background, an assessment of the constraints African entrepreneurs operating at different levels face against the economic and commercial imperatives of the 1990s follows.

Constraints on Indigenous Entrepreneurship

Entrepreneurship—in all its diversity—in Africa provides a dynamic and potentially efficient means of meeting many of the emerging challenges of development in the region. The question that therefore arises is, quite simply, what is holding African entrepreneurs back? What are the constraints on African entrepreneurial success in the 1990s? What can be done to remove these constraints? The main constraints—distilled from a number of sources on this question[6]—are presented below. First are general constraints that apply to existing and potential entrepreneurs operating at all levels, with an elaboration and discussion of these constraints. Following those are specific constraints that apply to particular levels of entrepreneurial activity, namely, informal sector microenterprises and formal sector small-, intermediate-, and large-scale enterprises. The second list is also followed by an elaboration and discussion. The question of what can be done to remove the constraints is a subject for later discussion in this chapter.

The general constraints on entrepreneurship are summarized below:

- Political instability
- Lack of business confidence
- Deteriorating infrastructures
- Uncoordinated policies on business
  promotion and development (financial policies, trade policies, and labour policies)
- Insufficient knowledge in government
  about the business sector

General Constraints

General constraints on entrepreneurship in contemporary Africa apply to existing and potential entrepreneurs. That is to say, aside from the obstacles posed by these constraints on businesses that are already in operation, potential investors may be deterred by what is perceived as an unfavourable business climate. An unfavourable business climate is difficult to define or, much more, to measure. But it refers to the willingness of investors and entrepreneurs to risk their capital, time, and other resources in the expectation of future returns. Hence the business climate is fundamentally a matter of perception of risk. As such, it cannot always be explained by objective conditions. Take the case of *political instability* in Africa.

Political instability can be defined "objectively" in terms of a breakdown in the normal functioning of government, civil unrest, or an acute condition of political disorder. Indeed, Liberia or Somalia in 1992 provide obvious examples of African political instability. But such clear-cut cases are the exceptions rather than the rule. Moreover, with a political settlement of the underlying problems, conditions in obvious instances of political instability could change very rapidly. What is more, where there are flash points of civil strife or other difficulties arising from conflicts over the legitimacy of government (for example in Algeria, Kenya, Malawi, Nigeria, Sierra Leone, Sudan, or Togo, also in 1992), the extent of the deterrent to an investor is ultimately a matter of personal judgment. The point is, however, that weakly institutionalised governments, challenges to the legitimacy of established authority, and civil unrest generate a psychology of fear. Africa is losing billions of dollars every year in both indigenous and foreign investment (and much more from multiplier effects) as a result of perceptions of risk associated with political instability. Such perceptions, of course, would deter a microentrepreneur wishing to set up an operation to produce kerosene lamps as much as it would deter a large investor wishing to establish a factory to manufacture office furniture.

Another dimension of an unfavourable business climate is *lack of business confidence*. Business confidence has been defined as a complex combination of objective "incentive" factors and subjective "confidence" factors.[7] As with political stability, a lack of confidence in any given country is related to objective conditions, in this instance, unhelpful policies or nefarious practices towards the business community. It is further related to fears—or subjective perceptions—that these policies and practices may change for the worse in the future. Misgivings are usually aroused by an established record of poor economic management and performance in the country in question. In such a context, business confidence shrivels out of fear of the chaotic state of economic management.

Business confidence may also flag in situations in which public statements accusing entrepreneurs of exploitation, profiteering, and other antisocial conduct are consistently made by politicians or influential public figures. Where public authorities fail to demonstrate a realistic understanding of the role of entrepreneurs in national development, the business community may feel vulnerable, exposed, and inclined to take their investments elsewhere.

Finally, lack of business confidence may arise when the public service bureaucracy is unhelpful, or even hostile, to investors. This can happen where bureaucratic inefficiency, incompetence, or red tape results in unnecessary delays in processing applications for licenses and permits or obtaining various types of clearances. An unclear or inconsistent division of responsibilities between departments, poor coordination among them, or the prevalence of corrupt practices can also frustrate bona fide entrepreneurs operating at any level.

The general business climate is also affected by the quality of *public infrastructure*. One of the casualties of Africa's intractable economic crisis of the 1980s is the deterioration of infrastructures, particularly in power, transport and communications, and water supply. Telephone and other communication facilities that work erratically, congested port facilities, and badly surfaced roads inevitably result in delays. As one assessment of contemporary African capitalism has noted, such inadequacies push up the cost of handling inputs and outputs.[8]

Uncoordinated policies on business promotion and development—especially finance, trade, and labour policies,[9] is another dimension of an unfavourable business climate and a source of many entrepreneurial frustrations. At the heart of this issue lies a practical problem: One agency of government does one thing; another agency (or perhaps even a division within the same agency) does the opposite. Contradictions abound; mixed signals are sent to investors. The solution, of course, is not to leave business development to "market forces." On the contrary, there is simply no alternative to sound institutional capacity in government for policy development, analysis, and review—if economic objectives are to be implemented with consistency.

Insufficient knowledge about the business sector in government is the final issue for consideration in the catalogue of general constraints on entrepreneurship in contemporary Africa. To be sure, efficient information flows between government and the business community is perhaps the most crucial element in improving the business climate, overcoming policy inconsistencies, and reassuring business confidence. Three areas of weakness are worth emphasising: inadequate institutional mechanisms for consultation and consensus-building between planners and policy-makers, on one hand, and different sectors and levels of the business community, on the other; shortcomings in national microeconomic databases and information systems; and insufficient appreciation in government of the role of market networks in business development and in enhancing the efficiency of business operations.

Specific constraints on entrepreneurship in Africa are summarized below:

- Informal sector microenterprises (limited, segmented markets; crude production techniques; and inadequate policy support)
- Small- and intermediate-sized enterprises (limited managerial capacity; constraints on technological development; weak policy or institutional support schemes)
- Large-scale enterprises (problems of investment design; excess capacity; weaknesses in technology adaptation; paucity of backward or forward links; and difficulties in the management of size)

Specific Constraints

A list of that apply at respective levels of entrepreneurial activity, informal sector microenterprises, small and intermediate-sized enterprises, and large-scale enterprises has been provided above. The focus now shifts to a discussion of the issues at these different levels.

Informal Sector Microenterprises

Among the constraints that apply to *informal sector microenterprises* are limited, segmented markets; crude management and production techniques; and inadequate institutional or policy support.

The size of market for many microenterprises depends on personal relationships between the owner and a small number of customers, or perhaps, on the service or product being custom-designed. In such cases, the potential for intra-enterprise growth is limited by market size. Hence economies from large-scale production cannot be achieved. This has often been the case in the metalworking trades and in tailoring and furniture making.

On top of this, management and production techniques in the informal sector are often cumbersome—a function of microenterprise entrepreneurs' lack of knowledge about more effective techniques. Although some incremental efforts have been made over the years by African governments to provide support services, such as workshops on low-cost sites, training, and access to loans, such efforts, have often lacked effective and strategic direction or have been inadequate.

Nonetheless, informal sector entrepreneurs, through two major routes, have been known to overcome these specific constraints of limited market size, cumbersome management and production methods, and government inertia. First, by link with formal sector businesses, microenterprises can achieve access to more sizeable markets and information or advice on such matters as improved management and production methods and better product design. An example of this is the wickerwork (*vannerie*) cane furniture trade in Abidjan. Much of the production of this beautiful and exotic furniture is carried out in the informal sector. Formal sector merchants, realising the profits that could be made from the product, have been keen to acquire a steady source of supply at wholesale prices for both local retail sales as well as overseas exports. As market networks develop, formal sector entrepreneurs have often been a source of information on product designs that are in demand and a source of advice on management and production techniques.[10]

A second way in which microenterprises can grow is through intergenerational expansion; the business gradually expands from one generation of family ownership to the other as experience and capital is acquired. In this way, petty trading among some Hausa families of northern Nigeria, for example, has grown through several generations into multi-store ownership or even manufacturing industry.[11] In Sudan, one study demonstrated the underlying continuity of business experience and capital accumulation over several generations, beginning with traditional office-holding and early access to land for commercial farming, through the education of sons, diversification from agriculture to trade, culminating, in the case of some families, in the establishment of modern industries by a more recent generation of Western-educated descendants.[12]

The extract on pages 152-153 and the profile in Box 11.2 illustrate the nature of small- and intermediate-sized enterprises. Such businesses are usually well established and managed by enterprising individuals with fairly sophisticated organisational skills. But among the constraints that apply to entrepreneurship at these levels are limited managerial capabilities; limited capacity for technological adaptation; and inadequate public provision of enterprise-level support.

The definition of entrepreneurship provided earlier emphasised its creative and innovative aspects. But a distinction can be made between the investment facets of entrepreneurship, identifying market opportunities and acting upon them, and the managerial side, running all aspects of the business once it is established and as it grows—finance, production, labour relations, marketing, advertising, research and development (R&D), and so on.[13] The investment side requires a flair or talent to perceive market opportunities and a willingness to take risks. The management side requires not only leadership and organisational competence but—in today's complex world—highly specialised knowledge and experience. As a business grows beyond a certain size, even if as in the cases represented in the extract and profile, it remains relatively small in the amount of capital or labour employed, it begins to require input from different management specialisations. At this point, the founder, or any individual, can seldom satisfactorily combine in his or her person all the skills required in the investment and managerial sides of entrepreneurship. It is well known that the supply of managerial skills and experience in Africa is limited. This remains a constraint at this stage of the region's development.

An underdeveloped capacity for technology adaptation and assimilation is also related to early stages of industrial development. Here again, as businesses grow in size, improvements in both productivity and the quality of the good or service usually require the application of more effective production methods. Accordingly, technological innovation (or the successful assimilation or adaptation of existing technology) is a necessary condition for productivity gains. The profile in Box 11.2 presents successful technology assimilation. Technical assistance from abroad was a key element in the success of the firm. It is clear that joint ventures and foreign investment and assistance will remain key mechanisms for the diffusion of technological know-how in Africa.

Entrepreneurs everywhere need advice, information, and various kinds of services to set up their businesses and deal with difficulties that arise in the course of operations. Technical and advisory services can be provided through market networks (via private consulting companies, finance companies, and commercial banks) and through the tertiary sector (via chambers of commerce, management professional organisations, cooperatives, universities, colleges, management training institutions, and NGOs). Though private (and some tertiary) sector provisions can be expensive, they are probably more professional and results-oriented.

There is clearly a role for market and tertiary networks to provide consulting and other services to entrepreneurs. But government intervention is required to establish a general framework for business development consistent with national economic objectives and priorities. Indeed, as part of post-colonial efforts to indigenise business activities in key economic sectors, many African governments established a range of support systems. These included facilities to provide start-up capital, technical advice and training, industrial estates, and related infrastructure. Sectoral development banks, investment promotion centres, industrial extension services, and export processing zones were among public institutions established to provide enterprise-level support. Specific country examples include Cameroon's National Centre for Assistance to

Small- and Medium-Size Enterprises (CAMPE), Kenya's network of industrial estates, and Mauritius' Export Processing Zone (EPZ). A systematic appraisal of the effectiveness of government schemes of enterprise support has probably not been undertaken. However, there is evidence to suggest that a few countries, such as Mauritius and Kenya, are way ahead of others in the provision of schemes that are better-coordinated, flexible, and performance-oriented. But in several other countries, evidence suggesting serious weaknesses in government support systems has emerged. In Nigeria, for example, one study found that only a few industrial development centres (established to provide extension services) are working as envisaged. Shortages of equipment and trained personnel were identified as serious weaknesses.[14] Again, these weaknesses underline the general African experience of poorly coordinated and implemented interventions.

Some of the specific constraints on African business that have been discussed up to this point also apply to *large-scale enterprises*. But at this level of entrepreneurship, constraints that are particularly related to size, scale, and complexity of the undertaking are especially relevant.

Designing investment in large-scale operations is a very complex undertaking. Mistakes are extremely costly and can easily result in industrial white elephants, as the profile in Box 11.3 readily illustrates. Indeed, problems in original investment design have been a common constraint on the performance of large-scale enterprises in both the public and private sectors. Shortcomings in attending to the details of initial investment design have been known to have bedeviled such operations as the steel, petro chemical, and pulp and paper industries in Nigeria and the textile industries in Tanzania and Somalia.[15] Although the expertise and experience in designing complex investments provided through foreign assistance or joint ventures is useful in overcoming the complexities, foreign experts cannot always be relied upon for the best possible advice. This is particularly so if they provide technology and equipment or if their remuneration is linked to the size of the investment. Another hazard in relying exclusively upon foreign experts is that local engineers gain little insight into how the technology works and how it can be modified or improved. The new learning that occurs in any project from adapting it to new settings or new raw materials accrues to the foreign experts, with little spillovers, to the local economy. Moreover, experience has shown that the lower the absorptive and adaptation capabilities of technology buyers, the higher is the total cost of technology transfer. East Asian experience, however, has demonstrated that local participation by design and engineering firms can quickly lead to development of the relevant skills.[16]

Closely related to the question of investment design is the problem of excess capacity. Significant excess capacity is known to exist in many African large-scale operations. One of the reasons for this is simply too ambitious an original investment design, resulting in structural excess capacity. But other reasons include operating difficulties, such as frequent shortages of spare parts, essential raw materials, inadequate provision for the maintenance of equipment, and infrastructural deficiencies such as frequent break down of power or water supply.

Weaknesses in the adaptation and assimilation of technology is a third constraint that is often a cause of excess capacity. As previously noted, an underdeveloped technological capacity is related to the early stages of industrial development. The turn key approach to technology transfer is simple, fairly straightforward, and, in certain industries, perhaps even the most efficient and cost-effective option. Once installed, however, the equipment requires maintenance and possibly adaptation to meet variations in raw materials or new product designs. Over time, the technology may also require upgrading. Current environmental concerns such as finding new uses for waste products and reducing energy consumption levels also demand thorough familiarisation with the technology.

All of these demands require an internalisation of production processes at several levels and from numerous disciplines. As one major study of structural problems in African industrial ventures has noted,[17] these demands rise with the inherent complexity of the technology, the scale of the operation, and the speed of technological advance in the industry. Such industries as food processing, beverages, textiles, or leather on one hand, have relatively stable technologies, simple process layouts, and easily transmitted skill requirements. On the other hand, mechanical and electric engineering industries, electronics, chemicals, and steel utilise fast-changing technologies.[18] The point is that African entrepreneurs operating or venturing into large-scale industrial ventures are compelled to assemble the capacity—in terms of technical personnel as well as hardware—to mount the sustained effort that is required. But these constraints can be overcome within an appropriate public policy framework and specific strategies on technology transfer and assimilation.

Another symptom of underdeveloped technological capacity in the region is the paucity of backward or forward links between firms in the same industry. Most industries (for example, vehicles, electronics, or chemicals) depend on a dense network of information, and technical and other cooperative arrangements. Any specific input, such as a particular component for a vehicle or a catalyst for a chemical process, has to be designed for a particular use, and its planned production must be geared to the quality required by the next stage of manufacture, with prior information on design specifications, price, and quantity.[19] The manufacture of such inputs is usually contracted-out to component suppliers—firms operating on a smaller scale within the industry.

A major constraint on African entrepreneurs venturing into manufacturing industry on a large scale is that the link-generating efforts have to proceed more or less simultaneously with the establishment of the lead enterprise. African industry is characterised by huge gaps in its link relationships. The motor vehicle industry in Nigeria, for example, has to import virtually all the components necessary for assembling the final product.[20] In the advanced industrial countries, however, these relationships between firms have evolved over a long period of time. The experience of the newly industrialising countries (NICs) has revealed that a carefully orchestrated effort is required by both the lead enterprise and government industrial development agencies to provide an appropriate policy framework and well-targeted incentives for small- and medium-scale entrepreneurs to enter into cooperative operations with entrepreneurs in large-scale industrial undertakings.

The management of size is the fifth constraint on large-scale entrepreneurship in contemporary Africa. There is growing consensus among management practitioners and academic commentators that the days of the "traditional" Weberian bureaucratic organisational form are over. In an increasingly competitive world economy, innovation has become the cutting edge of comparative advantage. Large organisations stifle initiative and creativity.[21] Large-scale organisation in Africa is especially prone to these problems.[22] But certain scale economies continue to be contingent on large size. Hence large organisations are being broken down into profit centres, quality circles, and work groups. These suborganisational units are then flexibly reintegrated into the overall organisational structure. It has been observed that the "Japanese have always based their continuing manufacturing miracle on tiny entrepreneurial component makers . . . and on surprisingly small . . . profit centres even within huge plants."[23]

From the general and specific constraints examined one can distill a number of recommendations for promoting African entrepreneurship as a vehicle for future growth, higher living standards, and sustained development.

Policy Measures, Recommendations, and Conclusion

Following the method of exposition that I have adopted in this chapter, two categories of recommendations can be identified: general recommendations and specific recommendations.

General Recommendations

The general recommendations I offer for building indigenous entrepreneurial capacity apply across-the-board.

Political Stability. Entrepreneurship at any level cannot thrive in a context of political instability. The whole African region is losing billions of dollars every year in both indigenous and foreign investment as a result of perceptions of risk associated with civil unrest and weakly institutionalised governments. To be sure, the causes of political conflict and instability in many countries are often complex and intractable. Although the current wave of democratic reforms in the region augurs well for the future, democratic structures of governance remain fragile. Both the business community and public officials bear a heavy responsibility to educate the public on the relationship between political stability and business confidence. Africa's development partners should also take concrete measures to foster the consolidation of democratic processes and political stability in the region.

Competent Economic Management, Efficient Civil Services and Sound Infrastructure. Business confidence is also affected by the level of competence in government economic management, the efficiency of the civil service, the attitudes of influential public figures towards private enterprise, and the quality of public infrastructure and services. Specific measures to promote entrepreneurship in the region must rest on a foundation of sound economic management, efficient public services, positive attitudes towards business, and reliable infrastructure.

Established Institutional Capacity for Policy Coordination. There are often profound contradictions among the range of policy measures on business promotion and development. Finance, trade, and labour policies are areas of particular concern. Policy objectives must be clearly defined and specific measures made consistent with overall priorities of economic management. Experience has shown that the provision of incentives to entrepreneurs must be subject to periodic review and the continuation of these incentives must be made conditional upon performance criteria established in advance.

A Reviewed Role of Lending Institutions. The role of commercial banks and development finance companies needs careful appraisal. Aside from a tendency to withhold credit from informal sector entrepreneurs and other small-scale businesses, there is evidence to suggest that financial institutions such as these generate an anti-equity bias. That is to say, as a source of investment capital, these institutions typically lend to sole proprietorships and partnerships. In the absence of (or where there are only fledgling) stock markets and merchant banks able to mobilise equity capital, this pattern of lending perpetuates itself. Thus joint-stock companies and equity markets have been slow to develop in African countries, and formal sector entrepreneurs are denied both the flexibility of tapping this source of finance and the discipline of working under pressure from equity markets. (See Chapter 7 also).

Sound Information Systems on Microeconomic Behaviour. Shortcomings in this important area of credit policy and practice is one indication that the overall framework of government-business relations in many African countries has fallen short of strategic direction. Lack of evidence of up-to-date knowledge in government about the business sector is another indication. This stands in sharp contrast with the East Asian experience. Planning and policy-making there is characterised by regular exchange of information on specific needs and requirements, including the critical area of technology transfer and development; a coordinated approach between different government agencies dealing with the business community; flexibility in response to changing circumstances; and emphasis on achieving high levels of performance. Any African government seeking to provide strategic direction to business within the overall framework of development priorities should take steps to ensure that reliable mechanisms for efficient information flows between businesses at various levels and government are put in place as the basis of the strategic direction of business promotion.

Specific Recommendations to Promote Informal Sector Microentrepreneurship

Market networks, government, and NGOs can play key roles in overcoming constraints and promoting informal sector entrepreneurship. Over the long term, of course, microenterprises can grow through intergenerational expansion, i.e., the business gradually grows as it is passed on from one generation of family ownership to another.

The Role of Market Networks. In the short term, microentrepreneurs can overcome the limitations of market size and other constraints through links with formal sector businesses. Beyond this, market networks are often more effective mechanisms for the transfer of know-how and assistance than are networks composed of government agencies and NGOs. The latter sometimes lack competitive pressures, the exigency of profit, and specialised knowledge to provide inputs that are most relevant to the needs of microentrepreneurs.

The Role of Government and NGOs. The foregoing does not, of course, deny African governments and the NGO community a proactive role in the promotion of microentrepreneurial activities. Markets often fail to generate links for a variety of reasons, including information gaps between potential collaborators. Through incentives and other measures, governments can encourage or facilitate links between informal sector entrepreneurs and their better-established formal sector counterparts. The NGO community, often a reservoir of knowledge and expertise on grass-roots activities, can also play an important role in linking informal and formal sector business. It is neither feasible nor desirable to provide a blueprint of government and NGO measures to assist and promote bona fide microentrepreneurs. But policy and institutional support should include, at minimum, three key measures: training, credit, enterprise-level support. The provision of facilities for technical and vocational *training* to upgrade the skills of informal sector workers and entrepreneurs is an important requirement. In this regard, the profile of a microentrepreneur in Box 11.1 vividly illustrates the association between training, entrepreneurship, and business development. Indeed, one of the many spin-offs of informal sector activities is the training of apprentices in the course of normal business operations. Government and NGOs can encourage this valuable service provided by microentrepreneurs through appropriate incentives to foster the practice of informal sector apprenticeships.

A second measure is the provision of *credit* facilities specifically designed to meet the needs of entrepreneurs operating on a very small scale, typically those without collateral or an established business track record. Because the management of small loans is time-consuming and expensive, conventional banks and financial institutions tend to shy away from dealing with microentrepreneurs. Hence the provision of credit facilities at this level requires unconventional banking practices. Grass-roots or community-level institutions are well placed to fill this vacuum. Banks could employ the model of the Grameen bank system, pioneered in Bangladesh and specifically oriented towards lending very small amounts. Another model that financial institutions could use is represented by Ghana's network of rural banks, which lend to informal sector businesses, small-scale farmers, and rural enterprises.

A third measure that can be adopted by governments or NGOs in promoting informal sector entrepreneurship is the provision of *enterprise-level support systems* such as business advisory centres, small-scale enterprise extension services, and physical facilities such as workshops, craft centres, water, electricity, and telephones. Advisory and extension services can provide valuable information and assistance to microentrepreneurs, especially in the areas of bookkeeping, management, and production and marketing techniques. These services can also play an important role in facilitating links between informal and formal sector businesses and may help to steer microentrepreneurs through the unfamiliar corridors of government bureaucracies with which they must sometimes deal.

<u>*Intergenerational Expansion*</u>. Although specific measures can be taken in the short or medium terms to promote business activity in the informal sector, it should be recognised that microenterprises also grow over time through intergenerational expansion. The business gradually expands as it is passed on from one generation of family ownership to another, and the family accumulates experience, know-how, and capital. It should not be forgotten that many of the world's leading corporations, for instance the Ford Motor Company, have grown from obscure, microscale ventures to the transnational corporations they have become today. There is evidence that this phenomenon is already happening among many African entrepreneurial families.

Measures to Promote Small- and Intermediate-Scale Entrepreneurship

Entrepreneurs operating on a small- to intermediate-scale usually exhibit fairly sophisticated organisational skills. But as their businesses grow along the small- to intermediate-scale continuum, they often face constraints that they must overcome: limited managerial capabilities; difficulties with technology adaptation; and, as in the case of microentrepreneurs, inadequate public provision of enterprise-level support.

Overcoming Managerial Constraints. In the context of Africa's relative early stage of economic development, the supply of indigenous managerial skills experience and expertise is understandably limited—although increasing numbers of Africans are acquiring management training and experience. National agendas of human resource development needs are already very crowded, but the expansion of management training facilities must be a leading priority. In this regard, approaches to management education and training are already undergoing a fundamental shift from "traditional," classroom-based methods to an increasing emphasis on in-house, on-the-job learning and training.[24] Dissatisfaction with traditional methods has opened the way for new arrangements that facilitate the acquisition and emergence of management skills directly relevant to the needs of business operations.

Surmounting Difficulties with Technology Transfer and Adaptation. As businesses grow along the small- and intermediate-scale continuum, they can make productivity gains from the application of more effective production methods, including improvements in technology. It is inevitable that foreign investment and technical assistance will remain important mechanisms for the diffusion of technological know-how in Africa for some time to come. This is clearly illustrated in the profile of an intermediate-scale enterprise in Box 11.2—a successful example of African technology assimilation and development. Government, as East

Asian experience has demonstrated, has a key role to play in facilitating and encouraging technology transfer, local adaptation, and development.

Enhancing Enterprise-Level Support Systems. Entrepreneurs everywhere need advice, information, and various kinds of services to set up their businesses and deal with problems that arise in the normal course of operations. Though technical and advisory services can be provided through market networks or through the tertiary sector, government intervention is also required to establish a general framework for business development as part of the planning and policy-making process. African governments should systematically appraise existing policies and measures on enterprise-level support systems to make them relevant to the needs of entrepreneurs.

Promoting Large-Scale Entrepreneurship

Many of the recommendations on promoting specific levels of entrepreneurship that I have advanced up to this point also apply to the promotion of African entrepreneurship on a large scale. The main constraints at this level, however, are principally related to size, scale, and the complexity of extensive undertakings. The profile of Morogoro Shoe Company of Tanzania (Box 11.3), an African large-scale enterprise, poignantly illustrates the issues raised by these constraints. Depending on the nature of the industry, African governments have essentially two ways to overcome these constraints: by encouraging the incremental and the turnkey approaches to investment in large-scale operations.

The Incremental Approach. There is evidence to suggest that an incremental approach to investment in large and complex undertakings provides a sound and effective basis for gaining the experience to cope with higher levels of managerial, organisational, and technological complexity. The textile industries in Kenya and Zimbabwe, for example, have grown during the last twenty-five years, from a few small mills in each country to a well-integrated industry encompassing several establishments engaged in cotton and raw materials production, spinning, weaving, design tailoring, manufacturing, and marketing. The incremental growth of the industry over time facilitated the evolution of links between production units and encouraged the foundation of a deeply rooted capacity to manage all aspects of the production process, including technology, quality control, and marketing. The experience of East Asia also suggests that through the establishment of links between firms and mastery of production and technological processes, most industries grow from the "infant" or "cottage" stage, to become, in many cases, world leaders. The East Asian electronics and motor vehicle industries are good examples of a successful incremental approach to the establishment of capacity in complex undertakings.

The Turnkey Approach. The turnkey approach to investment design and management of large-scale operations is a viable alternative to incremental growth, particularly in certain industries, such as those involving food processing, beverages, tobacco, and soaps and detergents. Indeed, indigenous entrepreneurship is well established in many similar ventures in most African countries. The turnkey approach has often been successful because the technology is relatively simple to acquire, install, operate, and maintain, and the product sales have been relatively stable.

It should be clear from the foregoing that the mastery of the complexities of large-scale operations by African entrepreneurs is clearly a long-term process. Business confidence and a favourable business climate are key factors in enhancing both the incremental and the turnkey approaches to investment in large-scale operations.

In conclusion, issues in promoting indigenous entrepreneurship in Africa continue to play a factor in the success of businesses there. There still exist many obstacles to entrepreneurship in Africa. The policy measures and recommendations I have proposed for overcoming the constraints holding back African entrepreneurs can be adopted and adapted by policy-makers in government and business leaders to their own specific circumstances. Future growth in Africa rests squarely on the shoulders of Africans, their governments, and their entrepreneurs. This is a truism that contains one of the foremost challenges in the economic development of Africa in the 1990s and beyond.

Notes

1. For an assessment of this debate see, for example, Christopher Colclough and James Manor (eds.), *States and Markets: Neo-Liberalisation and the Development-Policy Debate* (Oxford: Oxford University Press, 1991).

2. See Joseph Schumpeter, *Change and the Entrepreneur: Postulates and Patterns for Entrepreneurial History* (Cambridge, Mass.: Harvard University Press, 1949).

3. Alexander Gerschenkron, *Economic Backwardness in Historical Perspective* (Cambridge, Mass.: Harvard University Press, 1962).

4. See Jacques Giri, "Formal and Informal Small Enterprises in the Long-Term Future of Sub-Saharan Africa," in *World Bank, Long-Term Perspective Study of Sub-Saharan Africa*, vol. 2, *Economic and Sectoral Policy Issues* (Washington, DC: World Bank, 1990), 111.

5. World Bank, *World Development Report* 1991 (New York: Oxford University Press), 1991, 70-71.

6. See, for example, Philip A. Neck and Robert E. Nelson, *Small Enterprise Development: Policies and Programmes* (Geneva: International Labour Organisation

(ILO), 1987); UN Development Programme (UNDP), *Creating a Better Climate for Enterprise* (New York: UNDP, 1987); UNDP, *Human Development Report* 1990, 1991, 1992, and 1993 (New York: UNDP/Oxford University Press, successive years); John M. Page and William F. Steel, *Small Enterprise Development: Economic Issues from African Experience* (Washington, DC: World Bank Technical Paper No. 26, 1984); Keith Marsden and Thérése Bélot, *Private Enterprise in Africa: Creating a Better Environment* (Washington, DC: World Bank Discussion Paper No. 17, 1987); Maryke Dessing, *Support for Microenterprises: Lessons for Sub-Saharan Africa* (Washington, DC: World Bank Technical Paper No. 122, 1990); Keith Marsden, *African Entrepreneurs: Pioneers of Development* (Washington DC: International Finance Corporation Technical Paper No. 9, 1990); Harold Lubell, *The Informal Sector in the 1980s and 1990s* (Paris: Organisation for Economic Cooperation and Development [OECD], 1991); Aga Khan Foundation, *The Enabling Environment Conference: Effective Private Sector Contribution to Development in Sub-Saharan Africa, Nairobi, Kenya, 21-24 October 1986* (Paris: Aga Khan Foundation, 1987); Economic Commission for Africa (ECA), *Enabling Environment for Entrepreneurship Development in Africa* (report of a Senior Policy Seminar on Enhancing Entrepreneurship in the Private and Public Sectors in Africa) (Addis Ababa: ECA/African Association for Public Administration and Management [AAPAM], 1990); ECA, *Mobilising the Informal Sector and Non-Governmental Organisations for African Economic Recovery and Development: Policy and Management Issues* (Addis Ababa: ECA/AAPAM/Special Action Programme for Administration and Management [SAPAM], 1991); Peter Kilby (ed.), *Entrepreneurship and Economic Development* (New York: Free Press, 1971); P. Marris and A. Somerset, *African Businessmen* (London: Routledge and Kegan Paul, 1971); Adebayo Adedeji (ed.), *Indigenisation of African Economies* (London: Hutchinson, 1981); and Paul Kennedy, *African Capitalism: The Struggle for Ascendancy* (Cambridge: Cambridge University Press, 1988).

7. See International Finance Corporation (IFC), *Measures to Promote the Role of the Private Sector in Caribbean Development: A Report to the Caribbean Group for Cooperation in Economic Development by the Task Force on Private Sector Activities.* (Washington, DC: IFC, 1980), 12.

8. On this point, see Kennedy, *African Capitalism,* 156.

9. See Marsden and Bélot, *Private Enterprise in Africa,* 21-32.

10. See Fluitman, *Training for Work in the Informal Sector,* 109-110.

11. See Kennedy, *African Capitalism,* 177-178.

12. Ibid. See also Fatima B. Mahmoud, *The Sudanese Bourgeoisie* (London: Zed Press, 1984).

13. See Walter Elkan, "Entrepreneurs and Entrepreneurship in Africa," *World Bank Research Observer* 3 (2) 1988, 182.

14. See T. O. Odetola, "Industrial Extension: A Neglected Factor in African Industrial Development" (paper Commissioned for the ECA/SAPAM Senior Policy Seminar on an Enabling Environment for Enhancing Entrepreneurship in the Private and Public Sectors in Africa, Cairo, 8-12 October 1990), 2-3.

15. See Sanjaya Lall, "Structural Problems of Industry in Sub-Saharan Africa," in World Bank, *Long-Term Perspective Study of Sub-Saharan Africa,* vol. 2, *Economic and Sectoral Policy Issues,* 100.

16. Ibid., 99.
17. Ibid., 101-102.
18. Ibid.
19. Ibid., 104-106.
20. Ibid.
21. There is a growing literature on the implications of this trend. See, for example, Faqir Mohammad, "Public Administration: Prevailing Perceptions and Priorities," *International Review of Administrative Sciences* 54 (1), 1988; Clive Kinder, "Organisational Excellence and Action Learning," *International Journal of Public Sector Management* 1 (2), 1988; and John W. Hunt, "Management Development for the Year 2000," *Journal of Management Development* 9 (3) 1990.

22. See, for example, Moses Kiggundu, *Managing Organisations in Developing Countries: An Operational and Strategic Approach* (Hartford, Conn.: Kumarian Press, 1989); and Peter Blunt and Merrick Jones, *Managing Organisations in Africa* (Berlin: de Gruyter, 1992).

23. See "Intrapreneurial Now," *The Economist*, 17 April 1982, 50.

24. On this point, see "Survey of Management Education," *The Economist*, 2 March 1991; "Leaner Times for Business Schools," *The Economist*, 8 February 1992, 65-66; and see also Hunt, "Management Development for the Year 2000."

12

The Challenge of Privatisation

Mostafa Rhomari

Today, in regard to policy on public enterprises, African governments are faced with the major problem of combining efficient resource allocation with productive efficiency. As African governments have in recent years experienced severe financial constraints, owing in most cases to a combination of debt and reduced domestic and foreign financial flows, this issue has assumed urgency more than ever before. One of the responses to these budgetary constraints is to reduce the scope of public sector activities through the privatisation of public enterprises. Indeed, privatisation has become a worldwide policy response to overcome government financial constraints as well as public enterprise inefficiencies. In principle, there are at least four potential efficiency gains from privatisation, as follows:

- greater financial discipline of the enterprise through operation in the open market and minimisation of subsidies;
- more freedom to pursue higher returns on capital through a profit-oriented management;
- elimination of the multiple problems of state control; and
- attraction of good managers through better incentives and higher wages

The question that arises is whether privatisation policies will enable African states to improve resource allocation and raise the productivity of public enterprises. Privatisation is a complex activity, and the ultimate test of its usefulness is whether it yields a net benefit to the economy as a whole.[1] Indeed, only a handful of African countries have transferred the

172

assets or capital of public enterprises to the private sector. Even then, the organisations affected have often been relatively small, and sometimes they have already been operating in competitive markets, such as in the manufacturing or service sectors. Furthermore, it remains to be proved that change of ownership alone is a necessary condition for increased enterprise efficiency in Africa. Yet, as Chapter 11 in this book suggests, it is also clear that private entrepreneurship provides a flexible, dynamic, and potentially efficient means of meeting many of the development challenges in the region.

But on this specific issue of transferring public enterprise into private sector ownership and control, most African countries lack the financial instruments and institutional environment for the effective implementation of privatisation schemes. Hence, the selection of the method of privatisation to be used—liquidation, contracting out, management contract, placement, public bidding, issue of shares, etc.—will depend on these financial and institutional factors. The specific circumstances under which the enterprise is being sold, such as, for example, the extent of financial disarray, will also affect the modality that is used. Drawing from selected experiences of privatisation in the region and elsewhere, this chapter complements Chapter 11 on entrepreneurship in examining some key problems and possible solutions in transferring public enterprises to private sector ownership and control. The discussion centres around three main themes: (1) an evaluation of the main means of effecting the transfer of public enterprises into the private sector; (2) an assessment of some critical financial questions; and (3) an estimation of the impact of privatisation on employment and income distribution.

Techniques of Privatisation

Privatisation techniques and procedures include stock exchange offer, increase of unsubscribed capital, invitation for competitive bidding, sale by mutual agreement, leveraged management buyout or redemption by management, direct stock transfer, sale of the government's or company's assets, management contract, and agreement with liquidator to manage the company in liquidation.[2] Through each or a combination of the above-mentioned techniques, it is possible to achieve both the general objectives of the privatisation process, such as reduction of state losses and improvement of productivity, and specific objectives, such as encouragement of popular shareholding. In Morocco, for example, in addition to giving new social classes of people access to share ownership, transfer techniques are also aimed at coordination of regional development programmes and ensuring job security.[3] Although there is a wide range of privatisation techniques, the determinant factor in the choice of any technique must be its chance of success in effecting the transfer of the enterprise to the private sector.

Essentially, privatisation techniques can be divided into two main groups: (1) transfers effected through stock issue and (2) transfers effected without stock issue. A third category that may or may not involve stock issue is employee buyout.

Transfers Through Stock Issue

Stock offers by prospectus or through the stock exchange can be used to encourage direct financial participation of a large part of the population in privatisation operations. Another technique of stock issue is through the offer of unsubscribed capital. This opens the way for distribution of the capital to private investors and signifies a reduction or dilution of government shareholding. Widespread participation by nationals in stock acquisition prevents majority foreign shareholding or excessive capital concentration. This has been variously considered shareholding democratisation and even popular capitalism. In effect, the process involves the gradual conversion of cash savings into financial savings in the form of investments in stocks and shares. Increased financial savings—and thus increased demand for interest income—invariably increases the liquidity of the local financial markets.

In general, privatisation through stock issue is a transparent and flexible system that potentially allows wide participation in shareholding. However, aside from the costs of privatisation and the low savings threshold, which have been noted for most African countries, privatisation by stock issue also requires financial market conditions, that African economies find difficult to provide.

Transfers Without Stock Issue

The main methods of transfer without stock issue include direct transfer through invitation for bids and sale agreement and non-asset transfers, including management and performance contracts. Direct transfer is a privatisation technique in which either partial or full equity in the enterprise is transferred from government to private investors for a fixed price. The main disadvantage of this method is that the transaction is often not transparent to the general public. This method could also potentially lead to a concentration of ownership.

Non-asset transfer is a technique that involves the privatisation of management but not the privatisation of assets. The most common way of effecting this transfer is through management and performance contracts. This technique facilitates managerial autonomy, but the enterprise remains in the public sector. It is a useful technique where outright privatisation is not feasible or when used as an initial step in preparing the enterprise for privatisation, but it requires capacity in government supervisory agencies for the formulation and monitoring of contracts.

Employee Buyouts

One common practice in privatisation transactions through stock issue is to reserve a given proportion of the stock for employees of the enterprise in question. Employee buyout involves at least two types of transactions: first, repurchase of most of the capital financed by shareholder's equity and, second, purchase of the enterprise's assets through a leveraged management buyout or through an employee stock ownership plan. Employee buyouts tend to apply to relatively small public enterprises, especially in the service sector, which usually require reorganisation of capital and labour relations. In principle, the employees of an enterprise slated for privatisation are an important target in encouraging popular shareholding. Employee-shareholding also promotes commitment to the enterprise and higher levels of productivity.[4]

In most African countries, however, employees wishing to buy out their enterprise will face liquidity difficulties owing to the narrow financial market. But the number of employee-shareholders may increase if financial measures are taken to assist them to acquire part ownership of enterprises slated for privatisation. To this end, a special assistance fund may be created to purchase stocks and shares on their behalf. The money for this fund may come from the voluntary savings of the employees as well as from bank loans repayable from the enterprise's eventual profits. Shares may be transferred from the fund directly to the employees or held there on their behalf. If the shares are non-negotiable (unquoted shares), effort should be made to repurchase them from the fund. Although employee buyouts are not very common in the region, there are a few instances of this method, for example, the case of a company called SOUVER in Tunisia. In eight privatised enterprises in Senegal, on one hand, a remarkable average of 23.35 percent employee shareholding was achieved. In Morocco, on the other hand, there is no provision in the law for a complete buyout of the privatised company by its employees. The law stipulates a share of 20 percent for the employees in the case of share capital transfer. In the case of direct transfer, their share is 10 percent. The law also provides for a maximum of 15 percent rebate in the transfer price for employees. This follows the practice in France, where transfer to employees is accompanied by advantages such as free shares, preferential prices, easy payment terms, and the possibility of exceeding the 10 percent capital limit.[5]

As the foregoing discussion of techniques implies, privatisation involves complex financial arrangements and transactions.

Financial Questions

Although privatisation should in principle yield income for the government, it also involves huge costs in effecting transactions, for discharging the enterprise's liabilities, and for restructuring or rehabilitating them. Social costs are also incurred. In addition, financial resources have to be mobilised by private sector agents, including nationals and foreign investors, for the acquisition of enterprise assets. This section examines some of the main issues that arise.

The Cost of Privatisation Logistics

The first cost that has to be borne by a government embarking on privatisation is the financing of the operations of the agency or entities responsible for managing the programme. This includes planning, research and diagnosis of enterprises slated for privatisation, the audit of accounts, valuation, banking, legal advice, marketing, and publicity and popularisation campaigns. To some extent, these costs can be met through technical and financial assistance from donors such as the World Bank. Indeed, the World Bank has provided such assistance, especially for the audit of enterprise accounts and for activities such as liquidation, in several African countries, including Benin, Mauritania, Togo, Madagascar, Niger, Senegal, and Zaire.

Paying Off the Liabilities

African public enterprises are often heavily in debt to local and foreign banks and suppliers. In such countries as Cameroon and Côte d'Ivoire, the exercise has involved having to pay up, totally or in part, the liabilities of public enterprises slated for privatisation. These accounts have been settled by a trade-off of debts owed to each other by the state and public enterprises, debt/equity swaps between the enterprise and its creditors, consolidation of debts owed to banks, and financial assistance from foreign donors.

The Cost of Restructuring

Public enterprises usually require capital restructuring, including new investment and internal reorganisation before privatisation. The aim is to ensure the profitability of the enterprise after privatisation. The cost of restructuring requires adequate financing. Here, again, the World Bank has provided assistance for the reorganisation of enterprises prior to privatisation in cases such as Morocco, Mali, Niger, Gabon, and the Central African Republic.

The Social Cost of Privatisation

Transfer of public enterprises to the private sector usually leads to such consequences as the laying-off of workers and staff, the withdrawal of subsidies, and increases in consumer prices. Accordingly, labour has to be redeployed, redundancy settlements have to be paid, and ways have to be found to mitigate the impact of increased consumer prices. These issues are taken up again below in the discussion of employment and income distribution.

Mobilisation of Financial Resources by Nationals

In Africa, it is often the case that indigenes have limited sources of funding to invest in privatised assets. It is therefore necessary to review this problem and to identify possible solutions. First, I review ways of mobilising savings through financial institutions before I turn the focus on how these institutions can channel savings to facilitate privatisation and private sector development.

Savings

Quantitatively, on one hand, national savings are generally low in all African countries. Indeed, there has been a downward trend in the average rate of net internal savings since the 1980s. In general, the accounts of the major transactors show varying levels of insufficiency, as follows:

- at the state level, the savings deficit is huge;
- at the public enterprise level, it is very low;
- at the private enterprise and household level, there has been a rapid decline in the savings ratio

This shortage of national savings is due to well-known structural factors in African economies. On the other hand, informal savings are high in Africa. This takes many different forms, including money hoarding, jewelry, wool, livestock, and direct investment in real estate. In order to raise the level of private savings, some measures need to be taken.

Savings Mobilisation Measures

For such objectives of privatisation as private sector expansion to be achieved, African governments should take appropriate measures to encourage savings to be held within the banking system. Although the impact of some of these incentives will only be felt in the medium to long term, it is necessary for a start to be made. Measures to encourage savings would include:

- Application of realistic interest rate policies: Policy should aim at allowing interest rates to reflect their market value, either by means of complete deregulation or by gradually removing controls.
- Reform of the financial sector: This should be aimed at increasing the range of securities offered to investors and at increasing the efficiency of the national banking system. The latter objective is essential for establishing the confidence of savers and fund investors, thereby providing a better alternative to the money hoarding widely practised in various countries. As in the case of Senegal, privatisation should be carried out within the framework of a restructured banking system.
- Increasing the percentage of household bank accounts: This strongly influences the proportion of private savings invested in financial instruments. Banks should be given incentives, such as tax relief, to open branches in rural areas, to adopt simple procedures, and to promote the use of cheques as payment instruments. This also facilitates the development of a savings network. In Morocco, for example, it has been observed that the extension of the network of

bank branches encouraged the opening of more household bank accounts. The banks now collect almost 90 percent of customers' time- and short-term savings deposits through a network of 850 branches covering the entire country. But there is still a concentration of banking facilities on the Atlantic coast of Morocco.

- Diversification of the financial instruments offered to savers: This will widen the scope of earning interest on savings, stimulate the demand for interest income, and will give rise to an increase in net transfers to financial institutions.
- Providing incentives for short-term savings: This requires the establishment of monetary and fiscal measures to encourage banks to collect this ready money and invest it properly, thus compelling the banking system to fully play its role of financial intermediary, and it requires the conversion of short-term capital into stable resources necessary for investment financing in Africa (but see also the recommendation on long-term savings below).
- Encourage banks to collect funds on a longer-term basis: Currently, most banks in Africa do little maturity conversion. To stimulate private sector activities, banks should be encouraged to extend their assistance on a medium- or long-term basis, that is, to consolidate their stated assets. This asset consolidation should be complemented by a concomitant consolidation of their liabilities, that is, by extending the average maturity date of deposits. To encourage banks to collect funds for longer-term deposits, interest rates in fixed deposits should be very attractive.
- Avoid periodic occurrence of real exchange rate overvaluation: This can help significantly to establish an enabling macro-economic environment for savings and investment.
- Establishment of subregional capital markets: This is important not only for savings and investment development but also for making securities and other financial instruments generally attractive.
- Creating awareness through information: Again, in Senegal, a campaign to raise the awareness of savers is steadily being pursued with the aim of persuading them to purchase transferable securities instead of keeping their savings in liquid securities or investing them in real estate.

The Role of Financial Institutions in Facilitating Privatisation

As previously noted, savings in most African countries is generally low. Since private agents cannot on their own immediately effect the takeover of public enterprise assets from the state, some bridge-financing

from the banks is necessary to facilitate the process of state disengagement. Two types of bridge-financing that can be employed in this regard
are as follows:

- Credit line for privatisation: Banks and financial institutions can
  provide lines of credit for the purpose of financing the acquisition
  of shares by private individuals. These loans should be granted
  under specified conditions and possibly guaranteed by the government or the subscribed stocks and shares. To facilitate this, donors
  can help to strengthen the resources of the banks. For example,
  Morocco and the International Finance Corporation (IFC) of the
  World Bank Group have held negotiations on the creation of a
  privatisation-support fund to be managed by the Interfinal Company
  established for this purpose. During 1993, the IFC was holding
  negotiations with Moroccan banks in regard to financing share
  purchases by investors in privatised public enterprises.
- Bank takeover: Banks and financial institutions can purchase the
  shares of the enterprises being privatised and resell them to private
  investors. In Tunisia, for example, the Banque Saoudienne Tunisien-
  ne (BST), in conjunction with the IFC, has been doing this. The
  formation of consortia may also be used by banks and financial
  institutions to pool resources for takeovers. This is the case of the
  Caisse National de Crédit Agricole (CNCA) and the Caisse de Depôt
  et de Gestion (CDG) in Morocco.

Mobilisation of Financial Resources from External Sources

Privatisation may be funded externally from bilateral and multilateral
sources, that is, by foreign investors or by joint ventures with foreign
partners or international and regional banks. In Mali, for example, a
three-year privatisation programme costing an estimated Communauté
Financière Africaine Franc (CFAF) 72.2 billion is to be financed by the
World Bank and the African Development Bank with assistance from the
Mali government, Saudi Arabia, France, and the Banque Centrale des
Etats de l'Afrique de l'Ouest (BCEAO). There are two main modalities of
effecting external funding of privatisation initiatives: foreign investment
and debt/equity swaps.

Foreign Capital. Most African countries provide for foreign participation
in privatisation initiatives. In Senegal, for example, people feared that
privatisation might only favour foreigners. But these fears have so far
proved unfounded. Out of twenty-four enterprises offered for
privatisation, nineteen were bought by Senegalese nationals and five

became joint ventures with foreign partnerships. Although some countries, such as Tunisia, have placed limits on the involvement of foreign capital, others are more flexible and provide very favourable terms for foreign participation. Still others, such as Morocco, have neither restricted nor fully opened up to foreign participation. The Moroccan law authorising the transfer of public enterprises to the private sector stipulates in the second subparagraph of Article six, that the minister responsible for the implementation of transfers can also fix the maximum percentage of shares that foreign individuals or corporate entities or those acting on their behalf could acquire. This provision was designed to encourage maximum participation by indigenes in the privatisation process and to prevent the eventual transfer of residual ownership to foreigners. But it has to be recognised that foreign participation can bring many benefits.

In the first place, foreign participation implies the injection of capital from external sources. At a time when net capital transfers have become negative, this is to be welcomed. Indeed, since 1980, the trend in Africa has been reduced foreign direct investment except in such areas as petroleum extraction and other mining activities.

Second, aside from bringing in foreign exchange, foreign participation can facilitate the modernisation of management and production techniques through technology transfer and know-how. It can also facilitate the penetration or improvement of sales in foreign markets.

Third, foreign capital can help expand private sector capacity. For example, few African industrialists are capable of mobilising the necessary funds and technology to launch a canning industry or an airline. But through foreign participation, the capacity of African entrepreneurs can be expanded considerably.

As welcome as foreign participation is, foreign investors are often discouraged from investing in Africa. One of the difficulties is the right to remit profits and even the invested capital out of the country. Appropriate safeguards must be put in place to overcome such difficulties.

Debt/Equity Swaps. It is often the case that public enterprises have accumulated considerable debt under such attractive conditions as negative real interest rate and untied loans. In some African countries, such loans have accounted for as much as 30 percent of the funding of public enterprises.

Since the early 1980s, agreements have been made between public enterprises and banks leading to a reduction in bank debt by way of debt/equity swaps. This facilitates the exchange of debt for a share of the enterprises equity. In some cases, debt/equity swaps also reflect acceptance by banks of depreciation in the value of their loans and therefore of a reduction of debt. The technique of converting debt into direct shares in public enterprises is currently on the increase. At the international level, several factors are responsible for debt/equity swaps. One of these is that international capital market transactors have developed an interest in investment income to cover long-term exchange and interest rate flows.[6] Swaps also result from the inability of the debtor countries to repay their loans. In this connection, debt/equity swaps are used to reactivate the role of foreign capital in these countries in financing investments and privatisation.

In Latin America, for example, the use of debt/equity swaps yielded mutually beneficial transactions. The pioneers of debt conversion into equity in this region have been Chile and Mexico (1985), followed by Costa Rica (1986), Argentina (1986), Ecuador, Jamaica, and Venezuela (1987), and then Brazil and Uruguay (1988). In Africa, the debt/equity swap technique was recently introduced in the Congo and Zaire, where creditors could only exchange their credit for the stocks and shares of privatised companies.

Debt/equity swaps have also taken place in Senegal. In one transaction, a foreign investor purchased 60 percent shares in a company called BICIS, which had an external bank debt, and two Senegalese investors swapped 100 percent of state debt for shares. The state transferred $770 million worth of its shares for a debt of $1.5 billion.

In Morocco and Tunisia, the technique of debt conversion into shares is certainly of interest to foreign creditors. Western banks are aware of the advantages that both countries can offer in terms of a modern communication network and a relatively developed industrial setup. Both countries are also better off than most Sub-Saharan African countries in terms of their more dynamic financial markets and banking systems.

In Morocco, the takeover of ownership of enterprises can be done through conversion of a part of the country's public debt. However, the transaction can only be worthwhile if the debt buyback is accompanied by a reduction in debt value, but this does not seem to be the current trend.

Assessment of Swaps

Swaps have become a preferred method of privatization, especially for privatising hotels, enterprises that export their products, or any other activity involving high national value added. In Latin America, some experts even consider swaps a universal instrument of solving the debt crisis. There are certainly some benefits to all the parties involved in the swap transaction, namely, the creditor, the investor, and the state.

Although a creditor such as an international bank may, on one hand, suffer some net loss from the reduction in debt value, the advantage lies in the fact that it is at least able to effect a partial recovery. The bank is thus able to balance its accounts. On the other hand, the investor purchases the debt and converts it into shares in a local company, thereby realising an investment at a reduced or subsidised cost. For the state, the benefits include reduction of indebtedness, and spin-offs such as job creation, increased tax earnings, and contribution to economic growth from the enterprise whose viability has been restored.

But swaps also represent a resource mobilisation method with disadvantages, including reduced transparency in enacting the transaction and undue benefits to the investor. Beyond this, swaps simply exchange one form of external financing with another or substitute a debt accompanied by a fixed servicing and pay-off at maturity for a direct investment (acquisition of shareholding) or other forms of obligations. This may have a negative impact in the long run if the allocations of share dividends are higher than the reimbursed interest that ought to have been used to pay for the debt.

Impact on Employment and Income Redistribution

Privatisation is often resisted as a viable policy option on grounds that it has a largely negative impact on employment and income distribution. As previously noted, the restructuring of enterprises is often a prelude to privatisation. Indeed, such restructuring has resulted in considerable staff retrenchment in such places as Morocco, Côte d'Ivoire, Senegal, Mali, Zaire, and Benin.[7] Privatisation also affects income distribution, since divestment operations generally raise the problem of the transfer of collective wealth to individual wealth. Privatisation may also set off an increase in the prices of goods and services, leading to a net loss for consumers. Yet the experience of many countries shows that the impact of privatisation on employment and income distribution is complex, as we shall see in the discussion that follows.[8]

Impact of Privatisation on Employment

Privatisation may have a positive or adverse impact on the labour market, resulting, in some cases, in job creation and, in others, in job losses. Jobs may be created as a result of expansion and new investments that sometimes follow the transfer of public enterprises into the private sector.[9] Examples of this can be drawn from the a review of specific privatisation experiences in some African countries.

In Côte d'Ivoire, two agricultural enterprises, SOGB and TRITURAF, increased their staff strength significantly after management privatisation and partial privatisation, respectively. In Senegal, the MBAO poultry farm created more jobs after privatisation to meet the demand caused by the reopening of a previously abandoned activity.[10] In Togo, eleven privatised enterprises planned to create a total of 7,300 jobs with effect from 1988.[11] In Tunisia, the privatisation of textile enterprises had a medium-term positive impact on employment following their restructuring and modernisation. The private enterprise BA COSPORT in three years created 700 jobs, an increase of 50 percent of its labour force. In Zaire, the demonopolisation of mass urban bus transportation also resulted in the creation of more jobs.[12]

Nevertheless, privatisation or restructuring of public enterprises—especially the highly labour-intensive companies—almost always results in the retrenchment of staff. African examples of restructuring can be found in a sector such as railways. In Cameroon, for instance, employment at the railway corporation, RNCF, declined from 6,200 to 4,100 within a period of eighteen months during the late 1980s.[13] Since the mid-1980s in Senegal, the national railway company cut its staff strength down to 2,200.[14] Similarly, in Nigeria, 19,000 out of 26,000 posts were abolished in the railway sector, and in Burkina Faso the reduction was 800 out of 1,600 posts.[15] Other sectors that have experienced considerable decline in employment levels following restructuring or privatisation include building and public works, shipping, power, and banking in such places as Côte d'Ivoire, Senegal, and Guinea.[16] But these job losses can be mitigated by various employment protection strategies. A brief review of some of these schemes follows.

Employment Guarantee

An employment guarantee can be provided in the legislation governing the privatisation process or incorporated in the sale contract between the buyers and the employees. But in practice this may be difficult to enforce once the privatisation process is complete. Nonetheless, Morocco is one of the few African countries to make such a legislative provision for this. A key provision of Law No. 39-89, the country's privatisation law, states: "Certain privileges will be granted to potential buyers in the light of one or more of the following objectives: access of new social classes to the property of state enterprises and the fight against monopoly; development and strengthening of the regional economies; employment protection." Efforts to guarantee employment levels and benefits as part of the sales contract have also been made in Tunisia, notably in the privatisation of a company called COMFORT.[17] It is not unusual for employment guarantees to include agreements to maintain wages and other forms of compensation at existing levels and to enhance productivity.

Redeployment

Reintegration of retrenched workers into gainful employment can also occur by finding them new jobs in both the public and private sectors. Examples of redeployment can be found in Senegal, Morocco, and Tunisia. In Senegal, for instance, 718 employees of the SODEVA company were retrenched during its privatisation, but many of them were subsequently redeployed.[18] Other redeployment schemes include training and supervision to assist redundant employees to make a transition to activities including entrepreneurship in the small- and medium-scale enterprise (SME) sectors.

Employee Buyback Schemes

As previously noted, employee buyback schemes tend to be applicable to small-scale enterprises in the service sector. They foster continuity of operations and job retention, as well as popular shareholding. The access of employees to shareholding is a major factor in stabilising employment and stimulating more efficient performance by the enterprise.[19] This is a powerful reason to offer employees all the necessary assistance, especially with regard to financing to participate in buyback schemes wherever feasible.

Protecting the Interest of Employees

Aside from schemes to maintain continuity of employment after privatisation, the interests of employees can be protected through the payment of redundancy, voluntary departure, or early retirement compensations and benefits. Tunisia, Morocco, and Guinea provide examples of such action. For instance, according to a survey conduced by the National Commission for the Restructuring of Public Enterprises (CNAREP) in Tunisia, out of some twenty cases of privatisation, 50 percent of the redundant staff preferred voluntary departure, 40 percent went on early retirement, and only 10 percent was laid off. In these cases, statutory compensation was paid in addition to other benefits.

Privatisation and Income Distribution

It is usually assumed that privatisation has a negative impact on income distribution by transferring income-generating assets into private hands. Yet one criticism that is frequently levelled at public enterprises in Africa is that they not only perform poorly in financial terms but they also fail to achieve their social objectives, such as reducing social disparities.[20] There is evidence to suggest that this criticism is valid in some cases.

For example, in the agriculture sector, public enterprise marketing boards have transferred income from commodity producers by paying less-than-market prices to them for their products. In the power sector, the subsidisation by government of the cost of generating and transmitting electricity confers a greater benefit on big consumers, such as industrialists and high-income households, than on small consumers in low-income households or small-scale businesses. Both of these examples show that public enterprise operations do not always contribute to social equity.

Nonetheless, the question that arises is how can the potentially negative impact of privatisation on income distribution be minimised? In theory, where privatisation improves productive and competitive efficiency, the cost of the good or service being produced is likely to fall. The owners of the enterprise, its employees, and consumers are all likely to benefit if the windfall from lower production costs are distributed equitably in the form of profits, wages, and lower consumer prices.[21] Beyond this, government can intervene to ensure that privatisation does not generate undue inequities. For example, excessive profits accruing to the privatised enterprise can be taxed, as has often been the case in private sector mining operations. Another measure that can be applied is to provide subsidies directly to low-income groups if the good or service in question is deemed essential and privatisation results in an increase in price.[22]

Conclusion

Privatisation in Africa has often been resisted on grounds that conditions in the region for its implementation are not satisfactory. This chapter has been concerned to examine some of the problems and issues that arise in implementing a policy of privatisation. In particular, it has been shown that there are several techniques of privatisation to choose from. It is possible to find short- medium- and long-term solutions to the typical problems that arise—namely, finance, employment, and income distribution. It is not at all clear that change in ownership alone is a necessary condition for increased enterprise efficiency in the region. At the same time, however, experience has shown that the private sector is generally better at bearing risks that require entrepreneurial dynamism. To this extent, as this book makes clear, development management in Africa can no longer be seen as a responsibility of the public sector alone. For this reason, privatisation initiatives are to be encouraged and practical solutions found to overcome the problems that sometimes arise.

Notes

Editors' note: Originally written in French, this chapter is a translation.

1. See Mary Shirley and John Nellis, *Public Enterprise Reform: The Lessons of Experience* (Washington, DC: Economic Development Institute/World Bank, 1991), 56.

2. See C. Vuylsteke, *Techniques of Privatisation of State-Owned Enterprises*, vol. 1: *Methods and Implementation* (Washington, DC: World Bank Technical Paper No. 88, 1988); Helen Nankani, *Techniques of Privatisation of State-Owned Enterprises*, vol. 2; *Selected Country Case Studies* (Washington, DC: World Bank Technical Paper No. 89, 1988); and R. Candoy-Seske, *Techniques of Privatisation of State-Owned Enterprises*, vol. 3; *Inventory of Country Experience and Reference Materials* (Washington, DC: World Bank Technical Paper No. 90, 1988).

3. See Philippe Bras, "Les Privatisations au Maroc," *Revue Française d'Administration Publique*, No. 59, July-September 1991.

4. See Peter Waterman, *Le Prix de l'Excellence* (Paris: Inter-Edition, 1983).

5. See Bras, "Les Privatisations au Maroc."

6. See M. Blackwell and S. Nocera, "Les Effets de la Conversion de la Dette en Prise de Participation," *Finances et Développement*, June 1988.

7. See Mostafa Rhomari, "Fonction Publique et Ajustement Structure en Afrique," *Revue Sciences Administratives*, No. 43, 1990; and *Revue Juridique Politique et Economique du Maroc*, No. 24, 1990; Y. Huang and P. Nicholas, "Les Coûts Sociaux de l Ajustement," *Finances et Développement*, June 1987; M. Kouadio Benie, "La Restructuration du Secteur Publique et Para-Publique et le Marché du Travail en Côte d'Ivoire" (Genève: Institute International d'Etudes des Sociétés, 1987, processed); M. Tall, "Le Désengagement des Sociétés de Développement Rural au Sénégal: Etudes de Reconversion des Agents Victimes des Mesures de Déflation du Personnel" (Dakar: Ministère du Developpement Rural, 1987); M. Traore, "La Restructuration du Secteur des Enterprises Publiques et Para-Publiques et le Marché de l'Emploi au Mali" (Genève: Institut International d' Etudes des Sociétiés [IIES], 1988, processed); J. P. La Chaud, "Le Désengagement de l'Etat et

les Ajustements sur le Marché du Travail en Afrique Francophone" (Genève: IIES, 1989, processed); and "Bénin: l'Etat, il faut le Décongestioner," *Jeune Afrique Economique*, No. 114, December 1988.

8. See O. Bouin and Ch-A. Michalet, *Le Rééquilibrage Entre Secteurs Publique et Privé: L'expérience des Pays en Développement* (Paris: Organisation for Economic Cooperation and Development [OECD], 1991); and La Chaud,"Le Désengagement de l'Etat et les Ajustements sur le Marché du Travail en Afrique Francophone."

9. See Mostafa Rhomari, "La Privatisation des Enterprises Publique en Afrique," *Revue Cahiers Africains d'Administration Publique 1989*; and Mostafa Rhomari, "La Privatisation des Enterprises Publique: Equilibre et Transparence," *Revue Morocaine de Finances Publiques et d'Economie*, No. 6, 1990.

10. See J. P. La Chaud, "Restructuration des Enterprises Publiques et Ajustements sur le Marché du Travail au Sénégal: des Possibilités à la Mesure des Expériences"(Genève: IIES, 1987).

11. See Adoglie Silete, "Impact du Désengagement de l'Etat sur le Marché du Travail au Togo" (Genève: IIES, 1991).

12. See J. P. La Chaud, "La Restructuration du Secteur Publique et Para-Publique at les Effets sur le Marché du Travail au Zaire" (Genève: IIES, 1986, processed).

13. See L. Ambelie and A. Jabi Abodo, "La Restructuration du Secteur Publique et Para-Publique et les Effets sur le Marché du Travail au Cameroon (Genève: IIES, 1987, processed).

14. See *Jeune Afrique*, No. 1641, June 1992.

15. Ibid; for Nigeria, see I. D. Taiwo, "Potential Effects of Privatisation on Economic Growth: The Nigerian Case," *Savings and Development* (Italy), 14, 1990; and Phil Ayinla, "Nigerians Show Faith in Privatisation," *Pakistan and Gulf Economist* 10, 29 June-5 July 1991.

16. See La Chaud, "Le Désengagement de l'Etat et les Ajustements sur le Marché du Travail en Afrique Francophone"; and *Jeune Afrique*, 4-16 December 1991.

17. See Ilya Harik, "Privatisation et Développement en Tunisie," *Maghreb Machrek*, 1991.

18. See J. P. La Chaud, "Restructuration des Enterprises Publiques et Ajustements sur le Marché du Travail au Sénégal.

19. See Waterman, *Le Prix de l'Excellence*.

20. See World Bank, *World Development Report* 1988 (New York: Oxford University Press, 1988).

21. See Bouin and Michalet, *Le Rééquilibrage Entre Secteurs Publique et Privé*.

22. Ibid.

Part Five

Fostering Popular Participation in Development and Governance

13

Democracy, Popular Participation, and Good Governance: The Expanding Role of People's Organisations

Sadig Rasheed and Getachew Demeke

Since the late 1980s, Africa has been experiencing a major groundswell of political change, with the people of the continent taking resolute steps to demand open and accountable systems of governance. Many autocratic African leaders have been forced to institute programmes of democratic change. Significant and far-reaching political reforms are currently underway in the majority of African countries. "Democracy movements," often manifested in the form of mass demonstrations and national conferences, have culminated in multi-party elections, the adoption of new constitutions, and the legalisation of opposition political activities in nearly forty countries. While many former rulers have managed to return to power through manipulated elections, about a dozen have been displaced by the electorate.

Although the degree of commitment to truly democratic principles and the speed of change have varied from one country to another, the movement towards institutional pluralism and political liberalisation has been the general trend. A complex experiment is unfolding in many countries which, despite formidable obstacles, could mean that an increasingly democratic order may gradually gain ground. Indeed, some observers are of the optimistic view that agitation for political reform cannot be easily suppressed by force and that current democratic trends show every sign of taking permanent hold.[1] Yet the short record of fragile democratic transitions in the region suggests that caution in arriving at such conclusion is warranted. At the same time, it is evident that the model of the so-called "one-party democratic system," has been discredited and is as good as abandoned. Many of its erstwhile advocates have recanted their views, recognising the inherent deficiencies of the one-party system in leading even to a semblance of democracy, facilitating development or alleviating the grinding poverty of the masses. Moreover, many have also come to recognize that it has also failed in achieving its claim as a guarantor of national unity in the face of the rising tide of divisive ethnic and linguistic affiliations.

While views do diverge as to the degree of optimism or pessimism that can be ascribed to prospects for the institutionalisation of democracy and accountable governance in contemporary Africa, there is little disagreement over the role which voluntary organisations could play in promoting that cause. Accordingly, we examine that role in the following sections. It should be noted at the outset that the terms "voluntary organisations," "NGOs," and "people's organisations" are used interchangeably in the discussion. This chapter is divided into three parts and begins with an outline of some of the main tenets of the *African Charter for Popular Participation in Development and Transformation* (Arusha Charter)[2] to underscore the role and rationale of voluntary organisations as promoters and watchdogs of democratic change. The second part reviews some NGO interventions and activities in this area. And, in the third part, some ways in which such interventions could be fostered and strengthened are discussed.

Because this chapter focuses on "internal" watchdog activities, it complements Chapter 14 which examines the core characteristics of good governance that enjoy wide acceptance internationally and how external development partners could foster such practices. Chapter 15 develops this theme further and outlines a new strategy for donor intervention in polities in which the private and voluntary sectors are recognised as legitimate partners of government in the development process. Chapter 16 deals with another aspect of this theme (in the discussion of the administrative and managerial arrangements required for establishing an African Economic Community [AEC]) and emphasises that the community must be built up from "below"—upon ongoing activities of African social and economic agents in all sectors.

Main Tenets of the Arusha Charter

The 1990 *African Charter for Popular Participation in Development and Transformation*—sponsored by the ECA and adopted by representatives of people's organisations, governments and regional and international organisations—affirmed at a critical moment in the struggle for democratic change that the crisis engulfing the continent is social and political, as much as it is economic. It gave impetus to the campaign for political change by emphatically declaring that one of the underlying causes of the crisis has been the inherent conflict of interest between the civil society and the state. It further underscored a fundamental truism, namely that economic growth and development cannot be sustained, nor can human conditions be meaningfully improved without the full contributions, creativity, and popular enthusiasm of the vast majority of the people. Accordingly, the Arusha Charter urged the African people to continue to seize the initiative and press for democratic participation at different levels of decision-making, establish autonomous and independent organisations to articulate their interests, as well as hold their leaders publicly accountable. Turning the spotlight on political elites, the charter called upon African governments to:

- create political space where people and their organisations can flourish by allowing freedom of opinion and dissent;
- adopt structures of accountability;
- give recognition to people's organisations and grass-roots initiatives, develop cooperative partnerships that reflect African priorities, and allow people to direct their own socio-economic transformation;
- work with people and their organisations in formulating development strategies, with the aim of achieving "self-reliant and people-centred development based on popular participation and democratic consensus";
- make genuine efforts to devolve power, adapt government efforts to people's initiatives, and create an enabling environment that makes the empowerment of people a reality; and
- end armed conflicts, reduce defence spending, and redirect resources to productive activities and social services.

The charter went on to suggest that the strengthening of popular organisations in Africa will help make the emerging democracies stronger, state institutions more efficient, and policies more acceptable and respected. It conferred on individuals the right to question official policies and to challenge government leadership in setting the directions of national development programmes. The charter urged governments to respect the right of the people to organise themselves and to create institutional mechanisms that would enable them to participate actively in political life. It affirmed popular participation in polity and economy are both a fundamental human right and a civic responsibility that required no permission from state authorities or sponsorship by official institutions. Moreover, it interpreted democratic practice not only in terms of the right to vote, important though this may be, but also in terms of a whole set of rights, among which is the citizens' right to have a say in the decisions and policies that affect their lives.

People's Organisations and Democracy

The Arusha Charter affirmed a number of principles which have universal appeal and applicability. In so doing, it provided a crucial collective backing and legitimacy at the international level to people's organisations that have been at the forefront of the campaign for democratic change. Today, all over the continent, a wide range of autonomous and independent organisations, which operate as channels for the expression of the needs and concerns of grass-roots and urban communities, are emerging. These organisations have galvanised democratic movements by openly challenging the ruling authorities and demanding major reforms of national institutions and systems of governance in many countries. In countries where political parties have been virtually or next to non-existent and other civil institutions have been weak, these organisations have succeeded in mobilising the broad masses to demand radical change in the structures of governance and the economy. They have increasingly assumed important roles as platforms for democratic expression and citizens' initiatives in the search for more accountable systems of governance, democratic reform, and institutional pluralism. In this section, we review some POs interventions in this context.

Professional association, student organisations, church groups and trade unions played a crucial role in the political change that took place in many countries such as Kenya, Zambia, and Malawi. Popular dissent, expressed and channelled through such organisations, has even succeeded in forcing the military to relinquish power to civilians twice in the case of Sudan (in 1964 and 1985) and also in Ghana (in 1977).[3]

Some NGOs, such as the Silveria House in Zimbabwe, the Democratic Institute in Namibia, and the Foundation on Human Rights Initiative in Uganda, have sought to advance the concept of citizenship and create popular awareness of constitutional rights and responsibilities. Through civic education and related programmes, they have promoted a clearer understanding of the provisions of constitutions and the functioning of the state, the mechanics of the democratic process, and the rights and obligations of citizens within it. They have also offered advice, counselling, and legal aid services to victims of human rights violations. Recognizing the struggle for citizenship rights and the proper exercise of these rights alongside the campaigns of mass movements for political participation is of particular importance in Africa, given the very weak and antagonistic links between civil society and the state.[4]

Although these organisations have been involved in direct political activities, others have contributed to the promotion of the democratic process through the participatory methods practiced in carrying out their normal functions. This takes different shapes.

First, they could tap the talents of the poor and encourage their participation in the initiation of projects and development activities. By emphasising the benefits of involvement and collective action, they are able to empower cadres of grass-roots people and unleash the potential of ordinary men and women in the villages. To the extent that these organisations assist the poor in gaining experience in participatory processes, they are able to provide a kind of a springboard for expanded political activities. Hence, because they initiate community-based and participatory activities among marginalised people, voluntary organisations do provide means of empowerment and enhance possibilities for participation in other spheres of decision-making in the larger society.[5]

Second, through their style of operations, these organisations promote group discussions, consultation and resolution of conflicts by the means of debate, dialogue, and practices that contribute to a better understanding and respect for the right of others to express contrary opinions. Their method of working, through local and popularly elected committees for the management of development projects, helps to create awareness of democratic procedures and values.

Third, these grass-roots initiatives facilitate the democratic process by helping to develop the intellectual, moral, managerial, and technical capabilities of leadership at the local level. In many ways, they do serve as training grounds for the preparation of future leaders by enhancing their capacity to operate in a pluralistic environment. In other words, they provide an alternative base for training and support structures that empower local leadership. More explicit awareness-building strategies have also been pursued. For example, the Organisation of Rural Associations for Progress (ORAP) in Zimbabwe has a standing policy of initiating welfare or poverty-alleviating projects only after taking the communities concerned through participatory training sessions in political consciousness and socio-economic awareness.

Fourth, the importance of such initiatives and interventions have to be seen from the perspective that in many rural areas, people's organisations are the only established lines of communication between state agencies and rural society. Though the primary goals of these organisations are to contribute to the socio-economic development of the local community, they also often assist in promoting political change by enhancing the capacity of the people to articulate and express their views on issues of vital concern to them. Because of their grass-roots base, they are well placed to articulate the needs and aspirations of local constituencies in an organised and coherent manner. In many instances, they are the sole organised force that can challenge the hegemony of local elites and domination by the structures of the state.

In the southern African countries of Namibia and Zimbabwe, for example, popular organisations have consistently struggled, on behalf of communal farmers and landless peasants, against the allied forces of commercial farmers and local agents of the state. Within this organisational context, peasants in these countries have been able to articulate and often defend their right to land and have also been assisted to seek legal protection. Similarly, in Kenya, NGOs, like the Green Belt Movement, have been in the forefront of the fight against local corruption in the protection of wildlife and encroachment on protected land. Numerous examples, such as these, can be cited in which indigenous NGOs have succeeded in mobilising the poor and marginalised to put an end to illegal actions of local agents of the state.[6]

Fifth, NGOs have also encouraged the democratisation of the decision-making process by facilitating citizen's engagement in public policy issues. Such intervention may take different forms. Some NGOs are innovators—creating new programmes to meet specific needs that are subsequently adopted by the government and other NGOs. For example, a Kenyan NGO, the Undugu Society, has been so successful in providing basic education for street children in Nairobi slums to the extent that its methods have been adopted by the Kenyan government as well as governments of neighbouring countries. Other NGOs act as catalytic agents in promoting cross-sectoral cooperation on intractable problems. The Saving Development Movement in Zimbabwe, for example, was created by a small indigenous NGO that linked village saving clubs to government credit facilities to improve rural access to credit. Taking on these and other roles has enabled NGOs to contribute to the implementation of well-targeted policies and programmes in several countries. Hence, the entry of these organisations into the realm of policy influence offers another avenue for wider participation in policy-making.[7]

Sixth, NGOs have also helped to advance the democratisation process by maintaining the crucial link between continuity and change at the local level. Since they are embedded in the local culture, they tend to be more sensitive to local norms and customs, thereby avoiding unnecessary disruptions and conflicts and improving the prospects for the sustainability of change. Many women's groups, for example, draw on traditional structures, and at the same time challenge patriarchal customs and social convention.[8]

Finally, voluntary organisations provide mechanisms for directing people away from parochial concerns with tribal or ethnic interests. In much of Africa, the conditions for nationhood are far from fulfilled. Basic loyalties are still based on tribal affiliations. Ethnic kinship and a common language constitute the primary forces of cohesion. As such, the polity in many African states is highly fractionalised. Through their efforts to organise communities on the basis of economic and social interests, these organisations contribute to the understanding of the commonality of interests along these lines. Accordingly, they are among the few institutions that have been relatively successful in breaking tribal identifications as the primary basis of identity. Hence, in some rural settings, community organisations with a membership base that cuts across tribal or ethnic cleavages have succeeded in constituting the building blocks for political movements that also cut across parochial interests.

These, then, are some ways in which voluntary organisations could contribute and have contributed to the emergence of democratic movements and wider participation in contemporary Africa. In the section that follows, the focus is shifted to examine ways of strengthening this role.

Strengthening the Role of People's Organisations in Democratic Transitions

Although voluntary organisations have achieved some success at the local level in promoting good governance and fostering democratic change, much remains to be done to strengthen their interventions in this context. Given that post-independence liberal democratic institutions and practices have been considerably weakened by authoritarian regimes should lead us to temper optimism about the prospective role of voluntary organisations with a dose of realism. At the same time, it is evident that among the reasons for the failure to establish enduring democracies were the lack of concerted efforts to strengthen the institutions of civil society, promote respect for human rights, and foster democratic values and practices at all levels of state and society.

A unique opportunity has now emerged to draw lessons from past failures. The sustainability of democracy depends to a large extent on the ability of the people, social groups and institutions to properly understand the rights and obligations of citizenship under democratic conditions and structures, exercise these effectively, and establish and strengthen democratic and civil society institutions. As leading institutions of civil society, people's organisations bear a heavy responsibility in making significant contributions to the promotion and consolidation of democracy within this frame. To this extent, the future of democracy in Africa will hinge, to an overwhelming degree, on the ability of NGOs and people's organisations to educate the masses on democratic values and practices and to seize the initiative to defend these values. In this regard, several modes of action can be pursued to consolidate the democratic transition.

Fostering Democratic Values

Although NGOs in various countries have initiated activities in civic education, these efforts need to be expanded and supplemented by more systematic endeavours designed to reach and inform the general public. This would require close collaboration with various organs of the media. Beyond this, voluntary organisations can assist schools and other learning establishments to incorporate in their teaching programmes and curricula fundamental concepts and practices of democratic governance.

Supporting Civilian Control over the Military

Africa has relatively large and overpoliticized military establishments with an unsavoury record of frequent intervention in and undue influence over the exercise of political power. The reasons for this are complex and often intractable. On-going current efforts in some countries to reduce both the size of the military and public spending on it ought to be vigorously advocated and encouraged. As part of their campaign to foster democratic values, people's organisations should support these initiatives and also affirm the right of popularly-elected civil authorities to exercise effective control over the military.

Strengthening Democratic Institutions

Democratic institutions provide a framework for expressing conflicts in society as well as for encouraging cooperation. As such, they act as representatives of different interests, while at the same time being sufficiently autonomous from any particular interest. The viability of emerging democratic structures in Africa will ultimately depend on the institutionalisation of appropriate equilibria between the countervailing forces of conflict and cooperation as well as representation and autonomy. Voluntary organisations can play a useful role in strengthening democratic institutions by helping to maintain these delicate balances, especially in such areas as monitoring elections and organising and conducting public debates on competing political views and perspectives.

Promoting Accountability and Transparency in Government

In collaboration with other civic institutions, POs have a crucial role to play in promoting the accountability and transparency of governance. To institutionalize this process they could support and facilitate the establishment of independent and autonomous research and policy centres that could help monitor and assess public accountability and transparency and the progress of the democratic experience.

Transparency and accountability of governance have many facets. One of these is the integrity of financial management and the prevention of corruption, embezzlement, and waste. Experience has shown that, in many African countries, considerable squandering of resources does occur through financial improprieties exercised by the ruling politicians and civil servants. Here, again, voluntary organisations can play a key role in supporting watchdog institutions, such as the auditors-general and ombudsmen, monitor the work of such institutions and mount campaigns to expose excesses and ensure the implementation of disciplinary actions.[9]

Promoting Respect for Human Rights

Gross disregard for human rights in Africa is one of the consequences of three decades of authoritarian rule. A great number of Africans have endured arbitrary arrest, torture, execution, harassment of families and friends, confiscation of property, and the destruction of careers. Little surprise, then, that the respect for human rights has been a ubiquitous demand of democratic movements. People's organisations are particularly well placed to promote human rights, both at the official and popular levels. They could engage in a wide range of activities, including legal assistance, research and publications, lobbying for the reform of laws, and the ratification and implementation of international and regional agreements.

Working closely with international and regional organisations within this frame can give both moral and financial support to national endeavours. The establishment of human rights watch organisations at the national level has been obstructed and banned by the state across Africa for obvious reasons. Two main organisations are operable in Africa at the regional level. These are the Banjul-based African Centre for

Democracy and Human Rights Studies and the OAU-sponsored African Commission on Human and People's Rights. Their impact on redressing human rights violations has, however, been minimal.

Strengthening Civil Society

The key to establishing an enduring democracy is the emergence of a strong, viable, and assertive civil society. A well-developed civil society widens democratic space and facilitates opportunities for citizens' partici- pation in political and social life at large. The contemporary reality of Africa is that the state is too powerful in the face of an embryonic and weak civil society. In this regard, NGOs have a special responsibility for strengthening the countervailing power and influence of the civil society vis-à-vis the state by supporting and building alliances with civic institutions and fostering practices that encourage the people to take responsibility for their own destinies. The forging of alliances among organisations and associations of civil society has been a key factor in toppling down autocratic regimes and facilitating the take over of power by alternative ruling interests.[10] Only a fundamental transformation of the relationship between the state and civil society will make democracies endure.

Mobilising International Opinion

Internal efforts aimed at consolidating democratic transitions tend to benefit from supplementary initiatives at the international level. The international community, particularly international NGOs, could contribute significantly to the strengthening of national and regional NGOs and POs in Africa and support their struggle for democracy. This, however, should ensue without compromising their independence and autonomy.

Democracy in Africa will not thrive without sustained economic development. External constraints such as debt, reduced levels of resource inflows, and an unfavourable trading environment have contributed a great deal to the precipitation and deepening of the economic crisis in Africa. Action at the international level to ease these burdens is vital if political reforms are to succeed. Through their activities in implementing various development and relief programmes, voluntary organisations are particularly well placed to acquire first-hand experience of the devastating impact of these constraints on the lives of ordinary people at the local level. International NGOs, in particular, have a special responsibility to lobby the international community for more effective solutions to these external impediments. Happily, mention in this regard can be made of the effective campaigns by international NGOs such as Partnership Africa/Canada (PAC), the Forum for African Voluntary Development Organisations (FAVDO), and Oxfam in lobbying donors and the major international financial institutions for effective action on the deep-rooted economic problems of the region. But the results of these efforts are yet to be seen, and much more remains to be done.

Conclusion

The main trend in the political history of post-colonial Africa is the emergence of authoritarian top-down styles of governance, with an urban-based power structure and authority radiating from the centre. As Chapter 6 also shows, efforts to devolve authority have constantly been subverted by the central authority or frustrated by the bureaucratic machinery, often resulting in policies and programmes that are detached from local realities. Over time, NGOs and people's organisations have emerged to fill the vacuum for policy and programme delivery at the local levels. These organisations have not only succeeded in equipping ordinary people with skills for political leadership and action, but, along with and as part of the movement for political change, they have been at the forefront in the campaign for more responsive forms of governance. There are many ways in which they could further contribute to the promotion and consolidation of democracy. This role should not be under estimated, and this opportunity should not be missed.

Notes

1. Sahr J. Kpundeh and Stephen P. Riley, "Political Choice and the New Democratic Politics in Africa," *The Round Table* No. 323, 1992. For a pessimistic assessment of democratic change, see Mick Moore, Introduction, *"Good Government?" IDS Bulletin* 24 (1), 1993.

2. See *The African Charter for Popular Participation in Development and Transformation* (Arusha Charter) (Addis Ababa: Economic Commission for Africa [ECA], 1990).

3. See Sadig Rasheed, *The Democratisation Process and Popular Participation in Africa: Emerging Realities and the Challenges Ahead* (forthcoming).

4. For an elaboration of this idea see Alan Fowler, "Non-Governmental Organisations as Agents of Democratisation"(unpublished typescript, 1992), 12.

5. See Getachew Demeke, *The Impact of Indigenous Non-Governmental Organisations* (Nairobi: Ford Foundation Report, 1991), 19-25.

6. For more details, see B. Schnerder, *The Barefoot Revolution: A Report to the Club of Rome* (London: Intermediate Technology Publications, 1988).

7. See John Clark, *Democratising Development: The Role of Voluntary Organisations* (London: Earthscan Publications, 1991), 170-174.

8. See N. W. Ng'ethe, "Non-governmental Organisations: Local Capacity Building and Community Mobilisation" (Nairobi: Nairobi Institute of Development Studies, University of Nairobi, Working Paper No. 469, 1990).

9. See Sadig Rasheed and Dele Olowu, *Ethics and Accountability in African Public Services,* (Nairobi: ICIPE Science Press, 1994).

10. See Sadig Rasheed, *The Democratisation Process and Popular Participation in Africa: Emerging Realities and the Challenges Ahead.*

14

Governance and the External Factor

Pierre Landell-Mills and Ismail Serageldin

Inspired in part by the remarkable success of the Marshall Plan, development economists in the 1950s and 1960s were confident of their ability to bring about sustained improvement in the welfare of poor nations. Many saw progress as almost inevitable. This somewhat naive optimism has given way to a sense of failure and doubt. Development is now viewed as an uncertain process and, by inference, highly correlated with the quality of governance.[1] A renewed attempt is being made to link the roles played by political science, institutional economics, and neoclassical economics to create a coherent theory of development management.[2]

Although by no means a new topic in the literature on economic development,[3] the growing focus on issues of governance has been given impetus by the collapse of the totalitarian states in Eastern Europe, by China's prodemocracy movement, and by the popular call for multiparty democracy in Africa and Latin America.

Public debate has centred on five underlying themes: the perceived success of market economies in contrast to the failure of central planning; the abuses of authoritarian regimes; the inefficiencies of state enterprises and public agencies; the widespread corruption that is siphoning away domestic and foreign aid resources; and a resurgence of ethnic conflicts. These issues have greatly complicated the task of nation building and can no longer be suppressed.

Moreover, increased attention is being given to issues of human rights and democracy in the context of a new world order.

In this chapter, we examine the role of external agencies in promoting good governance and attempt to clarify the basis for their intervention in such a politically sensitive area. The discussion is intended as a contribution to the debate on the efficacy and modalities of different external interventions. There is no a priori presumption that such interventions are either desirable or effective.

The Meaning of Governance

"Governance" is not a word that has been used extensively in the past by political scientists, and its recent appearance in popular usage has not been very rigorous. It has become, in many ways, both all-embracing and vague. According to the *Oxford Dictionary*, governance means "the act or manner of governing, of exercising control or authority over the actions of subjects; a system of regulations." In essence, therefore, governance may be taken as denoting how people are ruled and how the affairs of a state are administered and regulated. It refers to a nation's system of politics and how this functions in relation to public administration and law. Thus the concept of governance includes a political dimension.

The World Bank report that raised the issue in the context of Sub-Saharan Africa defined governance as the "exercise of political power to manage a nation's affairs."[4] This is the interpretation used here. It encompasses the state's institutional and structural arrangements, decision-making processes and implementation capacity, and the relationship between government officials and the public. It implies that public authorities play an indispensable and potentially decisive role in the distribution of assets and benefits. Conversely, it also implies the possibility that the government may be "captured" by a self-seeking elite intent on plundering the nation's wealth. From time immemorial, societies have struggled to establish governments that promote the public interest, only to find that public resources have been diverted to private benefit and that power is being retained by violent and arbitrary means.[5]

In most societies, social and ethnic divisions—and the tensions they generate—may make compromise inevitable. Consequently, not all the conditions for good governance can be achieved, even by a competent and well-intentioned government. Sheer lack of capacity also limits the ability of public authorities to fulfil their responsibilities. But too often problems are deliberately exaggerated to mask the rapacious and exploitative actions of the ruling elite and its supporters.

There is also the more profound issue of the precise relationship between the different components of governance and development. Though it can be argued that freedom of expression, institutional pluralism, transparency, accountability, and the like (all seen as key ingredients in the process of democracy) are important aspects of good governance, there is no convincing evidence that multiparty democracy, which is being urged on developing countries by some donors, is necessary for social and economic development.[6] The performance of the Republic of Korea, Taiwan (China), and Singapore in the 1960s and 1970s, and Chile in the 1980s stands out not only in terms of economic growth but also as regards social indicators and poverty reduction. In these economies, spending on education and health was higher and the poor benefited to an increasing degree at the expense of the rich.[7]

There are, of course, numerous examples of economies ruined by dictators, but there are also inept or corrupt democratic regimes. Examples can be found, too, of well-run democracies, such as Botswana, Malaysia, and Mauritius. The best that can be said is that the evidence is mixed. On one hand, benevolent dictators are rare, but, on the other hand, democracies have an unfortunate tendency to degenerate into a crude populism that is equally inimical to good governance and sustainable development.

Economic and social progress is not the only objective of development. Freedom from fear and arbitrary arrest, free speech, free association, and the right to run for and hold political office can all be viewed as important elements in living a fuller and more meaningful life.[8] It is therefore arguable that actions in these areas can and should be subsumed under a broadened heading of development well-being.[9] Indeed, despite the economic success achieved by Chile's military regime in the 1980s, the regime was voted out of office in the first open elections because of its systematic transgressions against human rights. The Chilean people have thereby unambiguously indicated their "utility function" and their perception of well-being.

Although in general terms the notions of freedom, transparency, participation, and accountability are key ingredients for good governance, in practice country situations are never identical. Moreover, significant improvements in some areas may be accompanied by failures in others. The "acceptable" level of deviance from an ideal remains a subjective matter.[10] Conceptually, it is almost impossible to reduce the complex social, cultural,[11] political, legal, economic, and other interactions that make up a modern society to a single measure of good governance—or even to a number of such indicators. The interpretation of the selected indicator poses problems too, except when measured linearly against itself (that is, whether the country is improving or deteriorating) and only by that particular yardstick.

Individual country circumstances make judgmental approaches inescapable. Is a government repressing its citizens by the use of force, or is it defending itself against destabilisation efforts? In practically every instance, there is a little of both, and judgments as to the legitimacy of the government, its representativeness, the adequacy of its policies, and the appropriateness of its actions are all inescapable.

A further complication is that governments frequently perform well in terms of one set of indicators and badly in others (the Chilean experience noted earlier is an example). And since there is limited ability, at least at present, to bring together the various elements of this complex social, cultural, political, legal, and economic reality, moving from this confused conceptual situation to an operational one is fraught with difficulty. The efforts of the UN Development Programme (UNDP) to refine its Human Development Index represents an important step in resolving these issues.[12]

Characteristics of Good Governance

Given the conceptual complexity noted above, the only viable approach to guide intervention by external actors is to identify and foster those aspects of governance that are least controversial. Although there are many different views about what constitutes good governance, some important aspects of which are culturally determined, we can agree on a minimum core of characteristics. In large measure these derive from, or are related to, the *Universal Declaration of Human Rights*, adopted by the United Nations in 1948. This declaration has been signed by the vast majority of countries and thus may be taken as representing the moral consensus of the international community of nations. These fundamentals include the following:

- The political rulers and government officials are both held accountable to the ruled for their actions through clearly formulated and transparent processes, and, more particularly that the legitimacy of a government is regularly established through some well-defined open process of public choice such as election, referendum, and so on. (Article 21).
- The safety and security of citizens is assured (Articles 3, 5) and the rule of law prevails, such that contracts can be fairly enforced both among private operators (individuals or enterprises) and between a private operator and the state. Moreover, citizens should be legally protected from arbitrary or capricious actions by public authorities (Articles 7, 8, 10, 11, 28).
- Public agencies are responsive to the needs of the public, and social and economic development is promoted for the benefit of all citizens in an equitable manner (Articles 22, 23, 24, 25).
- The ready availability of information that will permit accountability to be practised, laws to be correctly applied, markets to function, and people to be creative and innovative (Article 19).

• Freedom of association and expression of opinion (Articles 19, 20).

These general principles were subsequently articulated in two covenants ratified by the United Nations General Assembly.[13] Their relevance to international institutions as well as to governments has since been the subject of scholarly study.[14] In applying these principles, it is important to note that governance consists of two distinct but intimately intertwined dimensions: One is political (and relates to the commitment, to good governance), and the other is technical (and relates to issues of efficiency and public management). Both must be addressed. Without political commitment little can be achieved, even with an efficient public administration. And without an efficient public administration, no government can be effective, however benevolent. Thus the performance of government depends on the role assigned to the state, the competence of public agencies, and the extent to which there is an enabling environment that facilitates and encourages growth-promoting activities by private citizens and honest behaviour by public officials.[15]

The trend toward disengaging the state from productive activities, while emphasising the state's role in providing social and infrastructure services, will have a major impact on issues of governance. A distinct through related trend is the parallel move toward decentralisation and the empowerment of local communities.[16] In what follows we discuss how accountability can be built into these processes; but neither empowerment nor accountability will assure better governance unless public agencies are made more competent. This brings to the fore issues of technical management and skill acquisition. It also highlights the need for institution-building in the broadest sense. A competent and accountable government dedicated to liberal economic policies will not alone ensure development unless public agencies simultaneously invest in infrastructure and human resource development.[17] When this is done, most elements are present to create an enabling environment in which private operators can flourish. This, then, is the challenge of good governance.

Sovereignty and Interdependence

Because the present international order is based on the concept of sovereignty, it can be argued that the quality of a nation's governance is not a legitimate concern of foreigners. This proposition merits careful examination, particularly because the quality of governance is usually raised by industrial countries in relation to developing countries. Yet accountability and bureaucratic failure must be central concerns for external agencies.

The concept of sovereignty underlies all aspects of the international order. It implies reciprocal noninterference in internal affairs and respect for territorial integrity and internationally recognised borders. The corollary of sovereignty is the recognition abroad of governments that exercise what Webster's dictionary defines as the "supreme power over a body politic" and a "controlling influence" over the affairs of society with "freedom from external control." In a word, autonomy.

All undertakings that commit societies, whether economically, militarily, politically or even concerning issues such as cultural exchanges and human rights, are entered into by national governments, not by some undefined society at large. Though idealists may posit a more perfect world based on a stronger international order, we must accept as our starting point the reality of a world made up of sovereign states.

The principal justification for building a world order of sovereign states is found in the recognition of the differences between societies and a belief in the inalienable right of self-determination. This sentiment was the basis of decolonisation, independence, and accession to membership in the community of nations. It also raises issues about the rights of minorities to secede from existing states, questions that are clearly beyond the scope of this chapter.

More pertinent is the fact that sovereignty is subjected to some internationally recognised constraints, enshrined in international conventions (such as the *Universal Declaration of Human Rights* and the *Vienna Convention*). There are also questions about the legitimacy or representativeness of existing governments that lead to issues of de facto and de jure recognition of governments, usually as a result of a change of authority. In South Africa, the legitimacy of the government was impugned by the UN General Assembly because of its systemic (not just systematic) violation of human rights. There was, however, no question about South Africa's sovereignty per se. Diplomatic and economic sanctions were debated and adopted within the existing international framework.

In this case we see the legitimation of collective action for dealing with individual situations and establishing a process for conflict resolution. States are bound together in an international community by a web of international, multilateral, and bilateral agreements that create mutually binding obligations within an established system of international law. We live in an increasingly interdependent world, in which each state must take into account the effect of its actions on others.

Developing countries are particularly vulnerable to events in the rest of the world and have come to depend heavily on the international community for financial and technical assistance. Donor agencies—and the public—are increasingly aware that whether or not assistance is used to promote development depends on the quality of governance in the recipient country. Consequently, they are concerned to promote conditions conducive to good governance and have become more proactive in this regard—although in a positive rather than a punitive way.[18]

In this context, the role of the international institutions is an expression of the will of the international community. But at the same time—and for this very reason—their mandate is strictly circumscribed and must conform to existing statutes.[19] An acceptable role is defined in terms of several key issues. First, is the role of international institutions to provide support to those governments whose policies and programmes the international institutions feel are consistent with their mandates, or do the international institutions have a responsibility to take an activist role in getting governments to adopt such policies and programmes? Second, if the international bodies are to pursue an activist agenda, what is the content of this agenda, and how does it relate to the statutes governing international institutions? Third, who determines the agenda? In the case of the World Bank, is the agenda determined by the member states? By consensus or simple majority? Would that "politicise" the agenda and poison the working atmosphere at the Bank? Clearly, the role of the international institutions is a function of the sovereignty of the member states and the mandate they have given to the international institutions.

Yet another question is what is the modus operandi? Ultimate authority (at least in the international financial institutions) rests with the representatives of the government. Staff members can only make proposals; the governing body and the government representatives must approve them—not NGOs, not the opposition, not the intellectuals, but the officially designated representatives of the government.

Although the ultimate beneficiaries may be "the people" or "the poor," given that international institutions are constructed as associations of member states, the channel of communication remains the government concerned. This does not imply that international institutions do not have the right to contact others in the country. The World Bank, for example, is obliged to form an independent judgment in deciding on an investment, and this calls for contacts with persons other than government officials and for field visits as well. Thus even though this requirement gives the bank some leeway to avoid excessive restrictions by governments of member states, it does not fundamentally affect the role of government or the sovereignty of its member states.

Because poor countries generally have fragile polities and weak systems of accountability, with few autonomous institutions and little power to offset that exercised by the central government, external agencies are potentially key political players, capable of exerting considerable influence. This brings out an important point: In its raising of the issue of governance, the external agency is calling into question the government's performance. This intervention goes further than a critique of a particular programme or project—which is generally regarded as a legitimate concern—and touches on the ability of a regime to govern effectively in the interest of its citizenry.

Beyond these considerations there is the fundamental issue of the link between the government and the governed, between the state and society. This issue is both culturally and politically sensitive. Few development questions are merely technical; typically, they involve political judgments that are inherently hostage to cultural and social particularities. Moreover, there are no accepted means of arbitration between competing views. This is an issue on which the government is likely to be defensive; the intrusion of external judgments may well be counterproductive.

Thus actions by the development community, if they are to be effective, must convince as well as assist countries to improve their governance without intruding on their sovereignty. If the partnership between external agencies and beneficiaries is to be successful, a frank recognition of interdependence is essential.

Although the government of a sovereign state has every right to resist the initiatives of donors, bilateral agencies representing sovereign states have an equal right to condition their assistance on measurable progress to improve the quality of governance. There is a growing appreciation among donors that improved governance is central to achieving development goals and that external aid will never yield lasting benefits unless concrete steps are taken to tackle the systematic causes of poor governance. But the right—and the willingness—to be proactive does not in itself ensure effectiveness. Modes of intervention that seem both justifiable and promising need to be explored.

One other issue must be addressed: How can donor agencies be held accountable by the international community for actions that will affect the welfare of millions of people? It can be argued that there are already established mechanisms for the control and supervision of the international institutions through their governing bodies. However, there is no comparable constraint on the activities of bilateral agencies, which are subject to considerable pressure from their own interest groups. To some extent, accountability could be achieved through the reinforcement of consultative group processes in which donors explain their actions as an integral part of the policy proposal. In addition, the Development Assistance Committee of the Organisation for Economic Cooperation and Development (OECD) encourages self-regulation and has done much to improve donor practices. Although peer pressure does, to some extent, constrain the blatant exercise of national self-interest by donors, it is a weak mechanism that needs enhancing. This topic merits further study.

Fostering Good Governance

It may be concluded that good governance depends on the extent to which a government is perceived and accepted as legitimate, committed to improving the public welfare and responsive to the needs of its citizens, competent to assure law and order and to deliver public services, able to create an enabling policy environment for productive activities, and equitable in its conduct. In our discussion of the ways in which external agencies address these facets of governance, it is important to bear in mind the distinction between the political and technical dimensions noted earlier and the need to address the operational capacity of government at the central, regional, and community levels. These correspond roughly to the macro, meso, and micro levels in economic analysis.

Given the risk of ethnocentric and cultural bias, external agencies need to be very cautious in proposing specific solutions or advocating particular arrangements. Through dialogue and analysis, options can be examined, but ultimately it is the responsibility of any government to determine its homegrown solutions. For their part, external agencies have a right (within the legal limits of their statutes) to judge whether the solutions proposed appear credible, to assist and to monitor their implementation, and to modulate their financial assistance accordingly.

Not all facets of good governance are conceptually independent or invariably complementary. Conflicts may arise, at least in the short run. Open, participatory processes may make governance less predictable and less efficient. Nonetheless, over the long term, homegrown solutions are likely to be more realistic in practice, because processes imposed on beneficiaries are generally less sustainable than those developed through a participatory process.

In practical terms, how can the development community encourage countries to perform better according to the criteria of good governance? For these conditions to be fostered, it is a necessary—though not sufficient—priority to have credible arrangements for political and bureaucratic accountability,[20] freedom of association, an objective and efficient judiciary, freedom of information and expression, and efficient public institutions.

Political Accountability

Ostensibly, governments exercise power for the purpose of promoting the well-being of the populace at large. In practice, there is always the possibility that political leaders and government bureaucracies will manipulate power for private benefit unless constrained.[21] The purpose of an electoral process is to ensure political accountability, stipulating limited terms of office. This does not necessarily mean a multiparty system. Nor does a system of democratic elections necessarily lead to good governance. But there is wide consensus that some system of popular choice is essential to legitimise a government, make it responsive to popular demands, and create an environment in which public agencies devote themselves to development rather than to suppressing popular discontent.

External agencies can assist, and indeed are assisting, in this effort. First, there is room for conflict resolution, such as that attempted by the Carter Centre (in Ethiopia and Sudan) and encouraged (as yet rather ineffectually) by regional organisations such as the Organisation of African Unity (OAU) and by the United Nations. Second, assistance can be given in organising and monitoring elections, as was done recently in Eastern Europe, Namibia, Zambia, and Nicaragua. An example of group decision-making occurred in early 1990, when donors withheld financial support from Benin because the government had lost popular support to the point where it could not govern effectively.

Although there should be no question of imposing a particular democratic system on any country, it would seem reasonable for the international community to withhold assistance from a government that cannot demonstrate that it enjoys some minimal level of popular support or that does not require those holding the highest political offices to submit themselves periodically to some transparent process of popular choice. On one hand, the willingness of some donors to continue to deal with regimes that lacked popular support (such as that of Jean-Bédel Bokassa in the Central African Empire or Idi Amin in Uganda) was largely ineffective in promoting development and, arguably, may have delayed rather than promoted good governance.

These matters are inevitably judgmental. To move more effectively toward a policy of aid sanctions will require a cautious, consensual approach that develops an international framework for collective action and that involves the key OECD bilateral agencies as well as the developing countries.

Freedom of Association and Participation

Closely allied to the above concern is the question of whether citizens enjoy the freedom to organise according to specific interests. Institutional pluralism can be seen as an important mechanism for diluting and disseminating political power.[22] But it is not always conducive to stability. As demonstrated recently in Africa and Eastern Europe, where people have shown a strong tendency to organise along ethnic lines, pluralism can be socially and economically disruptive. This is no reason to oppose freedom of association, but it involves certain risks that may call for special countermeasures.

At the national level, freedom of association means the freedom to establish religious groups, professional associations, women's groups, and other voluntary organisations to pursue political, social, or economic objectives. Donors can provide valuable financial and technical assistance to empower groups that are otherwise marginalised within the existing political and economic system. Surprisingly little has been done in this sphere, not so much because of official opposition, simply because this aspect of institution-building has not attracted significant donor attention.

The situation is different at the local level. Considerable assistance has been provided by donors to grass-roots community organisations and cooperatives that directly address the needs of the poor (often channelled through NGOs). The success of such initiatives is evident from the political impact that local NGOs have in a number of developing countries. The risks, openly acknowledged, are that the leadership of NGOs and community associations may be captured by local elites that are not responsive to the needs and interests of ordinary members.[23] The involvement of foreign NGOs may mitigate these risks, but, ultimately, systems of accountability must be built into the institutional design of each organisation. For instance, cooperatives in Cameroon are self-policed through cooperative unions.[24]

This leads to the broader role of external agencies in promoting the active participation of the ultimate beneficiaries of development programmes in both the design and the implementation of projects.[25] There is now a wide consensus in the development community on the desirability of such participation, and few governments would openly oppose the concept. Nonetheless, even regimes that are not notably repressive frequently regard such grass-roots initiatives as potentially threatening. This makes it important for external agencies to seek effective and genuine participatory arrangements, while giving due attention to the possibilities of local abuses. And external agencies, by deliberately supporting the development of plural institutional structures, can help to create an environment that will tend to constrain the abuse of political power.

A Sound Judicial System

There are few aspects of governance on which consensus is more firmly established within the development community than the need for an objective, efficient, and reliable judicial system. To achieve this goal, the emphasis has been on creating a strong and independent legal profession, capable of defining and imposing professional and ethical standards. This suggests that it is essential to institute a process for the selection of judges based on professional criteria and to guarantee a specified period of tenure. An essential concomitant is the creation of honest law enforcement agencies that effectively carry out court decisions and a court administration that ensures that cases are dealt with expeditiously and at reasonable cost to the plaintiff.

Public acceptance of a legal system is in part a function of perception about fairness not only in the administration of established laws but also of the laws themselves. Who enacts the laws and whom do they benefit? Achieving the rule of law is inseparable in a fundamental sense from the issue of political legitimacy.[26]

Typically, development aid agencies have been reluctant to assist in strengthening judicial systems, because the link to development is seen (incorrectly) as indirect. The involvement in law enforcement is seen to risk association with inequitable or unjust legal systems. Although very real, these risks can be exaggerated. The urgent need for solid legal training and technical assistance in improving court administration poses no risks. Nor does assistance in publishing and disseminating a country's body of laws. These are simple matters that are nonetheless a prerequisite for the efficient administration of justice.

Ignorance of the laws, unpredictable legal administration, delays in handling court cases, and a failure to enforce court decisions all tend to increase business costs, discourage private investment, and obstruct development. And most seriously, they imply injustice and inequity. Moreover, there can be no legal accountability (a prerequisite for effective political and bureaucratic accountability) without a sound judicial system.[27]

Inefficiencies in the judicial system can be systematically tackled by a committed government, and improvements can easily be monitored. Governments unwilling to address these problems may be viewed as lacking commitment to good governance and hence may be justifiably penalised by external agencies whose financial assistance is being sought.

Bureaucratic Accountability

To be fully effective, measures to achieve political and legal accountability need to be accompanied by arrangements to make bureaucracies accountable. The performance of public agencies and officials requires monitoring, and an effective system must be put in place to correct bureaucratic abuses and inefficiencies. The issue is how to design arrangements that are not subject to political interference or manipulation by officials whose behaviour is being controlled. This is in part a technical question, but equally a political, social, and cultural matter. The political commitment to establish honest and effective systems of bureaucratic accountability can only be achieved through effective arrangements of political accountability and a sound judicial framework. Without strong political commitment, bureaucratic accountability cannot be achieved. And even with it, success is not an easy technical matter because much depends on the social and cultural environment that underlies the behaviour of bureaucrats. Nonetheless, considerable experience suggests that bureaucratic systems must incorporate an incentive system that is compatible with local social values. Japan provides a model; it has adopted Western technology, yet has successfully kept its institutions Japanese in spirit.

A critical dimension of accountability is transparency, which implies making readily available for public scrutiny all public accounts and audit reports, a practice that some governments strongly resist for obvious reasons. This is not a question of sovereignty, but simply a matter of good governance. Every citizen, as well as every donor, can and should insist on it.

At the core of bureaucratic (and political) accountability is the need for rigorous systems of financial management and procurement, with swift and tough penalties for malfeasance. Sound methods of accounting and auditing, and of customs duty and other revenue collection, are readily available, and there can be no excuse for laxity. The same is true for procurement. External aid agencies have been extraordinarily tolerant of financial abuse and, indeed, have at times indirectly shown complicity in corrupt practices by responding to improper pressures from their own suppliers. The practice of export credit agencies financing "commissions" paid to individuals for securing a contract is but one example.[28]

There is a considerable technical literature on other aspects of accountability. Much of it has focused on monitoring inputs rather than outputs, although the latter are equally important. As Samuel Paul has recently stressed,[29] there are in essence two ways to promote accountability in the production of goods and services: exit and voice. Where the supposed beneficiaries have a choice, as is the case with competitive markets, expenditure switching (exit) effectively disciplines the suppliers. In the case of public goods and monopolies, however, the only way for beneficiaries to protect their interests is by making their voices heard—ultimately through elections, but on a day-to-day basis through special interest organisations, such as parent associations and trade unions. As previously noted, donors can play an invaluable role, directly or through local NGOs, in building mechanisms that give beneficiaries an effective voice in the delivery of public services. Here, again, vigilance is needed to discourage powerful interests from capturing these mechanisms for their own benefit.

Fostering markets and helping to create quasi-market mechanisms is also useful. Contracting out the provision of such services as refuse collection or road maintenance through competitive bidding procedures fosters accountability. Other instruments that can be considered include the appointment of an ombudsman, watchdog committees, public hearings, and public opinion polls. Loosening controls and simplifying the regulatory framework, if it facilitates competition, will also increase opportunities for exit. Less regulation, however, may increase monopolistic abuse, and much care must be taken in designing arrangements to fit specific circumstances. Nevertheless, there is a happy coincidence in that depending more on markets and less on administered systems is likely both to improve economic efficiency and to reduce the opportunities for rent seeking.

Freedom of Information and Expression

The free flow of information is crucial for accountability. Efficient markets depend on good information—as does the exercise of "voice." The need for the free dissemination of information goes well beyond facilitating accountability. Vital data on national accounts, trade, balance of payments, employment, cost of living, and household expenditure are frequently withheld from the public. Yet such information is essential to permit public debate about the performance of a government and its public agencies. Informed policy discussions lie at the heart of a healthy political process. And good social and economic data are important for efficient management of the economy; without them businesses find it hard to plan.

External agencies can assist in the collection and dissemination of economic and social data and other information needed for informed public debate, but until now their efforts have been remarkably slight. Building a national capacity for data collection and dissemination and encouraging public debate by financing seminars and public information programmes are complementary efforts. It is not enough for the information to be available; analysis and research are also needed, and this exercise should not be a monopoly of the state. Donors can contribute by funding independent research organisations and by supporting the autonomy of universities.[30]

Capacity Building

Good governance requires competent public agencies. Aid agencies have been active in this area for many years, but the results have been negligible, in part because of the lack of political commitment and in part because the interventions have been poorly designed. This is not the place for a detailed review of public management reform, but it is clear that much more imagination and determination are needed. Two aspects merit attention: first, capacity building is a long-term venture and external agencies need to create approaches that will enable sustained, long-term support programmes to be adopted. Second, external agencies cannot be fully effective unless they collaborate with the governments involved. An acceptable role is to help governments define clearly a single comprehensive programme of administrative reform and capacity building that can command widespread bureaucratic and public support.

The Differing Roles of External Agencies

External actors, depending on their varying missions and mandates, have a distinct role in fostering better governance. External agencies can more easily address the technical aspects of governance, for example, but by no means exclusively. Thus it is important to discuss the possible contributions of different categories of external agencies. Most of what is set out below has already been tried, but in most instances rather half-heartedly. Only by pursuing these opportunities more energetically will progress be made.

International and Multilateral Institutions

Because the statutes of international and multilateral institutions (with the exception of the new European Bank for Reconstruction and Development) expressly rule out political considerations; actions must focus on the technical aspects of governance. Thus the World Bank and the UN agencies have worked to strengthen public administration (including the judiciary), to reform public sector enterprises, and to build institutional capacity. This is entirely the right focus, although much more could be done to improve effectiveness and sustainability. In addition, there has been increasing effort to promote institutional pluralism by fostering local government, NGOs, and grass-roots organisations, with the objective of mobilising local human and financial resources to provide community services. There is no reason that this support for institutional development cannot also be extended to a whole range of NGOs, including professional associations and chambers of industry and commerce. Institutional organisations are already a major (and sometimes the only authoritative) source of basic social and economic data. This invaluable service could be expanded.

Bilateral Agencies

Although international agencies have a particularly strong role to play in the areas noted above, bilateral agencies can also contribute significantly in similar ways. In addition, bilateral agencies can use their influence to promote political accountability and respect for human rights, particularly by encouraging the rule of law. Helping to organise fair elections by furnishing resources and observers is another possibility. Support for particular political parties, however, clearly calls into question the motives of the donor.

Important opportunities exist for bilateral donors to promote honest government by channelling funds in ways that reduce the chances of corruption. These include untying aid, insisting on open competitive procurement procedures, and outlawing bribes or payments of "commissions" by suppliers. The United States has taken the lead here, but other OECD countries have so far been reluctant to follow.

Non-Governmental Organisations

Industrial-country NGOs can promote better governance in two ways. First, they can support their counterparts in developing countries. Such interventions by small agencies can be more effective at the community level, where they are less constrained by their relationship with central government authorities. This distance gives them more credibility with the groups they are assisting. Second, they can address human rights abuses in a manner that is seen to be completely apolitical. Amnesty International's strong reputation for professionalism and objectivity has been rewarded with considerable moral authority in international affairs.

It is not unimaginable that a comparable institution—perhaps called Integrity International—could be established to expose major corruption. Such an organisation would need to be evenhanded in its treatment of industrial and developing countries and would address the practices of both public officials and transnational corporations.

NGOs can also play an active role in conflict resolution, as discussed earlier, as well as engage in various other humanitarian actions to relieve suffering and reestablish civil order in war-torn zones. Another role is to set up twinning arrangements or networks between groups with common concerns, for example, professional associations, trade unions, chambers of commerce and industry, and other special interest groups.

Conditionality

The issue of conditionality is often raised, on the one hand, by representatives of some external agencies that believe an element of coercion is needed to counterbalance the private agendas of the ruling elites and, on the other hand, by developing country officials and many others who view coercion as either counterproductive or an unacceptable infringement of sovereignty. As a general principle, institutional reforms are not likely to be sustained unless underpinned by a genuine political commitment. Thus it is evident that a collaborative approach is likely to be more effective than coercion in the long run. However, setting a timetable for specific actions (that are considered crucial for achieving programme objectives) linked to the release of external funds has been found useful in the context of structural adjustment lending. But conditionality should be regarded as a judgmental matter depending on the circumstances and the actions being sought.

Conclusion

Although the world order remains strongly anchored to the principle of the sovereignty of nations, external agencies can contribute significantly to fostering good governance in countries seeking their assistance. Let us reemphasise that we are talking about governance and not a specific form of government. Without better governance, aid resources are likely to be largely wasted. Though concerted action among agencies would achieve the desired results sooner, not all agencies have the same role. Bilateral agencies can press for political accountability, and NGOs and some international agencies can address issues of human rights abuse and conflict resolution. The international financial institutions have a mandate to promote only the narrowly defined development aspects of governance. But all agencies can insist on more effective systems of bureaucratic accountability and can provide more targeted assistance programmes aimed at strengthening the capacity of public and private institutions. A pluralist institutional structure, better information flows, the rule of law, and a more participatory development process are likely to result in more political accountability.

At one extreme, donors will confront governments committed to improving their effectiveness. At the other extreme, entrenched elites will resist reform. The majority will be somewhere in between. The goal is not to attain some theoretical ideal but to further painstaking and systematic improvements. To this end it would be useful to set benchmarks for each country with respect to each of the components of governance discussed above, against which progress could be measured.

The effectiveness of these interventions will reflect their sensitivity to local conditions and the degree of popular participation. Although close coordination among agencies is a prerequisite for a concerted and coherent approach, success is likely to depend less on coercion and more on persuasion, and on progressively changing the internal power structure through education, income growth, and pluralist institutional development.

Good governance is a fragile plant that needs sustained nourishing. It requires a fundamental change in mentality and social expectations that will change only gradually. But the pace of change is likely to be strongly influenced by economic circumstances. Economic crises can precipitate radical political changes and lead to a rapid change in the perception of what is and what is not possible. We are living in such a period.

The possibilities for action by external agencies do not mean that more research into the conceptual and cultural issues related to governance would not be fruitful. Some efforts are already under way, for instance, the governance programme at Emory University and the United Nations Development Programme's (1991) follow-up to the first Human Development Report. In the context of such thinking, the complex matters raised in this chapter—the relationship between the state and society and the link between governance and effective development—should be the subject of further inquiry. Thus more thorough and complete analyses by scholars, combined with pragmatic and collaborative operational initiatives by donor agencies and recipient governments, should make it possible to achieve significant improvements in governance.

Notes

This chapter was originally published in the *Proceedings of the World Bank's Annual Conference on Development Economics*, 1991. Copyright is held by the World Bank. It is reproduced here by permission. The views expressed are the authors' own and should not be attributed to the World Bank, its Board of Executive Directors, or to the countries they represent.

1. See Douglas North, *Institutions, Institutional Change and Economic Performance* (New York: Cambridge University Press, 1990).
2. See also Thrainn Eggertsson, *Economic Behaviour and Institutions* (New York: Cambridge University Press, 1990).
3. See Gunnar Myrdal, *Asian Drama: An Inquiry into the Poverty of Nations* (New York: Twentieth Century Fund, 1968).
4. World Bank, *Sub-Saharan Africa: From Crisis to Sustainable Growth, A Long-Term Perspective Study* (Washington, DC: World Bank, 1989).
5. See, for example, Samuel Huntington, *Political Order in Changing Societies* (New Haven, Conn.: Yale University Press, 1968); Patrick Chabal (ed.), *Political Domination in Africa* (Cambridge, U.K.: Cambridge University Press, 1986); Goran Hyden, *No Shortcuts to Progress: African Development Management in Perspective* (Berkeley: University of California Press, 1983).
6. See Samuel Huntington and Joan Nelson, *No Easy Choice* (Cambridge, Mass.: Harvard University Press, 1976).
7. See World Bank, *World Development Report 1990* (New York: Oxford University Press, 1990).
8. See A. K. Sen, "Values, Capability and Well-being in Development Assistance" (paper presented at the Swedish International Development Agency [SIDA] Workshop on Development Assistance, Stockholm, 26-28 April 1989); and A. K. Sen, "International Freedom as a Social Commitment" *New York Review of Books* 37 (10), 1990.
9. See A. K. Sen, *Social Welfare and Collective Choice* (Amsterdam: North Holland Press, 1979), and A. K. Sen, *Resources, Values, and Development* (Cambridge: Harvard University Press, 1984)
10. See Leigh Grosenick, "Research in Democratic Governance," *Public Administration Quarterly* (fall, 1984) and Herbert Spirer, "Violations of Human Rights—How Many?" *American Journal of Economics and Sociology* 48, 1989.
11. For recent contributions to the cultural dimensions of development, see Daniel Etounga-Manguelle, *L'Afrique a-t-elle Besoin d'un Programme d'Ajustement Culturel?* (Ivry-sur-Seine: Editions Nouvelle du Sud, 1991); and Ismail Serageldin, "Culture, Empowerment and the Development Paradigm" (Washington, DC: World Bank, 1990 processed).
12. See successive issues of the UN Development Programme's (UNDP) *Human Development Report* 1991, 1992, 1993 (New York: Oxford University Press/UNDP, successive years).
13. *The International Covenant on Economic, Social, and Cultural Rights* (General Assembly Resolution 2200 A [XI] of 16 December 1966) entered into force on 3

January 1976. *The International Covenant on Civil and Political Rights*, adopted and opened for signature, ratification, and accession by General Assembly Resolution 2200 A (XI) of 16 December 1966, entered into force on 23 March 1976. (Cited in Ibrahim Shihata, *The World Bank in a Changing World* [Dordrecht, Netherlands: Nijhoff, 1991]).

14. See Ibrahim Shihata, "Issues of "Governance," in "Borrowing Members: The Extent of their Relevance Under the Bank's Articles of Agreement" (memorandum of the vice-president and general counsel) (Washington, DC: World Bank, Dec. 21, 1990).

15. See Anthony Killick, *A Reaction Too Far* (London: Overseas Development Institute, 1990).

16. See Robert H Bates (ed.), *Towards a Political Economy of Development* (Berkeley: University of California Press, 1988).

17. See World Bank, *Sub-Saharan Africa: From Crisis to Sustainable Growth, A Long-Term Perspective Study* (Washington, DC: World Bank, 1989).

18. On this point see the record of December 3-4, 1990, Development Assistance Committee Meeting; French president Mitterrand's speech at La Baule, France, 20 June 1990, and British Minister Douglas Hurd's 6 June 1990, Overseas Development Institute (London) speech in "The Emergence of the "Good Government" Agenda: Some Milestones," *IDS Bulletin* 24 (1), 1993.

19. See Ibrahim Shihata, "Issues of "Governance" in Borrowing Members."

20. See John Lonsdale, "Political Accountability in Africa," in Patrick Chaabal (ed.), *Political Domination in Africa.*

21. See Jean-Francois Bayart, *L'Etat en Afrique* (Paris: Fayard, 1989).

22. See Claude Aké, "Sustaining Development on the Indigenous," in World Bank, *Long-Term Perspective Study of Sub-Saharan Africa*, vol. 3 (Washington, DC: World Bank, 1990); Goran Hyden, "The Changing Context of Institutional Development in Sub-Saharan Africa"; and "Creating an Enabling Environment," in Hyden, *No Shortcuts to Progress*; and David Korten, *Getting to the 21st Century: Voluntary Action and the Global Agenda* (Hartford, Conn.: Kumarian Press, 1990).

23. See Joan Nelson, "The Politics of Pro-Poor Adjustment," in Joan Nelson, (ed.), *Fragile Coalition: The Politics of Economic Adjustment* (Oxford, U.K.: Transaction Books, 1989).

24. World Bank, *Sub-Saharan Africa: From Crisis to Sustainable Growth, A Long-Term Perspective Study* (Washington, DC: World Bank, 1989).

25. See David Korten and Rudi Klauss, "Rural Development Programming: The Learning Process Approach," in Korten and Klauss (ed.), *People Centred Development* (Hartford, Conn.: Kumarian Press, 1984); and Lawrence Salmen, *Institutional Dimensions of Poverty Reduction* (Washington, DC: World Bank Working Paper Series No. 411, 1990).

26. See Joost Kuitenbrouwer, *Reflections on the Genesis and Dynamics of Accumulation in Europe and Its Implications for Social Justice and Human Rights* (The Hague: Institute of Social Studies Working Paper No. 33, 1986).

27. See Samuel Paul, *Strengthening Public Service Accountability* (Washington, DC: World Bank Discussion Papers No. 136, 1991).

28. See Pierre Pean, "Corruption and Sous-Developpement," *L'Argent Noir* (Paris: Fayard, 1988).

29. See Paul, *Strengthening Public Service Accountability*.

25. The African Economic Research Consortium, sponsored by the Rockefeller Foundation, SIDA, and several other bilateral donors, is a good example of donor-sponsored research.

Part Six

The Way Forward

15

Toward a New Model of Managing Development Assistance

Goran Hyden

Africa, like the rest of the world, finds itself at a point where public confidence in the state is in serious doubt. As a result of a variety of shortcomings in the management of public affairs, the state has become the object of widespread distrust. This is a new situation that requires both fresh ideas and fresh approaches to the task of managing development. As the main theme of this book suggests, development management is no longer the prerogative of the public sector—the predominant viewpoint in the 1960s and 1970s. It is now clear that it is the responsibility of institutions both of state and civil society. As various chapters of this book have also established, institutional weakness is pervasive in Africa: public sector institutions because they have been run down; the private and voluntary ones because they are young and inexperienced. The biggest challenge in the 1990s and beyond, therefore, must be how these institutions can be strengthened in the shortest possible time and in the most cost-effective manner. In this exercise, Chapter 14 has suggested, external resources have to be related to local needs and opportunities in new and creative ways. Above all, outside assistance has to be revamped so that it challenges individuals and institutions in Africa to take themselves seriously and gives them back a sense of identity and direction.

This is a tall order, but accepting the challenge is inevitable if Africa is ever going to find itself on the road to a better future. Given the magnitude and complexity of the task, it would be presumptuous to suggest that what needs to be done can be formulated in the pages of a relatively short chapter. Yet here I have outlined the basic features of an approach for managing some—though not all types—of external assistance that attempts to meet the emerging challenges.

The Politically Independent Fund
as Development Catalyst

Development management in the 1990s is a multifaceted task that involves both politics and administration, both state and civil society. It is no longer adequate to focus on the public service only. Equally important are actors in the private and voluntary sectors. How can external donors respond to the challenge of this inclusiveness? An answer requires, first, a recognition that, for a variety of reasons, development management in the 1990s and beyond cannot be conducted on a "business as usual" basis. It is no longer possible to identify the answers by only recommending better techniques. Nor will it do to assume that one set of institutions are more important than others. Both intellectual and political boldness is badly needed to restore lost confidence in Africa's ability to chart its own future course of development. Nothing less is required than a formidable catalyst for getting both Africans and the donor community to recommit themselves to such a belief. At the same time, such a move must be administratively simple, economically cost-effective, and politically opportune. Bearing these factors and Africa's current short-comings and problems in mind, I believe that the future approach to managing certain types of foreign assistance should centre on the model of the politically independent development fund. It has a lot of promise and offers new and exciting opportunities for all serious actors involved, as the review of experience with the "fund model" that follows shows.

Experience with Existing Funds or Foundations

The idea of a development fund is new neither to donors nor to African governments. This particular institutional mechanism has been in place for over two decades. Rural or regional development funds have been especially common. Many bilateral donors have been placing money in these funds, which have typically been used to finance small-scale development projects in the countryside. A general feature of these funds is that they have operated without a board of trustees of their own. Instead, responsibility for these institutions has typically been vested in the office of the president or some other branch of government. Although no systematic evaluation of these funds has been carried out, anecdotal evidence suggests that (1) performance has been disappointing; (2)

political patronage rather than economic feasibility considerations have guided decisions regarding allocation of money; and (3) accountability has been very weak or nonexistent. As a result, many bilateral donors have ceased to support such funds.

In this perspective, it is interesting that more recently the World Bank has been instrumental in establishing so-called Social Action Funds to help finance social development programmes. These funds, which have been set up in several African countries, e.g., Burundi and Nigeria, are meant to cater to the many private and voluntary initiatives that have been taken to mitigate the worst social effects of recent macroeconomic reform programmes. They support a broad range of projects dealing with nutrition, child development, education, and public health care. They are more targeted than the rural development funds but, like the former, they are not autonomous but under political control. The appointing authority, for example, is the head of state or a senior minister. The same is true for other funds recently established under the auspices of multilateral agencies. For example, the United Nations Development Programme (UNDP) has a Village Development Fund in Gambia operating under these auspices. Among the bilateral agencies, the United States Agency for International Development (USAID) seems to be in the forefront in pushing the fund model, especially to finance the activities of non-governmental organisations (NGOs).

Despite problems and poor performance in the past, the fund model is still very much present. It is also being given a further boost by private philanthropic organisations like the Ford Foundation, which, in recent years, has been involved in setting up private foundations in such countries as Egypt, Mozambique, and Zimbabwe. These funds have been established as legally independent entities, but because they became too closely associated with particular persons in politics, they lost their original course of direction. As a result, public confidence in these foundations has declined.

In addition, private African foundations, capitalised by local individuals or communities, are being established. They are especially significant in Nigeria, where, at present, foundations bear the names of such prominent individuals as Obafemi Awolowo, Ibrahim Babangida, and the Sardauna. There are also a good number of foundations centred on specific communities or areas, e.g., Kano. Their records have been mixed. In particular, the task of making the foundations independent of the "founding individual," his family, and most immediate entourage has proved problematic. For community-based foundations, the challenge has been to get trustees to realise that their responsibility involves not only dispensation of funds but also decisions about how capital can yield more capital.

The proposal builds on the lessons learned from efforts such as those outlined above. Three issues about the "fund model" stand out as particularly important: (1) its legal and political status; (2) its scope of operation; and (3) its constituency of clients.

Legal and Political Status

The legal and political status of the model takes on special importance in the 1990s for two reasons. The first is the growing concern with pluralist politics. With the institutionalisation of multi-party systems of politics in Africa, partisan views that in the past, were accommodated in single ruling parties or military juntas are now being propagated in a transparent fashion. This new form of competitive politics puts great strains on Africa's already fragile social structures. Recent elections in such countries as Angola, Cameroon, and Ethiopia indicate the difficulties associated with shifting to an open and pluralist system in circumstances where no institutions are seen to enjoy the status of being independent of partisan politics, especially of the ethnic variety. The second reason is the decline—in some cases breakdown—of public authority that has occurred across Africa in the last decade or so. This has been well documented in many studies.[1]

The tendency is clear: Public servants have increasingly used their office to secure private benefits; citizens distrust public officials and seek alternative ways of dealing with their problems. Although this trend towards greater local self-governance on an informal basis is encouraging, its benefits will be realised only if there is a simultaneous growth of central institutions capable of serving local development efforts on professional rather than political grounds.

In a situation, therefore, in which the backbone of African countries is weak and easily broken, it is imperative that priority be given to institutions that can help strengthen it. The independent development fund model has this potential. It, by standing outside ethnic and patronage politics and being free from ties to the state, can restore confidence in public authority. This model, by professionally serving both state and civil society, helps in repairing fissures.

Scope of Operation

At a time when greater transparency and accountability is being called for, the scope of operation of the fund becomes especially significant. The tendency in recent years has been for funding agencies to promote institutions outside the state, especially those fostering multi-purpose community development. Although these measures are steps in the right direction, they reinforce the decline of central institutions. Thus, instead of multi-purpose development funds that cater only to one area or group of people—and thus reinforce their sense of being sovereign and separate— African countries need development funds that are *national* and *sectoral*. In the interest of better governance, African countries must prove to themselves and others that transparency and accountability are possible not only in the context of face-to-face relations within a given community but also at a higher and more abstract level of social action. At the same time, in order to give such funds a more manageable operational mandate, they should be sectoral, focusing on issues such as food security and public health or education, which have been identified as national priority concerns.

Constituency of Clients

The constituency of clients is an important issue because there has been a tendency among donors in the past decade to polarise government departments and NGOs. The latter have been the "darlings" of the donors, governments the "villains." Even though this may be somewhat of an oversimplification, the point is that development management in the 1990s must address the challenges of both the public and the private or voluntary sectors. The fund model proposed here does so by catering to funding needs in all sectors. Its constituency of clients consists of government departments, cooperatives, NGOs, community-based associations, and private firms. The fund, by not a priori discriminating against any particular actor, has an integrative role in a situation in which the pressures are otherwise centrifugal.

Implementing the Development Fund Model

The principal challenge in implementing this model is how to secure the necessary legal and political autonomy of the funds. Three issues are of special significance: (1) Who should appoint the board? (2) how can trustees be made to comply with the principle of autonomy? and (3) how can money be used to secure it?

Appointment

The appointment of members of the board of these funds—hereafter referred to as "trustees"—must be independent of any political authority, including the head of state, in order to minimise the risks of political interference in their operations. Legal provisions for the establishment of independent institutions of this kind may or may not exist in individual countries today. Where they do not, a necessary first step is to introduce new legislation to that effect. The basic principle must be that the institution should be self-governing. This means that the board should be a self-appointing body. It is accountable to the public through the means specified in the law. Building up confidence in such measures is an important aspect of the transition to more democratic forms of governance. In this respect, the attitude of governments and donors to this model can be used as an indicator of how seriously they are committed to democratic governance.

Compliance

Compliance with the law cannot be taken for granted, and additional measures are needed to secure it. The most important is to have all trustees sign an oath upon appointment, which asks them to declare that they are not actively engaged in politics or have any economic interests that run counter to their position as trustees. If a government has them sign such a document, this will help to "insulate" the fund from the well-known centrifugal and debilitating forces in African societies. In addition, the public will have a definite measuring rod against which to assess their performance. Finding people in African countries that meet these requirements is easier in the current context than it was before. There are an increasing number of officials who have retired from politics or public service who may qualify. With religious organisations taking a greater interest in public and developmental affairs, leaders in such bodies may also be potential nominees. To the extent that doubts may exist about the potential for impartiality of such a board, there is a case for having respected international figures appointed to serve as trustees. Since these funds are meant to be conduits of donor assistance, these external agencies may want to have such international representation on the board. These appointees, however, should not be anything but a minority because anything else would take away the value of having these funds serve as catalysts for strengthening development management from within.

Money

Money can also be used to secure the autonomy of these funds in various ways. One possibility is to endow the funds in such a way that their operational costs are being paid for by their own dividends. This presupposes the existence of well-functioning financial markets, and these are still rare in Africa. Capital investments in foreign funds is an alternative, but it does raise questions of transparency and may contradict the objectives of the project. Another possibility is that the funds receive capital through special debt swaps. Such initiatives have already been taken on a trial basis in a few African countries. Because the funds proposed here are public and, in principle, accessible to any actor, they constitute attractive targets for accelerating the implementation of such swaps and turning Africa's severest debt burdens into developmental opportunities. Should a particular fund prove incompetent in using such additional capital, the capital would be stopped and placed instead in another more promising fund. The same would apply to assistance received directly from donors. They would deposit their aid for a given sector in the relevant fund and continue making such payments on a contractual basis as long as the payments are being applied in a professional manner. If the trustees of that fund fail in this respect, the donor would discontinue its support and instead look for another fund to assist, either in that country or elsewhere.

Operational Features

As a national institution with a specific sectoral mandate, the fund must be equipped with a variety of policy instruments that enables it to serve all potential clients. For maximum versatility, it may be advantageous to have the funds operate through separate "windows." One such window may cater to project requests that are not expected to yield any financial return on investment. Through this window, the grant mechanism would be used to support activities such as education and training, which are important for development yet do not yield immediate returns. A second window ought to cater to the many individuals and groups that are not capable of attracting credit on commercial terms. Here the "soft loan" mechanism would be the most appropriate. Special care would have to be paid to striking an adequate balance between risk and opportunity. To ensure that support of such individuals and groups is viable, it becomes important to check how well rooted any project is in the local community and what its matching contribution might be. A third window would provide credit on regular market terms and thus cater to those individuals and organisations in society that can afford to operate on these terms. This window would be no different from a regular bank or credit institution, except that its loans would be targeted on a specific sector or set of issues.

Each fund, within its mandate of operation, would advertise its services publicly and invite individuals, groups, or organisations to apply. To make sure that project proposals are as well prepared as possible, it may also advertise what exactly the proposals should contain and what conditionalities, if any, there are to receiving the fund's money. Many projects will still be poorly formulated and many others will fail to meet feasibility criteria. As a result, a number of proposals will no doubt be rejected outright, but it should be the policy of the fund's professional staff to be as helpful and responsive as possible. Thus, for example, rather than rejecting outright a particular proposal, the staff may send it back to its sponsors and request them to rework it in certain ways.

Advantages of the Model

The greatest advantage of the model is that it responds to many of the most critical concerns in development management today: (1) development from within; (2) localisation of accountability; and (3) institutional viability.

Development from Within

The fact that the fund model encourages an enabling environment in which development is being driven by demands from within African society rather by than the whims of the donors. To be sure, there will still be constraints on what can be done, but the model enhances the social and political space for local actors, whether they are based in the public, private, or voluntary sector. As such, it has the potential of making a major contribution toward more democratic and effective governance. Particularly significant is that the fund becomes a local intermediary between donors and recipients with the capacity to direct external resource flows into more manageable and suitable financial packages. The prospect for better utilisation of both external and domestic resources is enhanced.

Localisation of Accountability

African countries have been extensively dependent on foreign aid, and for a long time they have been used to responding to conditionalities set by the donors. These conditionalities have now reached the point at which they cannot be taken further. In particular, it has become clear that policies and programmes that have not been designed locally, on one hand, cannot, in the final analysis, expect to secure whole-hearted or full local support. On the other hand, if existing political and economic conditionalities do not work, the frustrations and difficulties of dispensing foreign assistance to Africa will multiply. The best way Africans can mitigate these problems is to rise to the occasion and demonstrate that they are capable of acting responsibly on their own. The fund model provides both Africans and donors with a way out of this dilemma. It encourages the use of both domestic and outside resources in new and creative ways and leaves management responsibility to an institution that is legally incorporated in the recipient country. In line with Africans' demands for more democratic governance, it gives them a chance to prove that they can handle development management issues in a responsible fashion on their own.

Institutional Viability

Institutional viability is encouraged by this approach because it rewards those who can stand on their own feet and penalises those who fail to consider what it means to do so. It encourages Africans to take themselves seriously and to impose conditionalities on each other, as opposed to waiting for outsiders to do so. The fund model starts from the premise that the principal shortcoming in Africa today is not shortage of technical or managerial personnel but of viable institutions. Thus, rather than advocating expensive training programmes with little or no payoff, this approach tries to achieve better resource utilisation by encouraging competition among public and private institutions in society. Against the background of ongoing public sector contraction, it is especially important that an institution's employees are provided with an incentive to restore its viability. The civil service in Africa has been the villain of development management for too long. But it is time that it is given a chance to prove itself. The fund model has the ability to facilitate such a turnaround in certain sectors in a cost-effective manner.

Why Should Governments and Donors
Accept the Model?

Development management in the 1990s and beyond requires a new compact between donors and African governments. Both sets of actors need to rededicate themselves to the belief that progress is possible in Africa. The institutional model discussed in this chapter invites everyone to engage in such a rededication. But why should African governments and the donor agencies accept this approach?

At first glance, African governments may think that they stand to lose from adopting this approach. Such an attitude, however, would be very shortsighted since external donors are loath to give large amounts of money without instituting mechanisms of accountability. Government departments stand as good a chance of receiving financial support from these funds as do other institutions in society. The only provision is that they demonstrate that they can make use of their resource potential as well as others. Another reason that African governments should consider this approach seriously is that it has the potential of reducing the weight of conditionalities imposed from outside by providing donor and recipient countries the opportunity to work together in a new partnership of equals.

Donors no longer find themselves under the same pressure to give aid on grounds of economic or military security. Justification for foreign assistance increasingly has to be sought on other grounds. Other than humanitarian considerations, performance is appearing as the single most important criterion for foreign aid to be continued to Africa. The fund model, if adopted along the lines proposed in this chapter, would go a long way towards reestablishing confidence in the foreign aid enterprise, under conditions that are compatible with current democratisation objectives. If the donors really are serious about their demands for Africa to democratise, a logical step is for them to delegate greater responsibility for handling funds to responsible institutions in the recipient countries. Another reason donors might be attracted by this model is that it is administratively simple and obliterates the need for large bureaucracies, either at headquarters or in the field. This approach helps to cut the overhead costs of foreign aid and, at the same time, enhances the prospects that it will yield results.

Conclusion: Where to Go from Here?

The approach I have advocated in this chapter rejects the notion that we can proceed in the field of development management as if business is as usual. Implied in the preceding discussion has been the assumption that a fair amount of new thinking is needed. Both African governments and donors need to review their positions.

Everyone who has tried to change procedures and practices within already established institutions know that it is difficult and time-consuming. It is necessary to take one step at a time. To implement the independent development fund model, one must first recognise that this model is not applicable to all forms of foreign aid. Humanitarian assistance on an emergency basis, large-scale infrastructural investments, as well as balance-of-payment support, for example, fall outside its scope and suitability. It is more appropriate for what we have come to accept as mainstream development aid, whether in the social or economic field. Employment of the model is now needed to learn from the experience and to take corrective steps, as might be required.

Notes

1. See, e.g., James Wunsch and Dele Olowu (eds.), *The Failure of the Centralised State* (Boulder, Colorado: Westview Press, 1990).

16

Achieving the African Economic Community: Implications for Administration and Management

H. M. A. Onitiri

The establishment of the African Economic Community (AEC) poses a major challenge for public administration and management not only at the continental level but also at the subregional and national levels. The Organisation of African Unity (OAU) and other African organisations are well aware of the immensity of the challenge, and efforts are underway on several fronts to find ways of meeting it. Two major 1993 studies have set the stage for more intensive debate on ideas and options for meeting the challenge. One makes proposals for the structural reorganisation of the OAU Secretariat into a single OAU/AEC Secretariat; the other examines the structure of the Joint OAU/Economic Commission for Africa (ECA)/African Development Bank (AfDB) Secretariat, and recommends measures to increase its effectiveness. (These two studies were being undertaken within the framework of two projects funded by the United Nations Development Programme (UNDP) to assist the OAU—Project RAF/87/101 to improve the management capability of the OAU and project RAF/87/104 in support of the AEC).

Against the background of these efforts in this chapter, I examine some of the public administration and management problems posed by the present situation as well as some of the policy options that may be considered for resolving them. I argue that the administrative and management problems arising from the establishment of the AEC can be eased considerably if there is a major attempt to evolve various mechanisms and management procedures at subregional and national levels as well as the public, private, and voluntary sectors and international organisations in the implementation of the AEC treaty.

The Main Issues

The treaty establishing the AEC provides for several implementing mechanisms and subsidiary bodies. For their effective functioning these require qualified and experienced technical personnel, to staff the specialised committees provided for in Article 25 of the treaty, as well as institutions established under the various protocols provided for in the treaty. However, the main task of administering and managing the AEC devolve largely on the single OAU/AEC Secretariat, which serves the Economic and Social Commission and the specialised committees of the AEC. The successful implementation of the treaty depends in large measure on several crucial factors, which follow:

- the structure of the single OAU/AEC Secretariat;
- the improvement of the administrative and management competence of the OAU/AEC Secretariat;
- the effectiveness of the mechanisms that will be established to mobilise the activities of other African institutions and organisations (intergovernmental organisations or [IGOs], non-governmental organisations [NGOs], the private sector, etc.) for the implementation of the treaty;
- the effectiveness of the coordination arrangements between the AEC and existing subregional and regional economic communities (RECs); and
- the effectiveness of the mechanisms established at the national level to focus attention on the regional and continental dimensions of national programmes and on the implementation of regional and continental programmes at the national level

Structural Reorganisation of
the OAU Secretariat

The Council of Ministers of the OAU, at its fifty-first ordinary session (19-24 February 1990), decided that the African Economic Community should be an integral part of the OAU system and that the OAU should be restructured to reflect this. To this end, the council requested the secretary general of the OAU, in close cooperation with the executive secretary of the ECA and the president of the AfDB, to undertake an in-depth study of all the implications of a single Secretariat for the OAU and the AEC. Although there had been various attempts in the past to restructure the OAU Secretariat in order to improve its operational efficiency, the decision to have a single OAU/AEC Secretariat has increased the urgency of implementing such reforms.

The onset of operations of the AEC has, therefore, added a new dimension to the functions of the OAU and to the relationship of the organisation to other African regional and subregional institutions and organisations. The organisation's new role means that the OAU's traditional structure has to be transformed to enable it to focus primarily on the implementation of the AEC treaty, along with its continuing involvement in issues relating to political stability, security, popular participation and respect for human rights, and its new role of conflict prevention, management, and resolution. New duties and functions have to be defined for the organisation and new relationships established with other African regional and subregional organisations. In particular, the organisation in its role as the Secretariat of the AEC is to implement, along with the treaty, a series of protocols to be annexed to the treaty, covering a wide range of subjects on Africa's socio-economic development. This calls for the emergence of a new organisation in terms of structure and working methodology.

The immense task of managing the AEC can be glimpsed from the wide-ranging objectives that it is expected to fulfil. Among these are the following:

- establishment, on a continental scale, of a framework for the development, mobilisation, and utilisation of human and material resources of Africa in order to achieve self-reliant development;
- the promotion and strengthening of joint investment programmes in the production and trade of major products and inputs within the framework of collective self-reliance;
- the harmonisation of national policies in order to promote AEC activities, particularly in agriculture, industry, transport and communications, energy, natural resources, trade, money and finance, human resources, education, culture, science, and technology;
- the harmonisation and rationalisation of the activities of existing African multi-national institutions and the establishment of such institutions, as and when necessary, with a view to their possible transformation into organs of the AEC.

Given these wide-ranging objectives, it should be obvious that the only structure that can enable the AEC to fulfil these tasks is one that makes it possible for it to mobilise the institutions and mechanisms that are available at continental, regional and, national levels. The situation, therefore, calls for minimum centralisation of activities and a good deal of decentralisation, devolution, and delegation. Within this framework, the IGOs, NGOs, and the private sector need to be encouraged to play an effective part.

The new organisation must aim at a clear division of labour within its own structures and develop an effective arrangement for cooperation with African IGOs, NGOs, and other sectors, in order to encourage them to undertake activities relevant to the implementation of the treaty. In this context, it needs to redefine the activities of the OAU Regional Officers so that they can play an effective role in administering the network of relationships that the new OAU/AEC structure establishes with African institutions at regional and national levels, geared to the implementation of the AEC treaty and its protocols. Such relationships could take the form of seminars, workshops, and so on directed towards research on specific issues and the generation of ideas and options relevant to the implementation of specific aspects of the treaty.

Three basic considerations have to be borne in mind in the search for a new structure that will enable the OAU to fulfil its new responsibilities effectively. First, with the establishment of the single OAU/AEC Secretariat, the activities of the OAU now fall under two clear divisions—implementation of the AEC treaty and performance of the political functions. Hence, within the framework of the division of labour in the OAU/AEC Secretariat, a senior functionary of the organisation (assistant secretary general or deputy secretary general of the OAU) will be in charge of matters relating to the AEC.

Second, since the AEC deals with matters relating to social as well as economic development, some reorganisation of the present structure is necessary so that all activities presently falling under the Economic Development and Cooperation (EDECO) and Education, Science, Culture and Social Affairs (ESCAS) departments will come under the senior official responsible for the implementation of the AEC treaty, under the overall direction of the OAU secretary general.

Finally, because of the new role of the OAU in conflict prevention, management, and resolution, it is necessary to enlarge the political department, under another senior functionary responsible to the OAU secretary general.

Structure of the Joint (OAU/ECA/AfDB) Secretariat

Another development that affects the structure and functioning of the OAU/AEC Secretariat is the structure that is established for the Joint (OAU/ECA/AfDB) Secretariat.

In recognition of the importance of the three foremost African institutions in the implementation of the treaty, the African heads of state and government in Resolution AHG Res. 179 (XXV) called upon the OAU and ECA Secretariats and the AfDB to coordinate and pool their efforts and resources so as to provide, in a Joint Secretariat, the required logistic and technical support to the Permanent Steering Committee in the process of establishing the AEC. The resolution also directs the OAU secretary general, in close collaboration with the executive secretary of the ECA and the president of the AfDB, to hold consultations with the executive heads of existing REC in order to:

- establish a permanent consultative platform for the coordination and harmonisation of activities, projects, and programmes related to economic cooperation and integration at all levels;
- exchange information about cooperation and integration experiences;
- adopt common positions vis-à-vis their partners in the international community in economic cooperation and integration of the continent;
- prepare joint periodic reports for the assembly of the OAU heads of state and government on the state of economic cooperation and integration in Africa

Since that resolution was passed, the three organisations have met regularly to discharge these functions and to coordinate their activities in connection with the implementation of the AEC treaty.

The other study reviewed the efforts made so far to coordinate, through the Joint Secretariat, the activities of the three organisations in relation to the implementation of the AEC treaty and examined how the present arrangement can be improved so that the resources of the three organisations can be mobilised effectively for the implementation of the AEC treaty and its protocols. Matters examined included the following:

- an appraisal of the management problems hampering the coordinated and efficient mobilisation of the resources of the three organisations in the service of the Permanent Steering Committee of the OAU and relevant organs of the AEC on matters relating to the implementation of the AEC treaty;
- proposals for the allocation of responsibility to each organisation in the overall responsibility of the Joint Secretariat in serving the Permanent Steering Committee and the relevant organs of the AEC on issues relating to the implementation of the AEC treaty;
- proposals on how the Joint Secretariat can be made to act as a think tank on economic integration issues and ways of enabling the Joint Secretariat to carry out this task, including the establishment of ad

hoc independent think tanks and modalities for their operation and financing;
- an examination of the feasibility of transforming the present Joint Secretariat into a formal mechanism, with adequate staff, for coordinating the activities of the agencies, through subcommittees, expert groups, etc., with respect to the implementation of the AEC treaty, and mobilising human and financial resources to support those activities;
- the possibility of institutionalising the Joint Secretariat in each organisation, including arrangements for the establishment of focal points, coordination of activities relating to the AEC, and follow-up of the decisions of the Joint Secretariat

At the time of this writing, the first draft of the consultants' report was under consideration by the Joint Secretariat.

Improving the Administrative and Management Competence of the OAU

Because of the additional burden imposed on administration and management at all levels, it is necessary to pay more attention to training and retraining of the relevant human resources and to facilitate the mobility of staff among the three foremost African organisations. This is designed to strengthen the OAU's management capability to undertake its new role effectively until it can put in place its own expanded structures.

On the face of it, the time span for the implementation of the treaty (thirty-four years, from 1991 to 2025) provides ample opportunity to undertake the necessary reforms of administration and management. However, much depends on the strength of the administrative foundation laid in the early years of implementation. The temporary secondment of staff by other African organisations to the OAU for this purpose may do much to strengthen that foundation.

Involving African Institutions and Organisations in the Implementation of the Treaty

Particularly in the first few years of the treaty, much depends on the effectiveness of the mechanisms established to mobilise the activities of other African institutions and organisations for the implementation of the treaty. Hence no effort should be spared to sensitise these organisations about the tasks involved and the contributions that they might make in this connection. For this purpose, a wide range of sensitisation programmes have to be worked out.

The establishment of the AEC should provide a new opportunity to step up the rationalisation of the activities of African IGOs. Such rationalisation has been a major preoccupation of African governments for many years, but so far the results have not been impressive; and many such organisations continue to struggle for their very existence against great odds.

Renewed effort to rationalise the activities of African IGOs should be accompanied by a major review of their regular conferences and meetings held at the levels of ministers and high government officials. These activities should be streamlined to make them more efficient and effective. The present round of conferences and meetings at high levels imposes too heavy a burden on high government functionaries, apart from the high costs, which many African governments can ill afford.

To implement the treaty successfully will necessitate maintaining a careful balance between two principles: the decentralisation of activities and the need for effective coordination of such activities. Decentralisation should aim at avoiding the growth of an unwieldy bureaucracy at the AEC Secretariat and should ensure wide participation by African institutions and organisations at all levels. Implementation also requires close coordination of interrelated activities by these African institutions and organisations.

Coordination Arrangements Between the AEC and the RECs

The treaty provides that the first five years of its implementation should be devoted to the strengthening of existing RECs. Hence the first test of the management capability of the OAU/AEC Secretariat will be how effectively it discharges this function.

Strengthening Existing Subregional and Regional Economic Communities

Strengthening the RECs is likely to involve three major activities:

- a fact-finding exercise directed at obtaining detailed information about the present state of affairs in the RECs—how far they have gone in fulfilling their objectives, what problems they are facing, what options for a resolution of those problems are being considered, and what they believe that the AEC can do to assist with the resolution of those problems;

- in cooperation with the relevant RECs and with the assistance of suitable resource persons and experts on the issues involved, organisation of seminars, workshops, and discussions groups to generate ideas and options that may be considered for implementation;
- establishment of appropriate mechanisms that will enable the OAU/AEC to participate in negotiations for resolving the problems in question

Detailed arrangements for the pursuit of these activities need to be worked out by the Joint Secretariat before the treaty is ratified (about a dozen African countries are yet to ratify the treaty at the time of this writing) so that no time is lost in mounting missions of the three foremost African institutions to the RECs.

Strengthening Sectoral Integration at the Continental Level

Essentially, sectoral integration involves the coordination of national policies at the sectoral level. This is perhaps the very heart of the integration movement, since, in the final analysis, the success of every integration effort depends on the extent of cooperation, coordination, or integration of national policies in critical economic and social sectors. But this implies the existence of effective mechanisms for the elaboration of policy options for integration at regional and continental levels and the administration of whatever options are finally chosen for implementation. At national level, the main issues are how regional and continental strategies (in the form of agreements, resolutions, etc.) should be reflected in national policies and how national economic and social needs should be reflected in the strategies and policies designed at the regional and continental levels.

The Need for Strong National Focal Mechanism

It would be virtually fruitless to attempt to improve or build continental administrative and management structures without ensuring strong mechanisms at the national level and promoting intense awareness of the role that regional and continental integration can make in the attainment of national economic and social objectives. It is important, therefore, that

African governments should make serious efforts to encourage the establishment of such mechanisms. Governments should associate NGOs, the business community, the trade union movement, and other organisations representing women, youths, etc., with these mechanisms. Indeed, the new development management paradigm presented in this book reinforces the importance of building the community from below.

In this connection, the recommendations of the *African Charter for Popular Participation in Development* should provide the basis for promoting popular participation in the implementation of the treaty.

Conclusion

The first few years of the implementation of the AEC treaty are going to be particularly crucial, because during this period the administrative groundwork has to be laid. That groundwork should include an effective mechanism for the mobilisation of the activities of African IGOs. In this connection, it is significant that the first protocol to be ready for ratification by African governments is that of the relationship between the RECs and the AEC. If a good start is made with the implementation of this protocol, it will set the stage for developing a favourable atmosphere for the implementation of the treaty.

17

Conclusion: Toward Dynamism, Empowerment, and Entrepreneurship

Sadig Rasheed and David Fasholé Luke

The preceding chapters have raised a variety of issues aimed at eliciting dynamic responses from the public sector and fostering and supporting entrepreneurial impulses and empowerment in economy and society at large. The reflections of these chapters must, however, be followed by action. To this end, within the framework of its work programme, the ECA has formulated a *Strategic Agenda for Development Management in Africa in the 1990s.*

Besides setting out the basis of the new development management paradigm, which has been the main focus of this book, and proposing mechanisms for coordination, exchange of information, and networking among all actors and supporters, the *Strategic Agenda* identified ten priority areas for action, as follows:

- improving the public policy-making process;
- enhancing efficiency and quality in civil services;
- promoting ethics and strengthening mechanisms of accountability;
- decentralisation for sustained development;
- improving resource mobilisation and financial management capacity of African governments;
- optimising the use of information technology;
- strengthening the participation and enhancing the skills of women;
- public enterprise sector reform;
- building entrepreneurial capacity and promoting private sector development; and
- ensuring popular participation in development and governance.

It should be emphasised that these priority areas should not constitute a blueprint but rather a framework for reform. As noted in Chapter 1, the specific challenges of reform vary from place to place, and country to country, although there are common elements. Moreover, African countries are at various stages in the reform process. In the light of these observations, different countries will and should have different blueprints, but it is still valid to identify common concerns and a common framework for dealing with them. Substantive chapters of this book have focused on these priority areas in some detail. The full text of the *Strategic Agenda* is reproduced as an essential frame of reference for the issues raised in this book.

In line with our theme of multi-actor involvement in the new development management paradigm, responsibility for action on the priority areas elaborated upon in the *Strategic Agenda* is a shared one: state and civil society; public, cooperative, and private enterprises; and public, private, and voluntary organisations. It is a burden shared by everybody, including external agencies and actors involved in the continent's development.

Implied in the reflections in this book is that a fair amount of new thinking is needed. As one of the authors suggests (in chapter 15), African governments and donors need to review their positions. Both intellectual and political boldness is badly needed to restore lost confidence in Africa's ability to chart its own future course of development.

It is the case, however, that future development efforts must accord the private and voluntary sectors and popular initiatives an expanded role. This is a strategy that requires deliberate action from "above" to foster dynamism in public sector management and practices, to facilitate entrepreneurial initiative and effect measures of empowerment outside the state sector. To this extent, as suggested in chapter 1, development management reform in contemporary Africa remains, in the final analysis, a political question with a political answer. But the cost of not acting or acting only half-heartedly would be high. For this reason, it is to be hoped that all actors involved in managing Africa's development, whether local or external, will embrace the analyses and recommendations made in this book and in the *Strategic Agenda for Development Management in Africa in the 1990s* with the seriousness they deserve and forge a committed partnership for their effective implementation.

Appendix

Strategic Agenda for Development Management in Africa in the 1990s

Preamble

After a decade in which most people in Africa have suffered a significant decline in their living standards and African economies have fallen further behind those of the rest of the world, development management has assumed a new and critical importance. This stems from a growing recognition that Africa is not lacking in physical and human resources. But their effective utilisation still remains an elusive task. If Africa is going to reassert itself, reverse economic decline and revitalise its economies, investment in these resources and the management of development are likely to provide the most effective returns.

We refer here to this challenge as that of development management. Unlike the earlier concept of development administration which centred on the public sector only, development management implies the involvement of all sectors and institutions in society: state and civil society; public, cooperative and private enterprises; and non-governmental, voluntary agencies and people's organisations. It is a burden shared by everybody, including external agencies and actors involved in the continent's development.

After a series of disappointments with past approaches to development and its management, the question of what can be done at this point is justified. Why spend money on an activity that in the past has yielded little? We believe that current political and economic reform processes in Africa provide a window of opportunity that its people can seize to their benefit. To do so, however, requires a readiness to think and act boldly and moreover in a manner that strengthens society as a whole. African countries have come to realise that there is no alternative to accelerating the process of growth and development on a sustained and sustainable basis; that such a process must be human-centred; and that democracy, popular participation, good governance and accountability are essential prerequisites of socio-economic regeneration. The answer to socio-economic revitalisation does not lie with the governments alone; nor with private entrepreneurs and voluntary organisations alone. Past strategies that have emphasised only one set of actors must be replaced with one that emphasises the role that everybody has and potentially can play and the interdependence of these roles. New strategies, approaches and institutions will be needed to achieve this kind of self-reinforcement and reintegration.

Having collectively assessed the experience of thirty years of development management in Africa in the light of emerging development challenges, priorities, and changing global and regional realities and situations, we became convinced of the need for African countries to articulate a coherent, pragmatic, imaginative and bold strategic development management agenda for the rest of the 1990s. And further, we commit ourselves to the implementation of this agenda.

In what follows, we have spelled out the components of this agenda, namely the priority areas for enhancing development management in Africa in the 1990s; the actions that are required to support the enhancement of development management capacity and the effective implementation of these priorities; and last, but not least, the mechanisms for coordination, exchange of information and networking among all actors and supporters.

The measures and modalities identified in this document will require a willingness on the part of both governments and Africa's partners to make adjustment in their approaches and operations. None of these, however, should be difficult to make, given the significant gains that can be made in the long run. In the interest of Africa's future, we believe that what is being asked of everybody here is very little and achievable. The costs of not acting now, however, are forbidding. For these reasons, we hope that all actors involved in managing Africa's development, whether local or external, will embrace the recommendations made in this document with the seriousness that they deserve and forge a dedicated partnership for its effective implementation.

Preparing for the Future: Priority Areas for Enhancing Development Management

Improving the Public Policy-Making Process

Recent economic and political reform measures have dramatised the need to strengthen skills for policy analysis, formulation, implementation and review. If African civil services are to guide and manage the public policy process effectively, the following are among the key measures required:

- Policy analysis units should be established and/or strengthened at appropriate levels of government with a view to build capacity for policy formulation, implementation and review. These units should be properly connected to each other and individually linked to information gathering centres and appropriate data bases.
- Policy units should have a critical mass of staff of high professional standing in the field of policy analysis and should have adequate capacity for data and information gathering, analysis and processing.
- Governments should take advantage of and nurture the reservoir of knowledge and skills available locally to benefit national policy-making by encouraging closer interface with local universities, training and research centres.
- The resources of universities and other relevant institutions, including private think tanks, should be developed with a view to strengthening their role in all phases of the policy-making process.
- Effective popular participation, transparency and communication in policy formulation should be ensured as this broadens the basis on which public policy rests and thus enhances the prospects for successful policy implementation.
- Independent evaluation of the outcome of policy decisions by legislative, judiciary and watchdog organisations should be encouraged.
- Governments and private sector organisations such as Chambers of Commerce should strive to provide formal institutional frameworks to support cooperation between researchers, policy-makers and representatives of business and entrepreneurial interests. In this connection, there should be institutional arrangements for regular interactions between governments, the private sector, and research institutions.
- Governments should establish formal institutional channels to support cooperation and regular interactions between researchers and indigenous "think tanks" on the one hand and policy-makers and implementers on the other hand.
- At the regional or sub-regional level, forums such as workshops and seminars should be organised on a regular basis at which researchers and policy-makers interact and discuss common policy issues and problems.

Enhancing Efficiency and Quality of the African Civil Services

Africa's problem is largely a production problem. Africa's civil services have been a drag on the productive process. Accordingly, attention should be directed in every country to restructure and overhaul the civil services so that they can be productive and also capable of facilitating the productive processes in the wider economy.

It follows from this that current political and economic reforms of the context within which African civil services operate should be pursued with greater vigour and imagination. Specific measures for improving the productivity and professionalism of Africa's civil services should include:

- *Improvement of the Organisation for Managing the Public Service:* There is need to streamline and rationalise civil service management systems by establishing or strengthening an authoritative system of decision-making on all civil service management issues. This will facilitate monitoring of management procedures and guidelines but leave detailed implementation to the operational units.
- *Raise Levels of Competence:* This can be accomplished through an integrated approach to human resource development in the civil service, covering both pre-service and in-service training and linking training with the specific needs of the formulation, implementation and review of national development policies.
- *Compensation:* Low, declining, non-market related levels of compensation have been a major factor constraining productivity and efficiency in the civil service—especially at a time when inflation and currency devaluations have reduced the real value of take-home pay. Low real wages and salaries have resulted in low levels of performance, wide-spread laxity at work, moonlighting, indiscipline, lack of care for public property, pilferage, brain drain, and a host of other problems. There is, therefore, a need to improve morale and commitment to duty, thus raising levels of performance by providing appropriate compensation. The following measures can be taken towards this end:

  - Use of market forces and collective bargaining to determine wage/salary levels within the context of prevailing economic conditions.
  - Periodic adjustment to cushion wages against inflation.
  - Establishment of linkages between pay and performance.
  - Rationalisation of fringe benefits.
  - Stringent efforts should be taken to maintain discipline and accountability through clearly established criteria of performance.

- *Improvement of the Knowledge Base of African Public Administration:* Available information on public administration systems in terms of structure, size and other variables in many African countries is patchy. There is need to build up-to-date and comparative data and information on African public administration systems.

Promoting Ethics and Strengthening Mechanisms for Accountability

Lack of accountability, unethical behaviour and corrupt practices have become entrenched, and even institutionalised norms of behaviour in their own right, in civil services across Africa, to the extent that the issue has now become a matter of major and general concern. Such practices in public office are not peculiar to Africa. However, deteriorating economic and social conditions in the region have intensified the problems.

In order to tackle pervasive ethical violations and institutionalised corruption in African public services, it is proposed that the following strategies be pursued as a matter of urgency:

- African governments should match the reduction in civil service employment levels with increased pay and commensurate incentives for those who remain in the service. This will help to reduce the incidence of corrupt practices arising out of personal hardship aggravated by economic reform and structural adjustment programmes.
- African governments should encourage the formulation of codes of ethics and accountability. Such codes should become the standard authority on "best practice" and should not only contain expected norms of behaviour but should also include the sanctions that will be enforced when the code is breached.
- Where appropriate, African governments should revise existing codes of conduct with a view to updating them, making them more relevant and realistic and to accommodate the existence of other ethical codes at group, professional and organisational levels. Generally, ethical codes should neither be too lenient nor too harsh.
- Watchdog organisations, such as the code of conduct bureaus, public complaint commissions and public accounts committees, should be given adequate resources and independence to perform their job of exposing unethical practices, prescribing preventive measures against abuses and investigating public complaints of administrative abuses.
- Budgeting, accounting and auditing practices and procedures should be improved or strengthened.

- Institutions, such as legislatures and judiciaries, should be better resourced so they can adequately discharge their responsibilities of enforcing codes of appropriate conduct in the public service.
- Ethical values are inculcated through the usual agents of socialisation. In this regard, institutions such as the family, schools, religious institutions, political parties, the media, professional associations, youth clubs, etc. have a role to play. Beyond this, innovative approaches in popularising ethical values through the use of television, drama, music, etc. should be enhanced.
- Public and private sector institutions and regional/international organisations should regularly assist educational and training establishments in developing comprehensive and relevant curricula on ethics. In this regard, the ECA, and other regional organisations should assist in developing specific training modules and packages appropriate for use in schools, training institutions and universities. In designing training programmes, care should be taken to reflect the requirements of employees at different levels.

Strengthening Resource Mobilisation and Financial Management Capacity of African Governments

Public and private expenditures and investments determine the level of activity in an economy. Financial resources and managerial expertise are key to fostering growth and development. To this extent, there is need to put in place effective mechanisms for resource mobilisation and utilisation. In this regard, the following measures are recommended:

- restructuring of taxation systems to reduce avoidance, promote efficiency and equity, and provide incentives for savings and investments;
- simplifying administrative procedures for tax assessment and collection;
- encouraging the channelling of informal sources of savings and credit such as community-based savings arrangements into formal community banking systems;
- instilling confidence in the banking sector and encouraging the growth of financial intermediaries and capital markets;
- taking appropriate measures to reduce the incidence of capital flight and encourage repatriation;
- facilitating the flow of external financial resources through an enabling environment of political stability and a sound macro-economic framework;

- utilisation of financial resources should be both effective and consistent with established national priorities;
- on-going programmes of training and management development of public financial personnel is required to enable them to keep abreast with innovations in public financial management.

Public Enterprise Sector Reforms

Public enterprises continue to occupy a central role in African economies. To this extent, their efficient management is critical to the performance of national economies. For this reason, economic considerations must be taken fully into account in setting public enterprise objectives. Indeed, these principles are being recognised in current efforts at public enterprise reform.

While these reform efforts are shrinking the size of the public enterprise sector through divestiture or privatisation, public enterprises will continue to be used as instruments of development management. Nonetheless, it is clear that government cannot be involved in every sector of the economy as an operator. It follows from this that a strategic agenda for public enterprise reform has two main components: (i) taking measures to improve performance without changing ownership and (ii) transferring into private ownership some proportion or all of the equity of those individual enterprises which should not remain in the public domain—privatisation.

Improving public enterprise performance

The following measures are considered essential in improving public enterprise performance:

Enterprise objectives should be clearly defined and autonomy established through such instruments as memoranda of understanding, performance contracts and strategic and corporate planning. This will facilitate managerial and commercial autonomy.

- clarification of objectives will make explicit the assumptions underlying corporate strategy;
- autonomy will give managers the freedom to fix prices of products, to vary the type of product, to procure funds for investment, and to hire, discipline and fire staff.

Sound mechanisms and procedures for the appointment of chief executives and measures for effective human resource management must be introduced and strengthened. This will facilitate:

• the emergence of a competent, experienced, professional, creative and committed top management team;
• the emergence of positive and responsive personnel policies based on merit and sound staff recruitment policies;
• the emergence of management development and training policies geared to the specific needs of the enterprise and designed to equip enterprise managers with skills required to analyse internal and external influences on performance and productivity;
• the motivation and development of employees including a competitive pay and benefits structure linked with productivity and job performance.

The financial viability of public enterprises must be enhanced to ensure their contribution to growth and recovery in African countries through the following:

• there should be conscious acceptance of financial profitability as a major objective of public enterprises. It is important to make policy-makers and managers aware that financial profitability is a necessary goal to pursue in the management of public enterprises to enhance generation of savings, capital formation, and ensure return on investment to the national treasury;
• there is a need to determine adequate capital structure for public enterprises given that undercapitalisation is a major problem of African public enterprises. This, in turn, requires monitoring of capital mix and profitability through application of modern principles and practices of financial analysis such as Return on Capital Employed (ROCE), debt/equity ratios, etc.; special financial indices should be devised as appropriate for measuring profitability;
• there is need to identify criteria for determining sick and potentially sick public enterprises through appropriate financial indices.

Opportunities for technological adaptation and innovation must be fully pursued with a view to achieving and maintaining full capacity utilisation. This will help to facilitate the strategic use of public enterprises for technological transfer and development.
Enterprise operations must be imbued with an entrepreneurial culture. This is vital for creativity and innovation, effective management styles

and practices, optimum utilisation of plant equipment, technology, materials and supplies and attention to the details of quality control.

Privatisation

Experience of privatisation in Africa and elsewhere points to the need for the process to be approached on an orderly basis. The following measures are considered essential for the success of the privatisation process:

- Privatisation must not be approached on an ad hoc basis. There must be a carefully designed plan of action based on detailed study of the public enterprise sector and analysis of the specific problems of each enterprise;
- The privatisation programme must be clearly linked to broader efforts at economic reform, private sector development and competition;
- Responsibility for the programme must be vested in an independent implementing agency. The calibre and technical competence of the professional staff of the agency must be of the highest order. There must be unambiguous political support for the work of the agency at the highest level;
- Valuation of the enterprise should be clearly established prior to divestment by independent experts;
- Every effort must be made to explain the programme to the general public. If transparency in the transfer of assets is to be maintained, the publicity aspects of the programme should not be under-estimated;
- As the privatisation programme proceeds, there must be periodic evaluation of what is being achieved in relation to the plan of action and changing economic circumstances.

Enhancing Entrepreneurial Capacity and Promoting Private Sector Development

It is increasingly recognised that future growth in Africa rests with entrepreneurs, markets, and a supportive policy framework provided by governments.

Private enterprise provides a dynamic and potentially efficient means of meeting many of the emerging challenges of development in the region including regional economic cooperation. This can be accomplished through joint ventures between African entrepreneurs from different countries.

One of the key lessons of economic management which has emerged in recent years and now informs global programmes of reform is that government intervention is most successful when policies flow along with —rather than go against the grain of—market forces. This must be the guiding principle of a strategic agenda for building entrepreneurial capacity and enhancing private sector development in the African region. Among the key measures or main policy priorities would be the following:

- *Political stability:* Entrepreneurship at any level cannot thrive in a context of political instability. Both the business community and public officials bear a heavy responsibility in educating public opinion on the relationship between political stability and business confidence. Africa's development partners should also take concrete measures to foster the consolidation of democratic processes and political stability in the region.
- *Competent economic management, efficient civil services and sound infrastructure:* Measures to stimulate, develop and promote entrepreneurship in the region must rest on a firm foundation of sound economic management, efficient civil services, positive attitudes towards business and reliable infrastructure.
- *Investment promotion:* Foreign investment and joint ventures must be encouraged to accelerate the transfer of managerial and other skills, technological capability and development. Sending missions abroad or advertising internationally should be preceded by the establishment of a satisfactory business climate at home. Moreover investment promotion agencies and other public service agencies must first establish a "service function" (rather than a purely screening or regulatory function) to assist entrepreneurs who are already doing business locally.
- *Establish institutional capacity for policy development and coordination and sound information systems on microeconomic and market behaviour:* There should be sound institutional capacity in government for policy development, sensitivity analysis (to project the likely effect of particular measures) and policy coordination. Any African government seeking to provide strategic direction on the promotion of entrepreneurship within the overall framework of development priorities and objectives must also first collect and disseminate basic information about the scale and nature of existing businesses operating at all levels including linkages (or lack of them) between

firms and the range of problems or difficulties that are being experienced as well as microeconomic and market behaviour.

- *Development of financial markets and institutions:* Joint stock companies and equity markets have been slow to develop in African countries and formal sector entrepreneurs are denied both the flexibility of tapping this source of finance as well as the discipline of working under pressure from stock or capital markets. Hence, careful attention must be paid to the role and development of financial institutions with a view to promote versatility, flexibility and efficiency of financial and capital markets and banking institutions.

Specific recommendations for particular levels of entrepreneurship include the following:

Measures to promote informal sector microentrepreneurship:

The role of market networks: microentrepreneurs can overcome the limitations of market size and other constraints through linkages with formal sector businesses. Informal sector entrepreneurs can achieve access to bigger markets and information and advice on such matters as improved management and production methods and better product design through formal sector linkages. Moreover such market networks or linkages are often more effective mechanisms for the transfer of know-how and assistance than networks composed of government departments and non-governmental organisations.

The role of government and NGOs: Markets often fail to generate linkages for a variety of reasons, including information gaps between potential collaborators. Through incentives and other measures, governments can encourage or facilitate linkages between informal sector entrepreneurs and their better established formal sector counterparts. The NGO community, often a reservoir of knowledge and expertise on grassroots activities and operations, can also play an important role in linking informal and formal sector business. Such policy and institutional support would at minimum include three key measures as follows:

- *Training:* the provision of facilities for technical and vocational training to upgrade the skills of informal sector workers and entrepreneurs is an important requirement. Government and NGOs can encourage and give recognition to this valuable service by making available grants and other incentives to foster the practice of informal sector apprenticeships.
- *Credit:* The provision of credit facilities specifically designed to meet the needs of entrepreneurs operating on a very small scale, typically

without collateral or an established business track record is an important requirement. Grassroots or community-level banking and financial institutions are well placed to provide these unconventional banking needs and practices to fill this vacuum and should be encouraged through deliberate policies.

- *Enterprise-level support:* The provision of enterprise-level support systems, such as business advisory centres, small-scale enterprise extension systems, and physical facilities, such as workshops, craft centres, water, electricity and telephones. Advisory and extension services can provide valuable information and assistance to informal sector entrepreneurs, especially in such areas as book keeping, management, production and marketing techniques, facilitating linkages between informal and formal sector business; steering formal sector entrepreneurs through the unfamiliar corridors of government bureaucracies with which they must sometimes deal; and the promotion of informal sector goods and services through exhibitions, craft shows and trade fairs.

Measures to promote small- and intermediate-scale entrepreneurship:

As businesses grow along the small- to intermediate-scale continuum, they often face constraints such as limited managerial capabilities; difficulties with technology transfer and adaptation; and, as in the case of informal sector micro-entrepreneurs, inadequate or inappropriate public provision of enterprise-level support. Measures to promote and develop entrepreneurial capacity at these levels of the business structure in contemporary Africa must seek to surmount these constraints.

Overcoming managerial constraints: Approaches to management education, development and training are undergoing a fundamental shift from "traditional," formal, classroom-based methods to an increasing emphasis on informal, in-house, on-the-job learning and training. Dissatisfaction with traditional methods has opened the way for new arrangements which facilitate the acquisition of management skills that are directly relevant to the needs of business operations to emerge. One of the implications of this trend is that private businesses will increasingly bear the cost of training their own managerial personnel. Planners and policy-makers in African governments will be well advised to carefully consider the implications of this trend for national manpower and human resource development strategies.

Surmounting difficulties with technology transfer and adaptation: Government has a key role to play in facilitating and encouraging technology transfer, local adaptation and development, by providing a policy framework consistent with national development objectives and priorities. Accordingly, efficient information flows between government and business on precise needs and requirements should be an essential part of the policy-making process and the targeting of incentives.

Enhancing enterprise-level support systems: Entrepreneurs everywhere need advice, information and various kinds of services in setting up their businesses and in dealing with problems that arise in the normal course of operations. While technical and advisory services can be provided through market networks (via private consulting companies banks and financial houses) or through the tertiary sector (via Chambers of Commerce, management professional organisations, universities, colleges and NGOs), government intervention is also required to establish a general framework for business development as part of the planning and policy-making process. But such intervention must be designed to be well coordinated, flexible, unbureaucratic and results-oriented. African governments should systematically appraise existing policies and measures on enterprise-level support systems to make them relevant to the needs of entrepreneurs.

Measures to promote large-scale entrepreneurship:

(i) Many of the foregoing recommendations on promoting specific levels of entrepreneurship also apply to the promotion of African entrepreneurship on a large scale. But the main constraints at this level are principally related to size, scale and complexity of extensive undertakings. African governments can adopt two strategies to overcome these constraints by supporting:

- *The incremental approach:* an incremental approach to investment in large and complex undertakings—within the context of a supportive public policy framework—provides a sound and effective basis for establishing capacity and the experience to cope with higher levels of managerial, organisational and technological complexity.
- *The "turn-key" approach:* the "turn-key" approach to investment design and management of large-scale operations is a viable alternative to incremental growth in certain industries. Food processing, beverages, tobacco, soaps and detergents are good examples of such industries. Indeed, indigenous entrepreneurship is well-established in many such ventures in most African countries. One of the explanations of the success of the "turn-key" approach in these cases is that the technology is relatively simple to acquire,

install, operate and maintain and the products have been relatively stable.

Ensuring Effective Popular Participation in Development and Governance

There has emerged a vigorous demand for full and genuine people's participation in the political, economic and social processes of their countries and for having a meaningful say in the formulation of policies and programmes that affect their lives.

Public policies and programmes have too often been framed without taking the people into account, the specific needs and preferences of the people who are directly affected by them or are supposed to benefit from them. The result is more often than not a failure of those policies and programmes because of apathy and indifference on the part of people.

It is clear that intentions to promote good governance, democratic pluralism and reverse Africa's economic decline require a process of broad-based participation and effective citizen's involvement in decision-making. A democratic political and economic order cannot be built without the popular support and participation of the people, nor can human conditions improve without the full and effective contributions, creativity and popular enthusiasm of the vast majority of the people. To this extent, popular participation in development can be consolidated in several ways as follows:

- creating the political space where people and their organisations can flourish and by actively seeking people's input on decisions;
- working with people and their representatives in formulating development strategies with the aim of achieving "self-reliant and people-centred development";
- devolving power from the state to the people, adapting government efforts to people's initiatives, and creating an enabling environment which makes genuine empowerment of people a reality;
- allowing people to direct their own socio-economic transformation by giving recognition to people's organisations and grassroots initiatives and developing cooperative partnerships that reflect African priorities; and
- developing creative and mutually beneficial partnerships between local government institutions and NGOs.

The role of NGOs, voluntary and people's organisations deserves further attention. Such organisations have a crucial responsibility in consolidating the movement towards political pluralism and democratic governance in Africa by undertaking initiatives and activities such as:

- *Helping to foster democratic values and practices:* NGOs and people's organisations can initiate activities in civic education and public service programmes and encourage constructive criticism and practices that would help to institutionalise democratic values and traditions.
- *Helping to build and strengthen democratic institutions:* NGOs and people's organisations have a critical role to play in helping to build democratic institutions especially in areas of monitoring electoral processes, organising and conducting public debates on competing political views and perspectives, and providing support for autonomous research and policy centres that monitor government accountability.
- *Helping to ensure respect for human rights:* NGOs and people's organisations, are particularly well placed to promote respect for the basic rights of the citizenry, both at the official and popular levels. They should engage in a wide range of useful activities, including human rights education, legal assistance, research and publications, sensitisation campaigns, lobbying for the reform of laws and the ratification of international and regional charters.
- *Helping to build and strengthen civil society:* As one set of institutions in civil society and as part of the public domain of governance, NGOs and people's organisations have the crucial role of strengthening civil society vis-à-vis the state and the ruling elite. NGOs and people's organisations should assist in the setting-up and strengthening of institutions, organisations and practices which encourage people to take responsibility for their own destinies.
- *Helping to sensitise and mobilise the international community:* NGOs and people's organisations can play a valuable role in improving North-South relations through the active lobbying of the international community to create favourable conditions for the solution of the debt problem, increased inflow of resources, more equitable terms of trade and greater support for emerging democratic institutions.
- *Helping in affirming democratically-elected authority over the military:* People's organisations can help in this regard by sensitising civil society to affirm the right of popularly-elected civil authorities to exercise democratic control over the military
- *Helping to guarantee the integrity, accountability and transparency of government:* NGOs and people's organisations can help guarantee the integrity of governments by playing a watchdog role and by strengthening the role of watchdog organisations. Potential NGO

activities include periodic assessments of the state of bureaucratic accountability; and support for a free press.

Decentralisation for Sustained Development

Decentralisation has long been recognised and advocated as a means of promoting socio-economic development. The result in many African countries did not match this expectation because decentralisation efforts have been limited to deconcentration and delegation of responsibilities rather than devolution of power from the centre to the sub-national units and local authorities.

Several factors, prominent among which are the poor record of the centralising tendencies of the African state, growing demand for genuine popular participation in development and governance, and the spread of democratic processes have combined to give new impetus to decentralisation.

If decentralisation is to contribute to fostering socio-economic development and responsiveness to popular will, some policy measures will be required. Among these are:

> *Enhanced commitment to devolution:* government at the central level should facilitate the transfer of power to sub-national units (regional or local authorities/communities). This should be backed up by appropriate legislation and commensurate revenues to the local authorities. Furthermore, definitive efforts should be made to empower local people to enhance local government management capacities and ensure that they actually make the key decisions to enable them to fulfil their responsibilities effectively.
>
> • *Promoting partnership between central government, sub-national units and NGOs:* genuine partnerships between central governments and sub-national units are required. Dictatorial tendencies by central authorities should be abandoned in favour of dialogue and compromise in dealing with potential areas of conflicts. Local government institutions should in turn promote mutually beneficial partnerships with people's organisations and NGOs operating at the local level.
>
> • *Strengthening the leadership capacity of local institutions:* priority should be given to management training for local government staff, urban and village councillors, community leaders and leaders of NGOs. This is necessary to develop both leadership capabilities and professional competence to better articulate needs, views, and perspectives from this level. Such training is also part of the process

of empowering local leaders to seize the initiative on alternative policy options, programmes, and plans.

Enhancing the Participation and Skills of Women for Effective Involvement in Development Management

In spite of the fact that women make up more than 50 percent of the African population and assume the larger share of responsibility especially in the food, agriculture and trade sectors, they have not been fully accorded the importance they deserve.

A human-focused development strategy cannot afford to ignore more than half of the population. While the marginalisation of women has spanned all areas, this has been even more so in their involvement in political life and public management.

African women have to be given equal opportunity as men to contribute to national development by exercising leadership and responsibility at the highest and other levels and to participate in the formulation, design, execution and evaluation of public sector policies, programmes and projects. This requires conscious efforts and measures to effectively ensure that women play a major role in political life and development management. Among such measures would be the following:

- Existing gender disparities in civil service and public sector employment should be recognised. Appropriate measures should be taken to guarantee equity and fairness in providing women with access to public sector employment, especially in executive, managerial and other key decision-making and implementation roles and specifically in areas traditionally not open to women such as ministries of planning, finance, foreign affairs, defence and national security, the judiciary etc.
- In the private sector where women have been engaged in a number of activities including trade and food production, they have generally failed to achieve full potential and productivity largely because of inadequate access to financial, technical and other resources. For this reason, facilitating women's access to credit, training in enterprise management, and technology should be supported and encouraged both by government, private sector institutions and NGOs.
- In particular, a large proportion of African women are engaged in a wide range of activities in the informal sector. This calls for conscious efforts on the part of African governments to provide an

enabling environment for this sector to thrive and more specifically the millions of women entrepreneurs within it. This will involve first and foremost a radical change in the way governments perceive the informal sector.

- Historically, women and girls have not had equal opportunity to education in general and even more so in scientific and technical fields. African governments should institute measures to increase the participation and performance of women in these areas. High-level training programmes should also be set up or supported to provide women with appropriate managerial skills and experience.
- Recognising the multiple roles, family responsibilities, and other constraints women face in pursuing higher education, governments should apply appropriate incentives, including the provision of scholarships, and family support structures, for encouraging and enhancing women's participation in higher education.
- At the same time, the alarming level of female illiteracy in African countries cannot be ignored. Neither can the necessity of supporting adult education efforts and encouraging the work of NGO's in this area.
- At the workplace in the public, private, and voluntary sectors, measures to guarantee equity and fairness in the access of women to employment opportunities should be promoted. Effective measures should also be instituted or strengthened and implemented to put an end to the sexual harassment of women at work.
- Beyond these measures, the heavy responsibilities accompanying the multiple roles of women in their reproductive and productive roles, should be recognised. African governments should promote support systems such as part-time employment, flexible working hours, day-care centres, maternal, and child health services for women at work or pursuing educational opportunities.
- Cultural attitudes and customary practices exert enormous influence in perpetuating myths about gender relations thereby reinforcing the barriers to women's advancement. In this regard, governments have a major responsibility in promoting public understanding of these issues. For example, gender sensitisation and awareness-raising programmes could be included in school curricula. Key non-governmental organisations such as the media, religious organisations, and women's organisations, should also play an active role in promoting public awareness and understanding.
- A closely related issue is the simultaneous existence of conflicting customary, religious and statutory laws which give rise to confusion and manipulation. African governments should carefully review

overlapping provisions with the view of harmonisation of all laws
that affect the status of women.

- Beyond this, all African governments which have not already done
so, are urged to review their constitutions and other laws with the
objective of explicitly outlawing all forms of discrimination on the
basis of gender. The instruments of enforcement should also
strengthened.
- Given the inadequacy of data and information on women's status in
most African countries, governments should also take appropriate
measures to create or support facilities for comprehensive research
and data collection to ensure the desegregation by gender of
development data as appropriate.
- The ultimate responsibility for creating public awareness of gender
issues and the merits of gender equity rests with women's
organisations and women themselves. But women's movements
seem to be weak in almost all African countries. Accordingly,
women must—with appropriate support—seize the initiative to
strengthen these movements in order that they may be more
effective in serving their cause.

**Optimising the use of Information Technology
in African Public Administration**

Information technology is vital for improved development management. Use of information technology facilitates the storage and retrieval
of information and data, and advances the efficient flow of information.
Key issues of a strategic agenda on the use of information technology in
development management would include:

- replacement of old and outdated equipment, particularly in the field
of mini- and mainframe-computers;
- elimination of the inconsistent, highly diverse equipment base
brought in by different external donors;
- improvement of the missing or inadequate standardisation and
harmonisation in data storage;
- creation of African data bases on the basis of user needs surveys;
- creation and improvement of text-oriented data processing;
- increasing the number and use of micro-computers in government
offices as well as in the private and voluntary sectors;
- promotion of computer literacy within the public service and more
generally within the educational system; and
- creation of micro-computers networks.

Implementation of this strategic agenda calls for action on the following:

- a national strategy on information technology;
- proper planning for the introduction or extension of information technology within the public administration system and with appropriate budgetary provisions;
- increasing the acceptance of the use of information technology at higher levels in the public administration system;
- provision of appropriate training and software development facilities within the country as well as by seeking external assistance;
- provision of appropriate salaries and incentives for specialised computer personnel.

The Role of National, Regional and External Actors in the Enhancement of Development Management Capacity in Africa

The Need for Concerted Action

The implementation of the *Strategic Agenda* will depend on the readiness of actors at different levels, individually and in concert, to step up their efforts in building and enhancing development management capacity. The main responsibility in this regard rests with member states. Much can be achieved by simply doing things more efficiently and with greater determination. Conditions in many parts of Africa are such, however, that it also requires bold and creative thinking and action. This means there must be the political will to do things differently, in some cases making room for new institutions. In a situation as difficult as the one facing Africa in the 1990s, despondency and inertia can only be challenged by initiatives that raise and sustain the hope for recovery and improvement.

In this context, it is important that more powerful institutions are ready to give enough space for initiatives by others. Future development efforts must accord the private sector and non-governmental organisations an expanded role; a strategy which implies the need for greater pluralism and decentralised decision-making.

Future progress depends on negotiating this transition to greater institutional pluralism and more broadly based participation in the mobilisation and management of development resources.

The idea of providing an enabling environment applies at all levels: donors vis-à-vis recipient countries; regional organisations vis-à-vis national ones; and governments vis-à-vis private business, NGOs and people's organisations. Enhancing development management capacity must increasingly be driven from below rather than from above as the case has been in the past. This not only means providing adequate incentives for such initiatives but also a legal and regulatory framework in which equity, fairness and professional considerations prevail. An independent judiciary becomes a particularly important guarantor of such an environment.

The Role of National Actors

A major challenge for actors at the national level is to ensure that the framework in which development is going to take place becomes more hospitable for private and public initiatives. More specifically, the following actions to enhance development management capacity are recommended to actors at the national level.

Governments should

- reassess existing legislation, policies and regulations so that they become more supportive of entrepreneurial activities but also protect the public realm from being exploited by illicit actions;
- encourage a political climate in which public debate about specific national policies is encouraged and strengthened so as to broaden the involvement of other actors in policy-making;
- maintain political stability and initiate the necessary steps to make governance more transparent and accountable;
- provide a favourable macro-economic environment;
- develop and strengthen national capital markets with a view to enhancing the capacity for domestic funding of development initiatives;
- ensure better and more effective use of public resources, for example, by using funds earned from privatisation to fund specific projects such as the reform of public enterprises retained in the public portfolio.

Business should

- facilitate the access of small-scale entrepreneurs to markets and credit facilities;
- encourage the development and use of technology that draws on domestic ideas and resources;

- develop and maintain ethical practices and social responsibility to ensure that its public image is one of propriety and concern with development as much as with profit;
- forge partnerships with institutes and universities to promote applied research and training;
- encourage and secure reinvestment of profits locally so as to build up confidence and attract foreign investment that is vital for national development.

The People, their Organisations and NGOs should

- be ready to seize the initiative and exploit new opportunities;
- foster partnership with government and business through appropriate frameworks to promote entrepreneurship and strengthen development management;
- help to create an environment conducive to investment and business confidence and activity by fostering democratic traditions, national cohesion and stability;
- form and strengthen institutions of civil society that play the role of watchdog on public institutions;
- mobilise local resources through self-help activities that match outside contributions for local development;
- educate grassroots opinion to benefit from entrepreneurial promotional schemes such as cooperatives, credit and saving facilities etc.
- establish viable and effective networks and communication structures to exchange information, disseminate innovations and success stories on entrepreneurial and voluntary initiatives.

Institutions of Higher Learning and Training and Research Centres should

- enhance the interface with government with a view to further the contribution of national experts and "think tanks" to the making, implementation and evaluation of national policies, strategies, programmes and projects.
- revise curricula to reflect current African realities and provide students with knowledge that is relevant to dealing with today's and tomorrow's problems in general and meeting the challenge of development management in particular.
- take the necessary steps in consultation with government and other relevant actors to retain faculty and provide them with incentives to be more productive in both teaching and research.

- initiate and participate in the development and promotion of indigenous technology drawing on ideas and resources both within and outside existing research institutes.
- network with managers, researchers, administrators and scientists in government, business and other sectors with a view to transfer knowledge for application in the world of business.
- promote inter-and intra-African cooperation among centres of higher learning.

The Role of Regional and Sub-regional Actors

Although each individual country must develop policies and capacities that are relevant to its own challenges and opportunities, regional and sub-regional actors have an important role to play as catalysts of new ideas, promoters of greater mobility of talents within the continent, and advocates on behalf of Africa and the African perspective in international fora.

Many of the specific proposals of the *Agenda* as well as its underlying philosophy of shared responsibility in development management will enhance the implementation of the *Treaty Establishing the African Economic Community*.

With specific regard to the implementation of the *Agenda*, regional actors are expected, *inter-alia*, to take the following responsibilities:

- promote the effective implementation of the *Agenda* and the *Treaty Establishing the African Economic Community*.
- co-operate in mobilising resources from the international community for the implementation of the *Strategic Agenda*.
- help foster human-centred development, democracy, popular participation, participatory institutions and good governance.
- help foster regional and national mechanisms for peacekeeping, peace building and conflict resolution.
- promote and facilitate the dissemination and adaption of successful entrepreneurial initiatives and effective development management techniques between African countries.
- facilitate the establishment of multi-country business ventures at sub-regional and regional levels.
- help improve efficiency and accountability of the public sector and business through regional seminars and workshops for managers, administrators, policy makers, etc. and encourage networking among national "watchdog" organisations and professional associations dealing with these concerns.

- help establish and maintain dialogue among African experts for assessing new concepts and approaches for development management and entrepreneurship.
- promote applied cross-country research and comparative policy analysis in areas of development management and entrepreneurship.
- encourage whenever appropriate the utilisation of African personnel by facilitating their participation in consultancies and other activities across the continent.
- create networks of indigenous experts from all over Africa and the diaspora.
- distil country-by-country experiences to evolve general principles and practices and disseminate these to trainers and policy-makers through conferences and other appropriate means.
- coordinate activities within the region and sub-region so as to avoid unnecessary duplication and poor use of scarce talents and resources.
- articulate the African perspective e.g. on debt recycling and international accountability and the priorities listed in the *Strategic Agenda* through participation in international fora where African development issues are being discussed.

The Role of External Actors (Governments, Business, Multilateral Agencies and NGOs)

The main objective of the *Strategic Agenda* is to enhance national and regional self-reliance and capacity. The primary responsibility in this regard is clearly that of African countries.

For some time to come, most African countries will require substantial external support to supplement their efforts. Africa's partners can make significant contributions towards enhancing development management capacity.

But it must be acknowledged that the manner in which technical assistance has generally been administered in the past has not had the desired impact. This has been largely due to the fact that such assistance has often been "donor-driven" and designed to execute specific projects and programmes according to donor specifications rather than to build and sustain local capacity. Part of the problem has also been due to the fact that the various aspects of development management—as demonstrated in this document—are interconnected and require simultaneous action on several fronts.

Among the key responsibilities of external actors, and notably the donor agencies, in implementing the *Strategic Agenda* are the following:

- provide support and substantial external resources to strengthen development management in Africa.
- co-ordinate funding and assistance which should be targeted to priority areas that promote capacity-building and self-reliance at the national, sub-regional and regional levels. Establishing a politically and legally independent development fund could be another modality. (see proposal.)
- provide the means for more effective use of external assistance. Imaginative modalities and institutional arrangements are needed. This could include debt for development management capacity building swaps.
- provide assistance in support of better governance. This should include the promotion of national and international accountability. In particular, the donors and international financial institutions should be ready to accept responsibility (including financial responsibility) for any failure of their policy advice.
- assist programmes that stem and reverse the brain drain from Africa.
- international NGOs should promote the need for adequate support of the *Strategic Agenda*.

Mechanisms for Coordination, Exchange of Information and Networking

There is a great number of institutions and organisations, at the national, sub-regional, regional and international levels, that could provide inputs and are expected to participate actively in the implementation of the *Strategic Agenda*. Mechanisms for co-ordination of their activities, exchange of information and networking will therefore have to be established.

- Overall co-ordination should be provided by the ECA and specifically by its Public Administration, Human Resources and Social Development Division. It is therefore essential that ECA/PHSD capacity be strengthened to oversee the implementation of the *Agenda* and to effectively liaise with African countries and also with the institutions and networks concerned.
- ECA and AAPAM (the African Association for Public Administration and Management) are urged to deal with issues concerning the *Strategic Agenda* and regularly review the status of its implementation at AAPAM's annual roundtable.

- ECA should take stock of existing national and regional development management institutes and their particular expertise and capacities. This information should be published in a sourcebook form and made it available to all user organisations, governments, donors, NGOs, development management institutes etc.
- ECA should also establish a roster of experts/consultants in the field of development management and make this available to member states and user organisations. The sourcebook and roster should be regularly updated through points of contacts to be established in each country.
- African governments, donors, management institutes and other agencies are urged to assist ECA in compiling the sourcebook and the roster by responding promptly to its request.
- To make better use of the broad range of valuable research on African development management issues, it is proposed that ECA organises a special African Research Clearing House on Development Management Issues.
- Technical assistance provided to individual African countries and at the regional level constitutes much potential for transfer of experience to other countries of the region. ECA is therefore encouraged to make an inventory of technical assistance to Africa in the field of development management.
- ECA should strengthen its co-operation with Africa's sub-regional and regional organisations, especially the Organisation for African Unity (OAU) and the African Development Bank (AfDB) and professional associations with a view to ensuring the effective implementation of the *Strategic Agenda*.
- The reform of the public enterprise sector which is under way in most of the African countries is considered to be one of the main issues in African development today. It should be regularly monitored at the regional level to provide information of comparative experience, successes and deficiencies. The International Centre for Public Enterprises (ICPE) and its African member countries are therefore encouraged to form an appropriate network to facilitate the exchange of experiences and information.
- *The Strategic Agenda for Development Management in Africa in the 1990s* should be made available to interested parties in the donor countries. Special fora, such as the annual meetings of the African Studies Association in the United States, and International Association of Schools and Institutes of Administration (IASIA) should be utilised to spread information about its content and progress of implementation. To this effect, special panels should be organised on a regular basis at these meetings to deliberate on the concerns of the *Agenda*.

- The ECA is invited to convene an International Conference to undertake a mid-term review of progress in the implementation of the *Agenda* in 1996 and also an End-of-Decade Conference in 2000, where progress in the implementation of the *Agenda* will be assessed and actions will be taken as appropriate.

As adopted by the participants of the Regional Conference on Development Management in Africa in March 1993 and endorsed by the 19th meeting of the UNECA Conference of Ministers in May 1993

About the Editors and Contributors

Editors

Sadig Rasheed is director of the Public Administration, Human Resources and Social Development Division (PHSD), ECA, Addis Ababa, Ethiopia.

David Fasholé Luke is currently at the EDECO Department of the OAU.

Contributors

Ladipo Adamolekun is principal management specialist, Africa Technical Department, the World Bank, Washington, DC.

M. J. Balogun is senior regional adviser in public administration and management, Multidisciplinary Advisory Group, ECA, Addis Ababa, Ethiopia.

Hamadan Benaissa is senior inter-regional advisor, Department for Development Support and Management Services, division of Public Administration and Development Management, UN Secretariat, New York.

Zeinab El-Bakry is principal WID officer, Central Projects Department, African Development Bank, Abidjan, Cote d'Ivoire.

Getachew Demeke is project coordinator, Popular Participation in Development Project, PHSD, ECA, Addis Ababa, Ethiopia.

Herbert Girkes is chief of Computerised Communication and Documentation Section, African Centre for Development and Strategic Studies (ACDESS), Ijebu-Ode, Ogun State, Nigeria.

Goran Hyden is professor of political science, University of Florida.

Peter H. Koehn is professor and director of International Programmes, University of Montana.

Pierre Landell-Mills is senior policy adviser, Africa Technical Department, the World Bank, Washington, DC.

Maria Nzomo is senior lecturer, Institute of Diplomacy and International Relations, University of Nairobi, Kenya.

Dele Olowu is professor of public administration, Obafemi Awolowo University, Ile-Ife, Nigeria.

H. M. A. Onitiri is formerly chief technical adviser of the OAU/UNDP Project on the African Economic Community, OAU Secretariat, Addis Ababa, Ethiopia.

Mostafa Rhomari is professor, Ecole Nationale d'Administration Publique, Rabat, Morocco.

Ismail Serageldin is vice-president for Environmental Sustainable Development, the World Bank, Washington DC.

Index